大学英语自主学习能力培养教程（第4版）

A College English Course for the Development of Autonomous Learning

严明 主编

黑龙江大学出版社
HEILONGJIANG UNIVERSITY PRESS
哈尔滨

图书在版编目（CIP）数据

大学英语自主学习能力培养教程 / 严明主编. -- 4
版. -- 哈尔滨：黑龙江大学出版社，2014.9（2024.8 重印）
ISBN 978-7-81129-800-0

Ⅰ. ①大… Ⅱ. ①严… Ⅲ. ①大学生－英语－学习方
法－教材 Ⅳ. ①H319.3

中国版本图书馆 CIP 数据核字（2014）第 203356 号

大学英语自主学习能力培养教程（第 4 版）
DAXUE YINGYU ZIZHU XUEXI NENGLI PEIYANG JIAOCHENG（DI-4 BAN）
严 明 主编

责任编辑	戚增媚　韩　健
出版发行	黑龙江大学出版社
地　　址	哈尔滨市南岗区学府三道街 36 号
印　　刷	哈尔滨市石桥印务有限公司
开　　本	720 毫米×1000 毫米　1/16
印　　张	15.25
字　　数	258 千
版　　次	2014 年 9 月第 4 版　2007 年 9 月第 1 版
印　　次	2024 年 8 月第 11 次印刷
书　　号	ISBN 978-7-81129-800-0
定　　价	29.00 元

本书如有印装错误请与本社联系更换。

版权所有　侵权必究

编委会

主　编：严　明
主　审：王　瑞
副主编：于　丽　　刘　辉
　　　　　　汪志涛　　陈庆斌
编　者：(按姓氏笔画排序)
　　　　　　于　丽　　王　瑞　　王天予　　王玉双
　　　　　　孔香玲　　吕晓轩　　刘　丹　　刘　洋
　　　　　　刘　辉　　严　明　　汪志涛　　陈庆斌
　　　　　　郑春梅　　胥　扬　　徐德凯

前　言

20 世纪 70 年代,联合国教科文组织在《学会生存——教育世界的今天和明天》中提出自主学习能力的初步概念,明确指出:"明天的文盲将不是目不识丁的人,而是不知道如何学习的人。"此后,1996 年,联合国教科文组织 21 世纪教育委员会在向联合国提交的报告中,把"学会认知"作为社会教育的四大支柱之一。

2007 年,教育部颁布实施的《大学英语课程教学要求》中明确规定,大学英语教学要以英语语言知识与应用技能、跨文化交际和学习策略为主要内容,在培养学生英语综合应用能力的同时,增强学生的自主学习能力。培养学生的自主学习能力不仅是国家教育政策的要求,更是学生自身发展和经济与社会发展的本体诉求。

为此,黑龙江大学应用外语学院以学生全面发展为本,落实国家关于培养学生自主学习能力的基本教育要求,以建构主义学习观为指导,结合我国大学生及其英语作为外语学习的实际情况和特点,全新修订了《大学英语自主学习能力培养教程(第 4 版)》。全书共十章,分为语言学习元知识体系和外语学习策略训练两部分,从理念、意识和训练三个维度系统培养学生的自主学习能力,使学生由"自觉"达到"自为"。

语言学习元知识体系部分是针对学生外语学习中存在的误区进行的新尝试,包括外语学习理论基础、语言知识、语言测试和应用语言学基础知识四章。目的在于使学生了解人本主义、认知学习理论、建构主义、多元智能理论、二语习得理论、自主学习、学习动机、学习风格、学习策略、元认知、语言评价、高端思维、语言观、语言能力的构成、语言技能测试范畴、语境、体裁、话语、言语行为、跨文化交际和特殊目的英语等与大学英语课程学习密切相关的内容,形成对语言和语言学习的基本认识,改变中学阶段外语学习的某些错误观念,走出外语学习的"误区"。

外语学习策略训练部分与前一部分不同。本部分以任务为驱动,包括词汇学习策略、听力学习策略、口语学习策略、阅读学习策略、写作学习策略和文化学习策略六章。通过系统的策略训练培养学生外语学习的策略意识,发展学生的自主学习能力。

教育的根本目的不再是掌握系统化的知识本身,而是让学生形成正确的学习理念,掌握正确的认知手段和方法,学会如何学习。面对社会与经济的高速发展,发展学生的自主学习能力,进而培养其终身学习的能力已成为教育领域不可回避的课题。

另外,本教程得到全国教育科学"十二五"规划2011年度教育部重点课题"基于体裁的高校学术英语写作能力评价体系研究"(课题批准号GPA115062)和2012年度学位与研究生教育教学改革研究项目"基于体裁的研究生英语读写一体化教学模式研究"(项目编号JGXM_HLJ_2012093)的资助,在本教程修订出版之际,特此感谢。

同时,限于主客观多方面因素,本教程中难免存在不足。恳请广大专家、教师和同学提出宝贵的意见,使我们能够不断完善本教程并使其更好地服务于外语自主学习能力的培养。

严 明
2014年7月

目　　录

第一部分　语言学习元知识体系

第一章　外语学习理论基础 …………………………… 3
　一、人本主义 ………………………………………… 3
　二、认知学习理论 …………………………………… 3
　三、建构主义 ………………………………………… 4
　四、多元智能理论 …………………………………… 4
　五、二语习得理论 …………………………………… 4
　六、自主学习 ………………………………………… 5
　七、学习动机 ………………………………………… 9
　八、学习风格 ………………………………………… 13
　九、学习策略 ………………………………………… 18
　十、元认知 …………………………………………… 22
　十一、语言评价 ……………………………………… 24
　十二、高端思维 ……………………………………… 26

第二章　语言知识 ……………………………………… 28
　一、语言观与语言能力 ……………………………… 28
　二、听力 ……………………………………………… 31
　三、口语 ……………………………………………… 33
　四、阅读 ……………………………………………… 35
　五、写作 ……………………………………………… 37
　六、翻译 ……………………………………………… 39
　七、语法 ……………………………………………… 40

第三章 语言测试 ... 42
一、雅思 ... 42
二、托福 ... 55
三、剑桥商务英语考试(高级) ... 57
四、全国大学英语等级考试(四、六级) ... 61

第四章 应用语言学基础知识 ... 65
一、语境 ... 65
二、体裁 ... 67
三、话语 ... 70
四、言语行为 ... 71
五、特殊目的英语 ... 74

第二部分 外语学习策略训练

第五章 词汇学习策略 ... 79
一、词汇学习中的元认知策略 ... 79
二、词汇学习中的认知策略 ... 83
三、词汇学习中的社交/情感策略 ... 95

第六章 听力学习策略 ... 99
一、听力学习中的元认知策略 ... 99
二、听力学习中的认知策略 ... 106
三、听力学习中的社交/情感策略 ... 116

第七章 口语学习策略 ... 119
一、口语学习中的间接策略 ... 120
二、口语学习中的直接策略 ... 124

第八章 阅读学习策略 ... 138
一、阅读学习中的元认知策略 ... 139
二、阅读学习中的认知策略 ... 147
三、阅读学习中的社交/情感策略 ... 166

第九章 写作学习策略 ... 168
一、过程写作论 ... 169
二、准备写作:开动脑筋,挖掘思路 ... 170

三、开始写作:字斟句酌,组织成文 …… 176
　四、结束写作:修订润色,最终定稿 …… 194

第十章　文化学习策略
　一、文化的定义 …… 196
　二、文化在语言学习中的重要性 …… 197
　三、文化学习的内容 …… 199
　四、文化学习策略 …… 201

附　录 …… 211
　附录一:英语学习情况调查问卷 …… 211
　附录二:学习策略应用调查问卷 …… 215
　附录三:学习风格调查问卷 …… 221

参考文献 …… 226

第一部分
语言学习元知识体系

第一章　外语学习理论基础

本章学习目标
1. 了解人本主义、认知学习理论、建构主义和多元智能理论的基本理念
2. 理解二语习得理论、元认知、语言评价和高端思维的内涵
2. 理解自主学习、学习动机、学习风格和学习策略的内涵

一、人本主义

人本主义认为学习包括四个要素：(1)学习是学生个人从情感和认知两方面，全身心投入的过程，具有参与性；(2)学习是学生自己发现、获得、掌握和领会知识，具有自我发起性；(3)学习会改变学生的行为和态度，乃至个性，具有渗透性；(4)学习具有自我评价性，学生最清楚学习是否满足了他们的需求，是否回答了他们的疑问，是否解答了他们原来不清楚的地方。由此可见，人本主义强调的是调动学生的积极性和主动性，学习是学生不断探索、主动发展的过程。

二、认知学习理论

认知学习理论认为学习过程是学习者根据自己的需要和兴趣，利用过去所掌握的知识、经验，对外界的学习刺激做出主动的、有选择的信息加工的过程。学习者头脑中原有的知识结构对将要获得的知识起着决定作用，新知识的获得以旧知识为基础，原有知识结构不断同化新知识。

对于学习者来说，头脑中的"原有知识结构"不断变化，知识水平不断上升，这样学习本身就具有了层次性，学习者的认知水平也具有了阶段性。在不同的认知发展阶段，学习者所能完成的学习任务具有显著的差异性。为此，学习任务的选择要依据学习者的认知发展水平。另外，认知学习理论重视学习主体——学习者的主观能动性，认为只有发挥学习主体的主观能动性，使其积极主动地投入学习，充分调动自己的内在动机——好奇的内驱力、胜任的内驱力、互惠的内驱力，才能实现学习目标。

三、建构主义

建构主义认为学习不是简单地从外到内的信息输入过程，而是学习者主动的知识建构过程。由于学习者背景各异，他们往往从自己独特的知识背景出发，通过新知识的学习与原有知识经验相互作用，在原有知识或经验的基础上建构对新知识的理解。

由此可见，建构主义强调的是学习者的主动建构，这种建构既包括学习者对新信息意义的建构，同时又包括对自己原有经验的改造与重组。学习者获得知识的多少取决于学习者根据原有经验、心理结构和信念去建构有关知识的能力，而不取决于学习者记忆和背诵教师讲授内容的能力，强调学生的积极主动性。

四、多元智能理论

美国哈佛大学心理学教授加德纳提出了多元智能理论，认为每个人至少有八种智能——语言智能、数理逻辑智能、音乐智能、身体运动智能、空间智能、人际关系智能、自我认识智能和自然观察智能。对于每一个个体来说，这八种智能的组合方式都是不同的，而且其发展也是不平衡的，有的智能项强一些，有的稍弱一些。因此，每一个人都有自己的优势智能和弱势智能。如果你的数学学得不及别人，这并不能说明你的智商低于其他人，只是因为你们的优势智能项不同而已，数学只代表了你的数理逻辑智能项，而这项智能恰好是你的弱势智能，所以你学起数学来有些吃力。不要错误地认为某方面的学业成绩偏低就是智商低。我们要善于发现自己的优势智能，不要用自己的弱势智能和别人的优势智能相比而妄自菲薄。而且我们要充分利用优势智能带动自己的弱势智能。

五、二语习得理论

作为二语习得研究的核心内容，Krashen(1982)的监控理论包括习得与学得假说、自然顺序假说、监控假说、可理解性输入假说和情感过滤假说。

(一) 习得与学得假说

二语习得的过程类似于儿童母语能力的发展,是一种无意识的,在自然语境中关注语言的意义,发展语言的过程。而学得通常发生在语言教学环境中,关注语言的形式和规则,是一个有意识的语言学习过程。

(二) 自然顺序假说

自然顺序假说认为,二语学习和母语学习一样,对语法结构知识的获得都要经历一系列可预测的阶段。有些语法结构先学会,有些则后学会。

(三) 监控假说

监控假说说明了语言学习与语言习得的关系,认为只有来自于语言习得系统的潜意识的语言知识才是语言能力。而有意识学习的语言知识,只有在二语学习者有时间并有意关注语言使用的准确性的时候,才起到监控作用。

(四) 可理解性输入假说

可理解性输入是语言学习发生的必要条件,指学习者接触到的语言输入应该略高于他们现有的语言水平,只有这样才能提高他们的语言能力。一般来,说如果学习者现有的语言水平用"i"来表示,那么他进一步的语言输入应该为"i + 1"。

(五) 情感过滤假说

情感过滤假说说明情感因素对语言学习起到促进或阻碍的作用,影响着学习质量。一般来讲,明确的动机、良好的自信心和低焦虑状态能够为外语学习提供良好的心理环境,使所学习内容易于接受与理解,达到较好的学习效果。

六、自主学习

(一) 自主学习的内涵

1981年,Henri Holect出版著作《自主性与外语学习》,他认为自主学习就是"能够对自己的学习负责",并且认为自主学习能力主要表现在能够:

(1) 确立学习目标；
(2) 确定学习内容和进度；
(3) 选择方法和技巧；
(4) 监控学习过程；
(5) 评估学习结果。

美国研究自主学习的权威心理学家齐莫曼(Zimmerman)自20世纪80年代中期就与一些心理学家致力于自主学习研究。他认为只要学生在元认知、动机和行为三方面都是一个积极的参与者，那么其学习就是自主的。元认知指的是学生能够在学习的不同阶段进行自我反思，包括计划、组织、自我指导、自我监控和自我评价；动机是指学生从被动的学习者变成主动的求知者，由"要我学"变成"我要学"，视自己为有效的自律者；行为是指学生能够自主地创设有利于学习的最佳环境。

庞维国(2003)认为，"自主学习是建立在自我意识发展基础上的'能学'；建立在学生具有内在动机基础上的'想学'；建立在学生掌握了一定的学习策略基础上的'会学'；建立在意志努力基础上的'坚持学'"。

从对自主学习的界定来看，自主学习以学习者为中心(相对以教师为中心)。学习中学生根据自身不同的需求，在整个学习过程中自我规划、自我管理、自我调节、自我检测、自我反馈和自我评价。通常包括以下几个步骤：
(1) 在不同需求的指引下，分清主次，设计自己的中长期目标；
(2) 选择适当的学习材料和学习策略；
(3) 控制好时间和进度；
(4) 根据不同的情况做出适时的调整和反思；
(5) 确立评价标准，衡量自己的学习效果。

(二) 自主学习的必要性

自主学习是整个社会发展的必然，主要体现在以下两个方面：

1. 自主学习是科技发展的必然

21世纪，科学技术飞速发展，知识更新周期大为缩短，知识总量爆炸式增长，学校教育不可能为学生提供一生的知识储备。为此，要想跟上时代发展的步伐，必须打破"一次性"教育定终生的观念，不断地多渠道、多方式、多途径地摄入信息，充实自己，终身学习。

2. 自主学习是个体发展的必然

自主学习有利于个人潜能的发展,是个人发展的根本保证。有效学习能否实现取决于学习者个人的积极主动性的发挥程度。学习者只有自觉自愿地学习,掌握学习主动权,才能作为学习的主体,积极、主动地对知识进行筛选、吸纳、加工、整合、改造和建构,实现有效学习。

(三) 影响自主学习的因素

影响自主学习的因素可归结为两方面,分别是智力因素(主要指学习者的语能)和非智力因素(包括学习态度、学习动机、学习意志、学习策略因素、文化因素和自我管理能力)。

1. 智力因素

智力是学习的前提。语能(语言智商)被认为是智力的一部分。智力是个体一般性的学习能力、理解能力和推理能力,而语能则是个体语言的认知能力。心理学家一般把语言的认知能力归纳为四种:(1)语音的编码能力:能辨别不同语音,形成语音和符号之间的联系,并加以记忆;(2)语法的敏感能力:能辨认出词在句子里的语法功能;(3)语言学习的归纳能力:通过例句能够推测和归纳语言规则;(4)语言的记忆能力:能快速而有效地形成文字与意义之间的联系,并加以记忆。

2. 非智力因素

(1)学习态度

态度是影响个人对特定对象做出行为选择的有组织的内部准备状态或反应的倾向性。(邵瑞真,2000)学习者如果没有正确的态度,自主学习就很难开展下去,也无法将学习坚持到底。就学习态度而言,学习者应具备良好的自我效能感,能够正确归因。

1) 自我效能感

自我效能感是指个体相信自己有能力完成某种或某类任务,是个体的能力和自信心在某些活动中的具体体现。(庞维国,2003)首先,学生的自我效能感会影响学生对任务的选择。学生倾向于选择那些自认为能够完成的学习任务,回避自认为难以完成的任务。其次,学生的自我效能感会影响学生在某项学习任务上付出多少努力、遇到困难时能够坚持多长时间、面临复杂的情境时有多强的适应能力。高自我效能的学生更有可能花费更多的努力去争取成功。再者,学生的自我效能会影响学生在完成某项学习任务时所体验到的紧张和焦虑感。高自我效能感的学生在从事学习任务时冷静、沉着,更多地关注学习中的问题,而低自我效能感的学生会感到紧张不安。

2) 归因

归因是个体对自己的成功或失败所做出的因果解释。一般学习的成败可归因于四类因素,即能力、努力、任务难度和运气。能力是一种内在的、稳定的、不可控制的因素;努力是一种内在的、不稳定的可控因素;任务难度是一种外在的、稳定的、可控因素;而运气则是外在的、不稳定的、难以控制的因素。学习成败归因不同,对学习产生的影响也不同。如果个体把自己的学习成功归因于能力,把学习失败归因于努力不够,就容易激发学习的主动性和自信心,自主学习;如果个体把自己的学业成功归因于外部不可控的因素——运气,把学业失败归因于自身能力不足,就会影响其情感状态,可能形成低效能感,降低学习的自主性。一般而言,自主学习者倾向于把自己的学业成败归因于可以弥补或纠正的原因,这种归因通常会引发积极的自我反应。

(2) 学习动机

动机对语言学习者有巨大的推动作用。只有当学习者拥有了强烈的学习动机,有了"我要学"的念头之后,才会积极主动地去思考"学什么"和"怎样学"等问题,才会制定明确的学习目标,克服困难,主动寻求知识。学习动机是培养自主学习的前提。若缺少学习动机则会妨碍和阻止自主学习的实施。

(3) 学习意志

意志在学习中主要表现为两方面的作用。首先,意志能够维持学习活动。在学习过程中一定会遇到各种各样的困难,而要想克服困难,将学习坚持到底,学习者的意志力就要发挥维持作用。这种维持作用主要表现为学习者的恒心,即持之以恒,能够不折不扣、矢志不渝地坚持学习。其次,意志能够调控学习活动。在学习活动中,学习者有时会产生某种妨碍学习进程的心理与行为,如当行不行、当止不止等。学习意志发挥的调控作用可以克服这种障碍,使得学习活动顺利进行。这种调控主要表现在发挥积极的心理成分,制止消极心理因素。

(4) 学习策略因素

学习策略的正确使用被认为与自主学习能力的提高有着最直接的关

系。研究结果表明,外语学习好的人经常使用某些特定的学习策略来提高外语学习效率和应用能力。

(5) **文化因素**

文化因素影响着学习者的行为、学习价值观、思维习惯,直接影响学习效果。现代外语教学模式从以教师为中心逐渐转变为以学生为中心,学习者应该为自己的学习承担责任,在学习过程中有更多的选择和更大的自主权。这种教育观和文化习俗的改变有利于学生的个性化发展与创新能力的培养,也是培养自主学习能力的前提条件。

(6) **自我管理能力**

大学的学习方式与以往的学习方式不同。学生要提高自我管理的意识,增强自我管理能力,具备能够明确学习目的、确立学习目标、统筹时间、制订学习计划和利用学习资源的能力。在妥善管理自己学习的同时,充分调动自身认知、情感、行为等因素共同参与学习的过程,发挥自身的主观能动性,真正成为学习的主人。

七、学习动机

(一) 学习动机的含义

学习动机是指个体由一种学习目标或对象引导、激发和维持学习活动的内在心理过程或内部动力。学习动机一旦形成,不仅对所学的东西有一定的指向性,而且也能使学习者在学习过程中的注意状态、兴趣水平保持下去,在遇到困难时有克服困难的意志力。

学习动机与学习目的不尽相同。学习动机指的是引起学习的原因,而学习目的则指的是学习活动所要达到的结果。学习目的相同的学生,其学习动机不一定相同;学习动机相同的学生,其学习目的也可能不同。学习动机与学习目的可能相互转化,在一种情境下的学习动机,也可能是另一种情境下的学习目的。

影响学习动机的因素主要有两个:一个是强烈的认知兴趣和求知欲。在这种欲望驱使下,学习者能够放弃其他一切,执着地探寻未知的东西,最终成就学业。强烈的学习动机,能转化为坚强的学习意志。意志的强弱决定了智力活动能否持续进行,能否克服困难,勇往直前。

另外一个影响学习动机的因素是改变自身生存环境的强烈要求。如有些家庭经济状况比较困难的学生,在他们改变自身生存环境的潜意识驱使下,学习相当刻苦,这类学生只要注意学习方法的正确引导,成绩一般提高较快。

  大量的事实表明,许多成功的学习者都具有强烈的学习动机,即他们总是怀着"我要学"的自觉要求,积极主动地进行学习,因此能够不断地提高学习效果。

(二) 学习动机的特点

1. 多元化

  多元化指学习动机多种多样,学习者的学习往往受多种动机支配。由于每个学习者的家庭背景、教育背景、生活经历及对未来的打算不同,学习动机呈现出多元化的特点。有的是对某一学科有着浓厚的兴趣,希望自己在学业上有所作为;有的是为了改变自己的生活现状,希望将来能谋求到一个理想的工作;有的是为了提高自身地位,获得他人的尊重;有的是为将来的进一步深造打基础;有的则是为了学到更多的知识和本领,将来能为国家建设和社会发展多做贡献;如此等等。在学习过程中,往往是几种动机同时存在,但在一定时期总有一个主导性动机起到支配作用。

2. 社会性

  随着对社会认识的不断深入和社会责任感的不断增强,越来越多的学习者能自觉地把自己当前的学习与国家建设和社会发展的需要联系起来,能认识到自己所学的专业知识和技能在未来社会发展中的作用,希望能尽快适应社会。学习动机的社会性意义日趋广泛,特别是大学高年级的学生,随着对所学专业的深入了解,学习动机的社会性更加突出,这也是当代大学生奋发进取、努力学习的主要动力。

3. 可变性

  学习动机在学习过程中并非一成不变,而是随着社会环境、教育环境、个人经历、思想、需要、兴趣、情绪及家庭等因素的不断变化而变化的。学习动机还存在着强弱变化的现象。但是,学习动机并非越强越好。学习动机过强,会使学习者的注意力高度集中,注意的范围相应变小。而且,学习动机过强,容易造成心情过分紧张,产生焦虑情绪,使记忆活动中的再现发生困难,反而影响正常的学习。

(三) 学习动机的分类

1. 社会语言学视角下的分类

(1) 融入型动机(Integrative Motivation)。具有这种动机的学习者喜欢并欣赏所学的语言以及与所学语言相联系的文化,希望自己能掌握和自由运用该语言。这样的学习者被认为拥有内在的、更加持久的语言学习动机。

(2) 工具型动机(Instrumental Motivation)。工具型动机学习者则是将目标语看作一种工具,希望掌握目标语后能给自己带来实惠,如提高自己的社会地位和经济收入等。这种学习动机在于将外语作为一种获得其他利益的工具。

2. 认知语言学视角下的分类

从认知语言学的角度,学习动机还可以分为内在动机(Intrinsic Motivation)和外在动机(Extrinsic Motivation)。所谓内在动机,是指外语学习本身能激发学习者的兴趣和愉悦。如日常生活中碰到的人、物、事,具有内在动机的学习者总会情不自禁地用英语表达出来。他们能在学习活动中得到满足,积极地参与学习过程,而且他们具有好奇心,喜欢挑战,在解决问题时具有独立性。内在动机能对外语学习产生更积极的推动作用,因为它能使学习者保持持久的兴趣。所谓外在动机,是指学习外语的动因存在于学习活动本身之外,是为了得到奖赏或避免惩戒才学习外语,如为了得到老师表扬或是为了避免批评、惩罚等。

(四) 激发学习动机

1. 明确学习目标,端正学习态度

首先要充分认识到英语学习的价值。对英语学习者来讲,可以把英语看成是一个目标,目标的价值越大,它给予个体的激励值越大。只有认识充分,有充足的思想准备,才能充分调动学习英语的热情,保持动机不减退。其次,确立学习目标是非常重要的,有了明确的目标,就会有学习的动力。有了学习动力就能有足够的心理准备克服各种挫折,做到锲而不舍。

2. 培养学习兴趣

在学习动机中,最为活跃和最为现实的心理成分就是学习兴趣,它往往决定着学习者大脑这部"机器"的工作效率。学习兴趣是人们渴求获得知识的一种愉快的情绪表现。有学习兴趣的学习者会对学习产生满足感,学习对他们来说是一种愉快体验,这种体验会增强学习动机;反之,对学习没有兴趣的学习者会对学习产生一种苦恼的情绪,这种情绪会降低学习动机的强度。

3. 正确对待成功与失败

一般地说,成功的体验有利于增加一个人的自信,激发学习的热情,增强学习动机;失败的体验容易使人产生焦虑感和自卑感,降低学习动机的强度。大学生应对自己在学习中取得的成功和遭遇到的失败做出正确的归因,不应因暂时的失败而失去信心,要学会克服学习中的各种困难和由失败造成的不良情绪。任何人在学习中遇到失败都是难免的,关键是要正确对待,找出原因,改进方法,坚定信心。

4. 充分利用学习反馈

评估和测试的一个重要功能就是提供反馈。反馈在学习中的作用表现在两个方面:一是激励作用。了解了自己学习的状况,奋发努力,增强自信。二是提供信息。反馈可以使正确或错误的认识得到证实,模糊的认识得到澄清。通过反馈也可以区分出已掌握的和尚未掌握的部分,以便把精力集中在学习的薄弱环节,提高学习效率。

教师提供的成绩单、评语或同学之间的评价、互评等都是反馈信息,都可以作为掌握学习情况的依据。学生要及时关注反馈信息,调整自己的学习。

5. 创设英语情景,积极主动地投入学习

英语语言情景是运用英语交流的必要因素。在学习一门外语的时候,除了教师的作用之外,学生自己也需要创造一个良好的学习氛围和情景。在现今的社会里,适合的语言环境是很容易得到的。比如,各种各样的英文网站、英语演讲、各类重要活动新闻发布会的英文翻译、英语广播、英语电

影、夏令营、英语角等都能让我们置身于英语的环境中。在良好的语言环境中，能够熟练地掌握那些你曾经不擅长的技巧，如听、说、表演，你会发觉其实英语离你很近，你很愿意接触它、学好它，这样才能最大限度地激发学习英语的动机，积极主动地投入到学习当中。

八、学习风格

（一）学习风格的界定

学习风格就像每个人的签名一样独特，它受到先天和后天因素的影响，具有生物学遗传和后天发展的特点，是学习者在学习过程中经常采用的习惯性学习方式和倾向。具有如下特征：

· 学习风格是学习者喜欢的或者经常使用的学习方式或者倾向；
· 学习风格相对比较稳定，很少因学习内容和学习情景而变化；
· 每个学习者的学习风格都有自己的特点，与别人存在差异。

（二）学习风格的分类

学习风格是一种自然的感知、认知和情感上的倾向。一般可以从感知方式、认知方式和个性特点三个主要维度进行分类。学习风格没有好坏之分，以下几种对学习风格的分类也并不是排他的，只是帮助我们从不同的角度全面了解学习风格。

1. 感知方式

按照学习者对外部信息的感知方式划分，共有三种倾向：视觉型、听觉型和动觉型。

（1）视觉型（Visual Type）

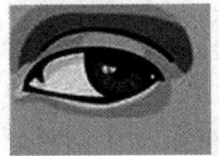

即喜欢用眼睛学习的人。视觉型学习者善于通过"看"来接收信息，直观形象的视觉材料能在学习者脑海中形成清晰的视觉形象。他们通过看书本、黑板与屏幕上的文字材料、图片、图表以及录像就能获得良好的学习效果。通过阅读能够更好地理解和记忆所学的信息。课堂上，如果老师只是单纯地口头讲授知识，视觉型学习者会感到很难理解，他们更愿意"看到"所学的知识，因此老师的板书会对他们十分有帮助。这种类型的学习者愿意记笔记,喜欢独自学习,擅长快速浏览学习材料,接受视觉材料效果好,易看懂图表,书面测验得分高。

（2）**听觉型**(Auditory Type)

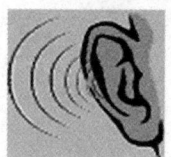
即喜欢用耳朵学习的人。听觉型学习者善于通过"听"来接收信息,听口头解释就能获得良好的学习效果。他们喜欢通过听录音带、听报告、听对话等方式获取信息。在学习新材料时,通过大声朗读或在阅读过程中进行默读可以更好地储存信息。课堂上,听觉型学习者能轻松地听懂老师的口头讲授,他们擅长语音辨析,口头表达能力强,但是书写对他们来说通常有一定困难。这种类型学习者喜欢在有背景声音的环境中学习,喜欢小组活动。

（3）**动觉型**(Kinesthetic / Tactile Type)

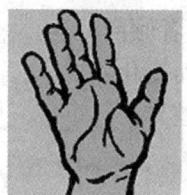
即喜欢通过实践和直接经验来学习的人。动觉型学习者喜欢通过参与活动、自己动手或亲身体验来获得知识。他们喜欢动手尝试,乐于在"做中学",善于执行计划并愿意参与新的富有挑战性的活动。动觉型学习者在操作性技能的学习中表现突出。他们的特点是运动感强,平衡感好。他们通过亲身参与课堂活动、角色扮演、实习活动和做实验等能获得良好的学习效果。

对于语言学习者来说,应该充分利用自己的感官偏爱和风格优势,多感官多渠道地接收语言信息,这样才能有效地将语言知识消化吸收。大多数优秀的语言学习者既善于通过"看",又善于通过"听"来获得语言输入。所以,在语言学习中,要了解自己感知方式的特点和倾向,尽量发挥自己的优势,同时又要有意识地扩展接收信息的渠道,最大限度调动自己学习的潜能。

2. 认知方式

认知方式是指人们组织、分析和回忆新的信息和经验的方式。在认知方式上,学习者表现出不同的倾向性,主要有以下几种方式:

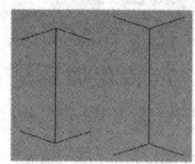
（1）**场依赖型与场独立型**(Field – dependent Type & Field – independent Type)

场依赖者往往依靠外部提供的有关信息,倾向于从整体上认知事物,他们易受外界因素的干扰,不善于独立分析问题。

Which is longer?

场独立者往往依靠自己内部具有的知识框架,倾向于自己独立分析问题,他们不易受外界因素干扰,能洞察出超越事物本身以外的事物间的相互关系,能够很容易地把重要细节从复杂的背景中区分出来,善于借助视觉和直觉线索。

一般来说,场依赖型学习者社交能力强,场独立型学习者分析能力强。场依赖和场独立是一个连续体,在连续体的一端是场依赖,另一端是场独立。大多数的学习者介于这两种类型之间。只要创造适当的条件,场独立和场依赖型的学习者都可以获得成功。

(2) **思考型与冲动型**(Reflective Type & Impulsive Type)

思考型学习者一般能够约束自己的行为,抗拒外界诱惑。他们在碰到问题时倾向于深思熟虑,用充足的时间考虑、审视问题,权衡各种问题解决的方法,然后从中选择一个满足多种条件的最佳方案,因而较少犯错误。他们在学习过程中的思维方式以反省为特征,逻辑性强,有较强的批判性,乐于在合作的情境中学习。

冲动型学习者则倾向于很快地检验假设,根据问题的部分信息或未对问题做透彻的分析就仓促地凭借自己的直觉推测答案,他们反应速度较快,但容易发生错误。冲动型学习者在学习过程中的思维方式以冲动为特征,直觉性强,乐于在竞争的情境中学习。这两种风格的学习者各有利弊如下表所示:

	思考型	冲动型
优势	口语表达中准确性高 阅读中准确性高 经过仔细的思考才采取行动	愿意在课堂上讲英语 阅读速度快 在限定时间的考试中表现突出
缺点	讲话之前犹豫太久 阅读速度慢 在限定时间的考试中完成得慢	口语表达不够准确 阅读中准确性低 没经过足够的思考就采取行动

(3) **整体型与细节型**(Global Type & Particular Type)

What do you see first?

整体型学习者学习时喜欢抓住重点或者大意,全面看待问题,思维的深刻性、准确性较低,直觉性、模糊性较高。即使遇到不认识的词汇或不懂的概念也能很好地与别人进行交流,他们能从几个角度对问题进行预测和观察,并与其他题联系起来考虑。

细节型学习者则关注具体的规则和细节,善于记住具体的信息,而且擅长逻辑分析和对比,善于以精细的逻辑形式理解各种信息,经常把宽泛的概念分解成若干小的单位来学习,擅长发现事物之间的差异。在语言学习中,细节型学习者关注语法规则,对新的词组和单词比较敏感。

(4) **左脑主导型与右脑主导型**(Left – brain Type & Right – brain Type)

根据人们左右脑处理信息的倾向,学习风格可以分成左脑型与右脑型。有人把语言学习比喻成可变焦距的照相机。你能通过放大镜关注每个词的意思及语法规则是如何应用的,你也可以通过广角镜头来识别别人讲话的大意。前一种学习者属于左脑型,他们喜欢使用放大镜来学习,喜欢关注细节,有很强的逻辑性和分析能力,擅长学习数学;后一种学习者属于右脑型,他们善于用广角镜头来学习,他们喜欢抓大意,相信直觉,有很强的灵活性,喜欢音乐和艺术。

左脑和右脑是一个统一的整体,无论学习什么,都会同时用到左脑和右脑。当我们在分析问题、发现规律、注意细节、利用直觉找出大意的时候,往往是左右脑并用才能找到解决问题的最佳答案。语言学习者要正确处理好学习中左右脑的关系,根据具体情况使用"放大镜"或者"广角镜"来解决问题,发挥两侧大脑的优势,这样才能成为有效的学习者。

3. 个性特点

根据学习者的个性特点,学习风格又可分为:外向型与内向型、封闭型与开放型、随机 – 直觉型与具体 – 程序型。

(1) **外向型与内向型**(Extrovert Type & Introvert Type)

外向型学习者关注外部世界,他们开朗、热情、喜欢与人交流,兴趣广泛,给别人以较好的印象。在课堂上,他们愿意参与游戏、对话、小组讨论、角色扮演等交际性的活动。内向型学习者一般关注内部世界,能够集中注意力,喜欢独处,不愿意与人多接触,兴趣不多但对个人喜欢者却很精通,沉默寡言,不善于表达自己的思想。在课堂上,他们喜欢独立思考,喜欢自己独立完成任务,或者与比较熟悉的同学做两人的学习活动。

外向型学习者善于利用一切机会使用英语,他们讲话多,在交际场合中显得自信大方,善于表达自己的思想,而且不怕犯错误,因此,口语表达更流利。内向型学习者一般因为怕出错而不愿意主动运用新学的语言,但是他们愿意集中注意力,独立思考解决问题,愿意花更多的时间研究和练习语言形式,因此对语言结构的理解更加全面和准确。

如果你是外向型学习者,那么你应该注意,仅仅注重口语的流利性是不够的,语言使用的准确性也同样重要。如果你是内向型学习者,那么你应该让自己在课堂上多"冒险"讲英语,增加自己使用英语的机会,提高语言使用的流利程度。

(2) **封闭型与开放型**(Closure – oriented Type & Open – oriented Type)

按照接收信息的方式划分,学习风格有封闭型与开放型之分。

封闭型学习者善于决策和行动,他们善于制订计划并按规定的期限完成任务,希望掌控并且尽快完成学习任务。学习刻苦有决心,不易受挫折,能够认真地对待所有的学习任务,在规定的时间期限内完成任务,而且会提前为学习任务做准备。

开放型学习者善于收集信息,不急于下结论,通常会在广泛地获取信息和经验的基础上才下结论。他们喜欢灵活、顺其自然的学习方式,喜欢放松地享受学习过程,把学习当成娱乐,能从语言学习中获得乐趣。他们偶尔也制订计划,但是不常检查计划完成情况,他们具有很大的灵活性和可变性,对歧义的容忍程度高,不关心规则也不重视规定的时间期限,喜欢通过自然的方式收集信息和发现式的学习。

(3) **随机 – 直觉型与具体 – 程序型**(Random – intuitive Type & Concrete – sequential Type)

根据加工信息的方式,学习风格又可以分为随机 – 直觉型和具体 – 程序型两种。

随机 – 直觉型学习者面向未来,爱推测可能性,善于发现事物的主要规律,常以随机的方式处理事情,喜欢抽象思考。比如要求随机 – 直觉型学习者给出5个例子,他们往往会给出4个或6个,不喜欢循规蹈矩的程序化的授课方式。

具体 – 程序型学习者面向现在,他们只关心眼前的任务,喜欢按部就班的学习活动,善于使用各种记忆策略。学习上讲究先后步骤,会严格遵照指令办事,往往将教师的话当成真理、刨根问底。如要求具体 – 程序型学习者给出5个例子,他们往往会严格遵照指令给出5个例子。课堂上,具体 – 程序型学习者喜欢分解式的课堂任务,一次完成一个步骤,而且希望能够在每个步骤中及时得到反馈。

学习风格总体上无好坏之分,每个人在学习风格上各有优势与局限性。任何一种学习风格都不是绝对的,不同的学习风格可以相互兼容和转换,优秀的外语学习者应该能够根据不同的学习任务,灵活地交替运用与语言任务相适应的学习风格,通过多种途径最大限度地接收信息,获得知识,从而全面提高外语水平。

九、学习策略

(一) 学习策略(Learning Strategies)的含义

学习策略是指学习者为了使学习的过程更成功、更愉悦、更自觉、更有目的而采取的行为或行动。(Oxford,1990)学习策略的使用是学习者有意识的行为,它不但包括学习者对语言学习的认识,也包括完成学习活动的具体做法或技巧。它与人们经常提到的"学习方法"有很大的不同。下表归纳了二者主要的区别:

学习策略	学习方法
操控层面	技术层面
大脑中的信息处理过程;不易观察	具体手段;更容易被观察和习得
有意识的行为	有意识或无意识的行为

首先,学习策略高于学习方法。学习策略的使用实际上是管理与协调技巧的过程,学习方法的使用主要是针对具体的活动而采取的解决手段。有人把方法与策略之间的关系与足球队作了形象的类比,二者的区别类似于足球中的"技术"和"战术"。一个足球运动员在一场比赛中可能会运用很多技巧,如传球、带球、射门等,这些都是技术问题。然而,要在比赛中取胜,他必须要知道什么时候使用这些技巧并把它们有效地组合。这要求他除了掌握技巧和方法之外,还要密切观察周遭的情况,如什么时候传球,把球传到左边还是右边,要根据实际情况做出恰当的选择。这就是战术的问题了。在语言学习中,学习者在学习过程中处理具体问题的技术或技巧,类似于足球中的技术;而对何时使用这些技术做出的决策以及对技术本身的认识,类似于足球中的战术。这里用一个例子来说明:我们遇到生词可以查字典,也可以通过上下文来猜测,还可以问老师或同学。这些都是具体的方法或技巧。但是,一般来说,这些方法并不是同时使用,而是要选择其中的一种,选择哪种方法需要根据自己的学习风格及当时的情况做出决策。这个决策过程就是学习策略使用的过程。

其次,学习策略与学习方法的外显程度是不同的。有些策略涉及计划、评价和目标的设定等,它们是大脑中信息的加工和处理过程,是无法观察到的。这就是为什么教师很难了解学生学习策略的使用情况,即使在录音机和闭路电视等仪器的帮助下也很难察觉。而学习方法是学习者为了解决某个学习问题或活动,或为了使学习过程更有效而采取的具体做法和手段。相对学习策略而言,学习方法具有外显性,更容易被观察和习得。

最后,学习策略的一个重要特征是自觉性和目的性。策略是发生在大脑中为特定的学习目的而采用的一系列的技巧。这就涉及对已有技巧的选择、排列,必要的时候还要做出及时的修正。

综上所述,学习策略比学习方法涵盖的内容要更宏观、更广泛,它处于指导和管理学习方法的层面。

(二) 学习策略的分类

由于分类标准不同,学习策略有多种不同的分法。其中具有普遍意义的是 O'Malley 和 Chamot (1990) 的分法,认为学习策略分为元认知策略、认知策略和社交/情感策略。

1. 元认知策略 (Metacognitive Strategies)

元认知策略是指学习者在学习过程中所采取的计划、监控及评估等手段,具体包括:确定和调整学习目标、选择学习方法和技巧、对学习过程和结果进行评价和反思等。一个有效的学习过程应该是这样的:首先,确立一个(或几个)明确的学习目标,这个(些)目标可能是长期目标或是短期目标,然后制订学习计划并执行计划来达到目标,在实施计划的过程中要采取必要的手段保证计划的顺利进行,如果出现了问题,分析为什么会出现问题,并寻求帮助来解决问题。常见的元认知策略有事先计划、指导性注意(事先决定把注意力集中在某个学习任务上)、功能准备(事先为将要执行的某个语言学习任务做好准备)、选择性注意、自我管理、自我监控和自我评估。

2. 认知策略 (Cognitive Strategies)

认知策略与元认知策略虽然仅有一字之差,但是二者有着本质性的差别。认知策略是属于信息处理和加工过程中直接和具体的行为,是学习者在完成学习活动的过程中用到的具体解决问题的方法。例如,在阅读中,很多人习惯通过上下文的线索来猜测生词的意思,这是一种典型的认知策略。

其实,外语学习者在学习过程中一直都在不间断地使用各种各样的认知策略,如重复、分类、关键词、推断、预测、联想和记笔记等。

3. 社交/情感策略(Social/Affective Strategies)

语言不是一种个人的行为,而是一种社会行为。它是发生在人与人之间的具体的交流。因此,在语言学习的过程中,使用社交策略是必要的,也是重要的。

(1) 社交策略

社交策略主要有三个:①提出问题;②与他人合作;③从他人的角度出发考虑问题。如下图所示:

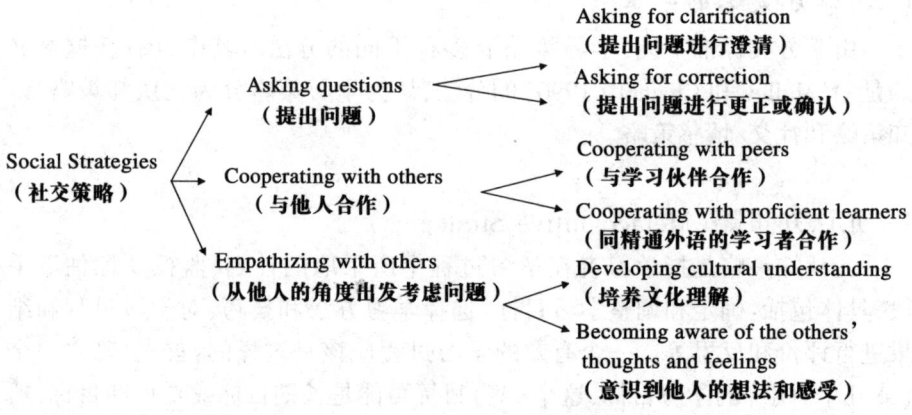

提出问题是最基本的社交策略之一。通过提问学习者可以弄清楚不确定的知识、证实自己的想法,同时可以获取更多的信息。一般来说,提问有两个目的:一是对不理解的内容进行澄清,二是确定信息是否正确。然而,很多外语学习者不愿意问问题,不敢问问题,甚至不懂装懂,这样就错失了许多巩固知识、更新知识的机会。

与他人合作也是一个重要的社交策略,学习者互相交流想法和经验,共同研究策划并完成一个共同目标。通过与其他学习者合作,可以促进相互依赖和相互支持。

为了达到成功的语言交际,学会从他人的角度出发考虑问题是一个重要的策略。对于外语学习者来说,由于文化差异,运用这个策略比较困难。

这就需要学习者增强文化理解,提高文化差异的敏感度,善于根据交际对象的文化背景来考虑问题。许多语言交际的失败并不是由语言的应用错误造成的,而是由文化差异引起的误解造成的。

(2)情感策略

情感策略指语言学习者在学习的过程中,通过自己的情绪、态度、动机和价值观等个体因素来影响语言学习。情感策略一般包括降低焦虑、自我鼓励和检测情绪状况。如下图所示:

降低焦虑感的一个重要策略就是采取一些放松的手段,如放松身体、听音乐、看电影。这些手段有的时候并不是学习者不了解,只是被忽视了。

自我鼓励也是一个非常有效的情感策略。它能够帮助学习者转变原来学习外语的消极态度,增强信心。

要控制好情感因素,外语学习者需要定期了解自己的情绪状况,以及为什么会有那些状况。并且最好把那些状况记录下来,以便日后对照不同时间的变化情况。要让自己来掌控自己的情感状况,而不是别人。

语言学习中学习策略的使用是一个非常复杂的过程,任何一类策略都不是孤立使用的。一般来说,完成一个语言活动会同时用到三类策略,在活动的不同阶段用到的策略也会不同。

由于学习活动性质的不同,再加上学习者学习风格差异等因素的影响,哪些策略适合于哪些活动并没有一个现成的答案。因此,如何选择恰当的策略需要学习者在实践中不断摸索,逐步找到适合自己的行之有效的策略。

十、元认知

元认知作为一种高端思维过程,支配人的认知过程,可以将其简单地理解为是关于思维的思维或者是关于认知的认知。(Wellman,1985:1)它以认知主体的认知系统为认知对象,对认知过程进行监控、评价、反馈和调节。

(一) 元认知与认知的区别

元认知与认知活动的区别主要体现在活动内容和作用方式方面。就活动内容而言,认知活动的内容通常是具体事物和心智意向,以取得认知进展为目的,例如在外语学习的过程中运用认知策略记忆单词,目的是为了记住单词,增加词汇量。元认知活动的内容则是关于认知的知识、技能和信息等,是对认知过程本身的认知,对认知过程进行监控、反馈和调节,以促进认知活动的有效进行,例如在单词的记忆过程中,思考记忆方式是否得当,是否还有更为有效的记忆方法,进而对认知做出调整。

无论是认知活动还是元认知活动,其目的都是取得认知效果和认知进展,使认知主体认识认知客体,但二者的作用方式截然不同。认知活动直接作用于客观认知对象,而元认知活动则作用于认知过程本身,通过对认知过程的监控、反馈和调节等,优化认知过程,提高认知效率,更好地促进认知发展。

(二) 元认知模型

元认知一直是心理学和教学领域关注的焦点。在对元认知进行解释和界定的同时,以 Flavell(1979)为代表提出了元认知模型,认为元认知主要包括元认知知识和元认知体验,系统解析了元认知的构成。

1. 元认知知识(Metacognitve Knowledge)

Flavell(1979)认为元认知知识是个体所具有的关于各类认知任务、目的、行为和经验的知识,包括个体元认知知识、任务元认知知识和策略元认知知识。

(1) 个体元认知知识

个体元认知知识是认知个体对自己和他人作为认知加工者所具有的本

质特征的认识,包括对个体内差异、个体间差异和认知普遍性的认识。对个体内差异的认识是指个体应该对自己的兴趣、爱好、学习习惯和能力等有较好的了解,同时知道如何克服自己在认知方面存在的不足;对个体间差异的认识指个体能够意识到个体间存在认知差异;对认知普遍性的认识指个体要能够意识到存在不同程度和种类的理解,理解有不同的水平,人的认知能力是可改变的。

(2) **任务元认知知识**

任务元认知知识是关于认知任务的信息,即任务要求、目的和认知材料的特点等。认知主体要能够意识到认知材料的性质、长度、熟悉度、结构特点、呈现方式和逻辑结构等内容对认知效果的影响,应该对当前的认知任务的要求和目标有明确的认识,以增强认知活动的针对性。

(3) **策略元认知知识**

策略元认知知识包括策略和策略使用的知识,使个体能在不同的认知任务中,恰当地运用各类策略,实现特定认知效果。一般个体要对策略的种类、各类策略的优缺点、应用条件和常见的应用效果等信息有所了解。尤其是要具备通过策略元认知知识,对认知过程进行监控、评价、反馈和调整的能力。

2. 元认知体验(Metacognitive Experience)

元认知体验在认知过程中产生,是伴随认知活动过程的认知或情感体验。认知或情感体验可以是瞬间的,也可以具有持续性,可以发生在认知活动的任一阶段,例如在认知活动开始之前我们可能会预感到活动是否能顺利进行,或在活动中我们能够意识到我们已经取得什么样的进展或者会产生什么情况等。同时,Flavell(1979)猜测元认知体验更倾向于发生在能够激发学习者有意识思考的情景中。通常这类情景中的认知决定具有重要性,认知行为需要大胆尝试,认知活动给认知者带来更多的认知或情感体验,需要有足够的时间进行事先计划和事后评价。

在认知活动中元认知知识和元认知体验相互交织作用。"元认知体验有助于人们确定新的目标、修改或放弃旧的目标(比如,困惑或失败的体验都可以产生这种作用),有助于激活认知策略和元认知策略,另一方面人们的元认知知识又大多来源于人们对认知活动的监控、调节的实际过程,善于对认知活动进行自觉或不自觉调节的人,自然会有更多的元认知体验和经验,从而具有更多的元认知知识。"(严明,2008:126)

十一、语言评价

语言评价的总体目标是改善语言教学和强化语言学习,包括信息(学习表现信息)、解释(对所获信息的解释)和决策(依据前两点做决策)三个基本要素。(Genesee & Upshur,1996)由于目的和功能的不同,语言评价分为终结性评价和形成性评价。

(一)终结性评价与形成性评价的界定

终结性评价在一定时间的教学后进行,考察学生在前一段学习中知识的掌握情况,测定并记录学生的成绩,学生以取得高分为目的,并认为分数越高学得越多越好。终结性评价通常以正规考试的形式进行,如期末考试、中考和高考等。重在考查学习结果,而不是调控学习过程。

形成性评价一般贯穿整个学习过程,通过多种途径诊断学习过程中存在的问题,为教与学提供即时的反馈信息,监控优化学习过程,提高学习质量。

(二)形成性评价的分类

依据评价主体的不同,形成性评价又可进一步分为学生自我评价、学生间互评和教师评价三类。

1. 学生自我评价

学生是评价的主体,肩负评价自我的责任。在评价的起始阶段,教师要对学生自我评价方式、方法、评价内容和标准等进行有效的引导,使学生有的放矢。在引导学生自评的过程中,培养学生对学习过程的自我反思、信息反馈、监控和调节意识。在评价的过程中正确认识自我,形成良好的学习和思维习惯。

2. 学生间互评

学生间互评不仅要求学生对自己负责,同时要对他人负责。客观公正地对他人的学习行为做出判断,对他人的学习过程进行及时有效的信息反馈。学生互评中教师同样要起到引导的作用,提供明确的评价内容和标准,明确评价的方式、方法,让学生知道评什么,怎么评。在互评的过程中培养学生的合作意识,学会客观公正地对待自己与他人,互相学习,互相促进,共同进步。

3. 教师评价

教师作为一个成熟的评价主体,要对学生的行为表现具有敏感性,能够依据学生细微的行为表现对学生的学习以及心理状况做出较为准确的推断,提供及时的信息反馈,对学生学习过程中出现的学习问题以及心理波动提出较为合理的解决方案,帮助学生有效地展开学习。教师评价渗透在学生学习过程中的各个环节,通过观察、访谈、提问和测试等多种形式进行。教师依据即时反馈,对教学计划和手段及时做出调整,给予个别学生以相应的关注,优化教学过程,提高教学有效性,服务于有效学习。

(三)形成性评价的特征

形成性评价是师生双方共同收集学习信息,反思、调整、优化教与学的过程,具有发展性、主体性、多元性和过程性等特征。

1. 发展性

形成性评价的目的不是针对学生的学业成绩对其进行区分,而是对教学和学习进行动态调控,优化学生的学习过程,实现有效学习,促进学生发展。

2. 主体性

终结性评价中学生是被评者,缺乏主动性。形成性评价中学生具有双重身份,既是评价的主体,同时又是评价的客体。学生参与评价过程,具有一定的主体性。

3. 多元性

多元性指形成性评价的评价方式、评价主体、评价内容等的多元化。形成性评价可以以观察、问卷调查、访谈、学习档案、测试、活动记录等多种方式进行;评价主体有学生、家长和教师等多重主体;评价内容不仅包括知识技能,同时关注学生的学习策略、文化意识和情感态度等。

4. 过程性

形成性评价贯穿教学的各个阶段、各个环节,渗透于整个教学过程,对教学进行监督、反馈和调整。

十二、高端思维

(一) 教育目标分类研究

1. Bloom 的目标分类

Bloom(1956)认为教育目标分为知识(knowledge)、理解(comprehension)、应用(application)、分析(analysis)、综合(synthesis)和评价(evaluation)六类。其中,除了应用,Bloom 对其他五类目标进行了更为详细的划分。

- 知识分为细节知识(例如术语或具体事实等)、应对细节的方式、方法知识和某一领域的普遍与抽象知识(包括理论、结构和原则知识);
- 理解分为转化(translation)、解释和推断;
- 分析包括要素分析、关系分析和组织原则分析;
- 综合分为独特交流的实施、计划的制订和一系列抽象关系的衍生;
- 评价又进一步分为依据内部证据的评价和依据外部标准的判断。

2. Anderson & Krathwohl 的目标分类

Anderson & Krathwohl(2001)对其教育目标分类进行了修改,保留了原来的六类。但将原来的名词称谓改为动词性称谓,分别为记忆(remembering)、理解(understanding)、应用(applying)、分析(analyzing)、评价(evaluating)和创造(creating)。

* 记忆指长时记忆检索相关知识,包括识别和回忆;
* 理解是指判定口头、书面或图表交际中的教育信息的意义,包括释义、示例、分类、总结、推理、比较和解释;
* 应用是在特定的情景中使用某一程序,包括执行和生效;
* 分析是指将材料分解为若干组成部分,探讨各部分之间以及各部分与整体结构和目标是是如何相关联的;
* 评价是依据标准做出判断,包括检查和鉴审;
* 创造是将各要素组合成新的、连贯的整体。

(二)高端思维能力

高端思维源自教育目标的分类研究,是一个相对的概念,需参照低端思维加以理解。高端思维能力的概念来自于 Bloom(1956)对认知能力的层次划分,其将认知能力由低到高分为:知识、理解、应用、分析、综合和评价。一般认为 Newcomb&Trefz 的"记忆"层对应 Bloom 的"知识"层和 Anderson &Krathwohl 的"记忆"层;"加工"层对应 Bloom 的"理解与应用"层和 Anderson &Krathwohl 的"理解与应用"层,这两个层面构成低端思维能力。"创造"层对应 Bloom 的"分析和综合"层和 Anderson &Krathwoh 的"分析和创造"层;"评价"对应"评价",构成高端思维能力。对应关系如下图所示:

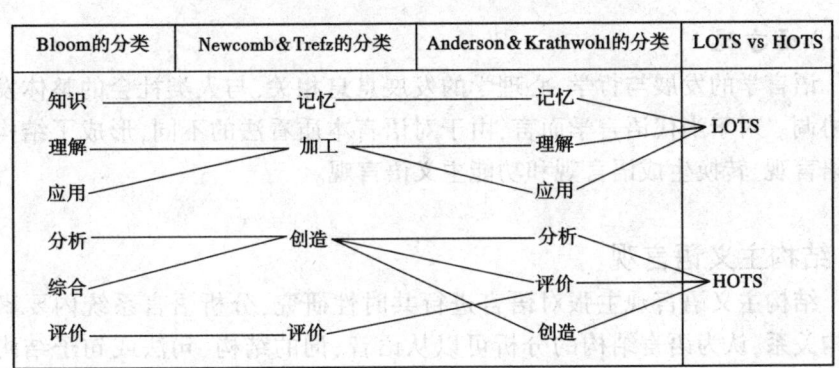

低端思维能力(LOTS)与高端思维能力(HOTS)

高端思维能力的发展以低端思维能力为基础,是个体在遇到问题或困难时进行的批判性的、反思性的、元认知和创造性思维。它与低端思维能力的界限并非泾渭分明,但对人类认知能力的层次划分却体现着人类认知能力随着知识阅历的增长而不断提高,思维由具体逐步过渡到抽象的发展过程。

本章学习心得:

第二章　语言知识

本章学习目标

1. 了解语言观与语言能力构成
2. 了解各分项语言能力的界定
3. 了解各分项语言能力的测试范畴

一、语言观与语言能力

(一) 语言观

语言学的发展与哲学、心理学的发展息息相关，与人类社会的整体发展相协调。对于当代语言学而言，由于对语言本质看法的不同，形成了结构主义语言观、转换生成语言观和功能主义语言观。

1. 结构主义语言观

结构主义语言观主张对语言进行共时性研究，分析语言系统内要素的结构关系，认为语言结构的分析可以从语音、词的结构、句法或句子结构层面进行。"语言学习的目标被认为是掌握该系统中各种成分，即音位、语法单位、语法和词汇。"（束定芳，1996：193）

2. 转换生成语言观

转换生成语言观以 Chomsky 为代表，在融合内在论、自然主义、普遍主义、个性主义和心智主义等哲学思想的基础上，在人类心智的背景下考察语言，认为语言是天赋的。语言能力体现于生成语法，语法的功能在于通过语形生成语句，因此语言的本质表现为语形结构。同时，转换生成语言学认为人类语言具有共同规则——普遍语法，这种语法是儿童与生俱来的，存在于语言习得机制之中，使人能够通过不断建立和验证假设来学习语言，并有能力利用有限的语言符号和规则生成无限的句子。

3. 功能主义语言观

功能主义语言观认为,语言是社会交往的工具,是社会系统的一部分。"人的言语行为就是从数量巨大的、彼此有关的、可供选择的各种成分中,同时地进行选择的过程。"(Thompson&Hunston,2010:D30)语言只有在社会文化语境中才能得到解释,不能与社会和文化脱节。语境决定语义,语义决定形式。(Thompson&Hunston,2010:D31)

(二) 语言能力

随着语言学理论以及其学科分支的不断发展,大致形成了结构主义、转换生成主义和功能主义语言观。语言观念不同,自然产生了对语言能力的不同界定和解释。目前,Bachman 和 Palmer(2010)的语言能力构成研究广泛应用于教学设计和测试开发领域。他们认为语言能力由语言知识和策略能力构成,具体为:

1. 语言知识

语言知识是语言使用者在建构和解读语篇时必然用到的信息储备,包括组织知识和语用知识。

(1) 组织知识

组织知识决定口头和书面语篇的构成,进一步分解为语法知识和语篇知识。语法知识包括语音、词汇、词法和句法等方面的知识,它决定如何组词成句。语篇知识决定话语或句子是怎样组织起来形成语篇的,即如何运用衔接和修辞组织规则组句成篇。

(2) 语用知识

语用知识从句子/话语、语篇、意义、语言使用者的意图和语境相联系的角度来建构和解读语篇,分为功能知识和社会语言知识。

1) 功能知识

功能知识解读句子/话语、语篇与语言使用者意图之间的关系,分为表意功能、操作功能、启发功能和想象功能。

① 表意功能

表意功能指使用语言传递、表达、交换想法、知识或感觉等信息,即用语言表达或解释自我经历和周围世界。

② 操作功能

操作功能是指人们能够通过语言影响周围的人或事,分为交换功能、规范功能和人际功能。交换功能包括要求、建议、命令和警告等形式,用于要求他人完成某事;规范功能是指通过规则、规范和法律等控制规范人的行为;人际功能是指问候、道别、赞美、侮辱和道歉等言语形式,用来建立、维系和改变人际关系。

③ 启发功能

启发功能指使用语言进行教学、学习、解决问题和获取信息等,使人们能够通过语言拓展对周围世界的知识。

④ 想象功能

想象功能指人们运用语言建构一个想象的世界或者以幽默、艺术的描写方式来扩展我们周围的世界。

2) 社会语言知识

社会语言知识能够使我们在语言使用情境中恰当地运用、解读语篇,分为体裁知识、语言变体知识、语域知识、习惯用语知识和文化指称与修辞认识。

① 体裁知识

体裁是按交际目的,对交际事件进行的分类。它对语篇内容、建构角度及形式有限制作用。体裁源自于话语共同体,体现话语共同体成员的社会行为的规约模式。掌握共同体内体裁范畴和体裁的组织结构,是成功组织交际行为的基础,同时能够建构共同体成员身份。

② 语言变体知识

语言变体是语言作为交际工具,在不同地域、不同社会团体和交际环境内产生的变体,分为方言和语域变体。方言进一步分为地域方言和社会方言。地域方言是由于地理位置的不同而形成的方言,如汉语中的北方方言、闽南方言和粤方言等。一般而言,社会成员依据自己的特点、利益和信仰等组成不同的团体,使用能够表示自己社会层次的语言,表明自己的阶层、职业、地位、年龄和性别等信息。

③ 语域知识

语域知识使交际者有能力识别交际的语域特征,依据不同的语域特征使用不同的表达方式完成交际。语域包括语场、语式和语旨三个维度的知识。语场表示实际发生的事,包括话题、事件背景和所进行的活动等。语式是交际的渠道或媒介,如口语和书面语。语旨是交际参与者之间的人际关系、角色分配和交际目的等。

④ 习惯用语知识

习惯用语知识是指应该具备的一定习语、惯用语的积累。习惯用语知识的恰当运用能够使交际更加自然得体,同时促进对信息的理解和判断。

⑤ 文化指称与修辞知识

文化的不同往往会使人对同一事件、制度、人或事物等有不同的理解,这就要求我们要了解相关的文化知识。修辞使用的规则以及修辞的意义具有特定社会文化和言语共同体的所属性。为此,我们在使用一种语言的时候要掌握该语言的修辞知识和文化指称。

2. 策略能力

策略能力指对交际起到高端组织功能的元认知策略能力,分为设定目标、评价和计划。

设定目标阶段通常需要完成确定一系列可能的交际目标、选择一个或多个目标、决定是否想达到上述目标三个任务。

评价从三个方面展开:首先,要对语言交际任务特征、完成任务所需资源和完成任务的可能性做出判断、评价;其次,评价自己所具有的关于主题或语言使用的知识构成,判断是否具备成功完成语言使用任务的知识储备;再者,评价语言交际任务的完成程度。

计划是对完成任务现阶段所具备条件的整体规划。一般包括三个阶段:一是选择有关的语言知识和话题知识来完成特定的交际目标;二是制订一个或几个计划以实施语言知识和话题知识,完成交际任务;三是选择一个计划来完成任务。

二、听力

(一)听力能力

听力能力是在相关知识背景帮助下,在语境中理解口头语言的能力。要求听者在听的过程中,能够辨认说话人发出的声音、感知表达信息焦点的语调模式、识别韵律,并解释听到的内容与当前话题间的关系。

听力是一个积极的认知过程,听者在听的过程中通常会用到自下而上、自上而下以及二者相结合的信息加工模式。

自下而上的信息加工是将以线性方式听到的各个部分一个一个地按顺序拼合起来。(Schimitt,2010:223) Anderson & Lynch(1988:99)形象地将这类听者喻为"录音机似的听话人"。

自上而下的信息加工是一个从整体到部分的整体性加工过程,关注所听内容的整体意义。这种信息加工方式一般要求听者具有内容图式和修辞图式两方面的知识经验储备。内容图式是个人在生活中,通过不同的渠道和经历形成的关于不同话题的知识网络。头脑中有较为完备的相关话题的知识储备,会易化话题的整体理解。修辞图式是我们所具有的关于不同体裁语篇的组织结构方面的知识。了解所听内容的语篇结构,能够帮助我们有效地在听的过程中进行预测和推理,促进语篇的整体理解。

一般而言,单独运用自下而上或自上而下的信息加工模式都不能完整、准确地理解信息,听力能力较强的听者通常会在无意识中将两种信息加工模式整合运用,以充分地理解所听内容。

(二) Hughes 听力测试能力考查范畴

一般听力测试通常要求受试者具备获取信息的能力和交互能力。(Hughes,2008:161—162)常见的获取信息的能力和交互能力如下:

(1) **获取信息的能力**

- 能够获取事实性信息;
- 能够理解指令;
- 能够理解信息寻求性语言表达;
- 能够理解需求性语言表达;
- 能够理解寻求帮助的语言表达;
- 能够理解请求允许;
- 能够理解致歉;
- 能够跟随事件顺序;
- 能够跟随观点论证;
- 能够理解信息比较;
- 能够识别、理解建议;
- 能够识别、理解评论;
- 能够识别、理解理由;
- 能够识别、理解喜好类表述;
- 能够识别、理解抱怨;

- 能够识别、理解推测。

(2) 交互能力
- 能够理解问候和介绍；
- 能够理解表示同意的表述；
- 能够理解表示不同意的表述；
- 能够识别讲话者的意图；
- 能够识别表示不确定性的标记；
- 能够识别、理解要求澄清的请求；
- 能够识别意见请求；
- 能够识别信息已被理解的标记；
- 能够识别信息理解失败的标记；
- 能够识别、理解讲话者对信息的改正；
- 能够识别、理解对陈述或评论的修改；
- 能够识别讲话者对听话者信息应答的期待；
- 能够识别讲话者对某一陈述的论证或支持；
- 能够识别讲话者对其他人信息的质疑；
- 能够识别讲话者的劝导性表述。

三、口语

(一) 口语能力

口语能力是指以口头的方式,依据当前的交际主题、目的和听众,清晰地传递思想和信息以及与他人展开讨论的能力,一般包括语音、语法和词汇知识等微观语言技能,常用的口头用语与信息传递方式和交流中解决问题以完成沟通的技能(Weir & Bygate,1992),表现为:

1. 能够清晰、准确发音,正确运用重音、节奏和语调；
2. 能够选择听者可以理解的话题词汇,准确地运用时态、语态、句型等恰当地表达意思；
3. 能够根据交际情境,选择正式或非正式的交际文体；
4. 能够依据具体语境,直接或间接地表达思想,建立和维持社会关系,同时遵守社会约定俗成的谈话方式和法则；
5. 能够调节交际双方在交流中的参与度,对语义进行协商,恰当地运用交际策略,克服交流中出现的困难,使谈话顺利进行,达到交际目的。

(二) Hughes 口语测试能力考查范畴

一般口语测试中会涉及报告、讨论、对话、采访等体裁,包括信息技能、交互技能和管理技能。(Hughes,2008:114—115)

1. 信息技能
   - 能够提供个人信息;
   - 能够提供非个人信息;
   - 能够描述事件;
   - 能够提供指令;
   - 能够进行对比;
   - 能够提供解释;
   - 能够进行辩论;
   - 能够提供所需信息;
   - 能够表述需求;
   - 能够引出帮助;
   - 能够寻求同意;
   - 能够致歉;
   - 能够详述想法;
   - 能够表达观点;
   - 能够论证观点;
   - 能够表达抱怨;
   - 能够表达推测;
   - 能够分析;
   - 能够表述理由;
   - 能够释义;
   - 能够总结;
   - 能够提供建议;
   - 能够表述喜好;
   - 能够下结论;
   - 能够评论;
   - 能够表明态度。

2. 交互技能

- 能够表明目的；
- 能够识别其他讲话者的意图；
- 能够表达同意；
- 能够表达不同意；
- 能够引出观点；
- 能够引出信息；
- 能够质疑他人的主张；
- 能够修改声明或评论；
- 能够证明或支持他人的观点；
- 能够劝说他人；
- 能够对交际中断进行修补；
- 能够检查自己是否被正确理解；
- 能够回应要求澄清的请求；
- 能够寻找、建立共同点；
- 能够引发澄清；
- 能够对自己或他人进行修正；
- 能够示意是否理解；
- 能够表示不确定。

3. 管理技能

- 能够发起互动；
- 能够改变互动话题；
- 能够分担互动责任；
- 能够在互动中转换话轮；
- 能够做决定；
- 能够结束互动。

四、阅读

（一）阅读能力

阅读不仅是一种语言活动，更是思维活动。阅读能力以阅读过程为载体,呈现读者在语音、词汇、句法和语篇结构的基础上,依据阅读目的,利用现有的知识资源和语境特征,提取、加工信息,解读语篇意义,监控和评价阅读过程的能力。

(二)Hughes阅读测试能力考查范畴

测试中,阅读分为两类题型,一类要求受试者对材料进行泛读,一类则是要求受试者对材料进行精读,所以一般要求受试者具备泛读技巧和精读技巧。(Hughes,2008:138—139)

1. 泛读技巧
(1)略读
- 迅速有效地获取主要思想和篇章主题;
- 迅速建构篇章结构;
- 迅速判断篇章内容与个人所需信息的相关性。

(2)寻读
- 能够迅速找到既定话题的信息;
- 能够迅速找到特定的词或短语;
- 能够迅速找到数字或相关百分比;
- 能够迅速找到索引中的特定条目;
- 能够迅速找到文献中的特定信息。

2. 精读技巧
- 能够识别代词指称;
- 能够识别话语标记;
- 能够解释复杂句;
- 能够解释主题句;
- 能够列出篇章的逻辑结构;
- 能够列出篇章论点的发展;
- 能够区别实例与概述;
- 能够识别篇章的主要意思;
- 能够识别作者意图;
- 能够识别作者的态度和情感;

- 能够识别篇章的受众；
- 能够识别篇章类型；
- 能够区分事实与观点；
- 能够区分假设与事实；
- 能够区分流言与事实；
- 能够依据语境推测生词的意思；
- 能够对命题信息进行推测，回答谁(who)、什么时候(when)或什么(what)等问题；
- 能够对命题进行动机、原因和结果等解释性推测，回答为什么(why)或怎么样(how)等问题；
- 能够进行语用推测。

五、写作

(一) 写作能力

写作是一项产出能力，与阅读构成互动关系。也就是说，写的目的是向读者传递信息。在写的起始阶段就已经有目标读者的存在。作为一个复杂的心理认知过程，它是一个作者、读者、语篇和现实的交互过程，不仅表达现实，而且通过语篇的建构，作者也在建构自己的语篇身份，同时通过语篇建构与读者进行思想的沟通和意义的协商。

一般而言，写作能力可以从词汇语法能力、语篇能力和社会文化能力三个层次加以界定。词汇语法能力是指作者能够在词汇语法知识的基础上，应用一定的写作技巧，写出准确、恰当、得体的句子，表达基本思想；语篇能力要求作者能够将句子组织成结构完整、连贯、观点明确的语篇；社会文化能力是指写作的语篇应该符合社会文化的常规要求，选择恰当的修辞模式、文体和体裁。

(二) 写作测试能力考查范畴

Sally Burgess & Katie Head(2005:45—49)将写作测试任务分为基于内容与程序性知识的任务、开放式任务和输入式任务三种类型。基于内容与程序性知识的写作任务是针对某种特殊的知识或经验而设计的，如依据做志愿者的经历，写一篇800字左右的文章；开放式任务，这类测试涉及的主题广泛，由受试者自己确定写作内容；输入式任务，受试者需要整合测试任务给定的输入信息来完成写作。

写作测试一般主要考查受试者八个维度的能力，具体为：

1. 完成任务
   - 写作文本的语言能够体现读者与作者的角色关系和交际目的；
   - 写作文本涵盖任务评价量表要求的内容；
   - 写作文本字数符合规定要求。

2. 符合要求
   这类技能针对输入式测试任务，要求受试者能够整合注释、图表、调查数据等给定输入信息，完成写作任务。

3. 原创性语言输出
   受试者要能够运用自己的语言表述给定的信息。对于高水平测试而言，受试者则需能够引入自己的观点和评分标准所规定的内容。

4. 词汇语法结构
   - 受试者应能够在词汇使用中，有词汇的变化，表现出一定的词汇量；
   - 受试者应能够熟练使用各种语法结构。

5. 组织与衔接
   - 篇章或段落组织合理恰当；
   - 段落应涵盖主题句，其他句子与主题密切相关；
   - 能够使用连接词、短语、代词、省略、替代等形式，使篇章语句衔接连贯。

6. 表述与语域特征
   - 应掌握不同体裁的表述方式，选择恰当的形式写特定体裁的篇章；
   - 语言使用符合特定语域，即符合人物关系、事件和文体的要求等。

7. 对读者产生预期效果

　　略

8. 主题拓展

　　高水平写作测试不仅要求受试者针对要求进行应答式写作，更需要受试者依据自己的世界知识和经验来支撑、论证自己的观点。

六、翻译

(一) 翻译能力

　　翻译是一种伴有社会文化语境转换的，源语作者、源语读者、译者、译文读者、源语语篇、译文语篇和现实之间的复杂的交互过程。语言能力只是翻译能力的一个维度，作为一种综合能力，翻译涉及各种知识和技能的协调应用。(苗菊,2007:47—50)

　　Roger Bell(1991:43)认为，"翻译能力是译者从事翻译活动必备的知识和技能"，是一种包括目标语知识、文本类型知识、源语知识、客观世界知识、对比知识以及解码和编码技能的交际能力。Christina Schaffner(2000:147)认为，翻译能力包括语言能力、文化能力、文本能力、语域能力、研究能力和转换能力。

　　PACTE(Process in the Acquisition of Translation Competence and Evaluation)将翻译能力界定为译者进行翻译所必需的潜在的知识、技能体系。(苗菊,2007:47—50)PACTE(2003)认为翻译能力是由双语能力、语言外能力、翻译专业知识、专业操作能力、策略能力和心理生理因素等一系列相关的、有层次的、可变化的成分能力构成。双语能力是两种语言交际需要的程序性知识，由两种语言的词汇、语法、文本、社会语言和语用知识构成。语言外能力指主题知识、百科知识和文化等陈述性知识。翻译专业知识包括翻译类型、翻译目的、翻译方法、翻译步骤、翻译伦理、翻译标准原则等知识。专业操作能力是使用翻译工具、信息、资源、通信技术的能力。策略能力是提高翻译效率，解决翻译问题方面的知识。心理生理因素是包括记忆、感知、注意、情绪、逻辑分析能力和创造能力在内的认知能力。

(二) 翻译测试能力考查范畴

　　翻译是一项语言综合运用技能，往往依据测试目的有不同的能力侧重。

综合多项翻译测试对能力的要求,翻译测试能力的考查核心为:
- 能够准确理解原文;
- 译文能够表达原文主题思想;
- 译文表达准确得体;
- 译文文本衔接连贯;
- 译文语域风格得体;
- 术语运用准确一致;
- 译法、策略应用灵活;
- 能够恰当运用百科知识。

七、语法

(一) 语法能力

语法是语言的必要组成部分,伴随着语言学习与应用的各个部分。对语法的理解与对语言本质的认识息息相关,不同语言观念的人会赋予语法不同的界定和解释。在结构主义语言观念主导语言学习的时期,语法被认为是关于语音、词汇、句法规则的知识。这一时期语言学习的重点就是掌握词汇、句法知识。随着语言学理论研究的发展,功能主义语言观成为主流,教学由"形式"导向转为"语言使用"导向,强调语言的运用。

结构主义语法观使语法单纯关注语言形式而忽视语言使用,而功能主义语法观在一定程度上忽视了形式的作用,使得交际中学生语言产出缺乏准确性。为此,随着研究的深入以及两种语法观在教学实践中问题的出现,Diane Larsen-Freeman(2003)从形式、意义和语用三个维度对语法能力进行了全新的界定,认为语法结构不仅包括(形态结构)形式,同时涵盖意义和语用。意义指脱离语境的意义,即某一形式的词典意义;而语用则使形式和意义与交际目的语言环境相联系,即用来表达语境适切意义。如下图所示:

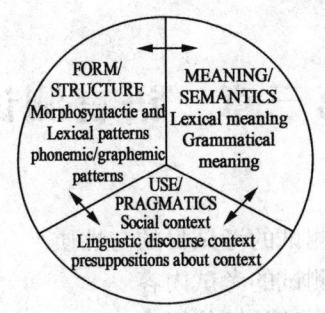

对于语法能力而言,形式、意义和语用三方面缺一不可。意义是要表达的信息,语用决定用何种形式来呈现信息。三个维度相互作用构成一个有机整体。

(二)测试中语法能力考查范畴

语法贯穿语言使用的全过程,通过词汇表达得以体现。Sally Burgess & Katie Head(2005:69—70)认为,测试中一般会考查如下几方面内容:

1. 词语搭配知识;
2. 固定表达和惯用语知识;
3. 语法结构和词汇知识;
4. 文体和语域意识;
5. 词语或短语的隐含意义;
6. 表达准确恰当。

本章学习心得:

_____

_____

_____

第三章 语言测试

本章学习目标
1. 了解国内外大型测试的考试目的与性质
2. 熟悉国内外大型测试的考试内容
3. 掌握国内外大型测试的评价标准

目前，社会上存在多种测试形式，它们服务于不同的目的。其中雅思和托福主要针对有留学打算的学生；剑桥商务英语考试针对修读商务、经济类的学生；国内最大规模的语言测试为大学英语四、六级测试，针对我国广大的大学英语学习者，其目的是检测学习者的学业水平，反馈于教学。本章将从考试目的、性质、内容及评价标准等维度，针对雅思、托福和剑桥商务英语资格考试、全国大学英语等级考试（四、六级）进行全面介绍。

一、雅思

（一）雅思考试的目的与性质

雅思（International English Language Testing System，IELTS）由英国文化教育协会、剑桥大学英语考评部和 IDP 教育集团三方共同合作开发、管理。雅思考试分为两类：一类是以留学为主的学术类；另一类是以移民为主的培训类。其目的在于测量申请赴英语国家留学或移民的非英语国家考生的语言能力。雅思考试为到英语国家和国外以英语为教学语言的高等院校学习的考生设计。通常考生想获得国外本科学位，或我国高校毕业生到海外进行硕士研究生阶段的学习，或已经获得硕士学位的想到国外工作或移民，都会参加雅思考试。雅思考试对这三类考生具有至关重要的作用。

（二）雅思考试（学术类）的评分标准

考核学生在日常交际及进行高等教育教学中的听力理解、阅读理解、写作和口语能力。具体测试的内容、题型及分值比例见表 3-1。

表 3-1 雅思考试内容

测试重点	分值	作答时间	材料	题型	题量
听力	25%	30分钟 + 10分钟	每段听力材料只播放一次，材料中会出现多种不同的英语口音，包括英式、澳大利亚式、新西兰式和美式。双向交流的谈话（如关于旅行安排的对话）	完成填表/记笔记/流程图/总结 选择题	10
			具有交流目的的独白（如介绍博物馆开放时间）	填空题 完成句子 为图表、计划或地图进行标记 分类、配对	10
			2—4人在学术环境下的讨论（如辅导或讨论会；老师和学生关于作业的讨论）		10
			在学术环境下的独白（如一般性学术话题的讲课内容）		10
阅读	25%	60分钟	阅读考试中所出现的文章是由真实的文章改写而成的。这些文章来源于诸如杂志、期刊、专著和报纸等途径。文章还包括非文字性的内容，比如图表、曲线图以及画图等。文章的写作方式多样，比如记叙文、说明文或者议论文等文体。文章的内容包含即将学习本科、研究生课程或进行职业注册的考生所感兴趣的、与其认知程度相符的常见话题。其中，至少一篇文章会出现详尽的论述形式。所有文章总计长度约在2000—2750词之间。	选择 填空 完成句子 完成笔记、总结、表格或流程图 对图表进行标记 为段落或文章的部分选择相对应的小标题 寻找信息 寻找作者观点、论点或文章中的具体信息 分类 配对	40
写作	25%	20分钟	在作文一中，题目中会给出一些视觉性的信息，如一个或多个互相关联的图表、图解或表格。	考生需对这些信息或数据进行描述，文章字数不能少于150词，建议考生用20分钟完成	1
		40分钟	在作文二中，题目中会给出一个看法、问题或议题，考生需就此进行论述。	在根据不同的情况，考生可能需要针对问题提出解决方法、论述和证明一个看法、对比和对照论据或看法、或者评价和反驳一个论点或观点。文章字数不能少于250字，建议考生用40分钟完成。	1

续表

测试重点	分值	作答时间	材料	题型	题量
口语	25%	4—5分钟	在进行自我介绍和考生身份核对后,考官会就考生熟悉的话题进行询问。	简介以及问答	3
		3—4分钟	考官会交给考生一个答题任务卡,卡上有一个相关的话题。考生有一分钟的准备时间(如笔记),然后需就此话题进行1—2分钟的陈述。	个人陈述	
		4—5分钟	考生将与考生就第二部分中出现的话题较为抽象的部分进行双向讨论。	双向讨论	
总计	100%	171—174分钟			85

雅思考试包括四个单项——听、说、读、写,每一个单项单独计分,最高9分,最低0分。总分数的计算方法为:将四个单项所得分数经过平均后,取最接近的整分或半分。总分和四个单项成绩均允许出现半分。雅思考试每个分数级别有相应的表述,见表3-2。

表3-2 雅思考试级别描述

分数	语言水平	说明
9分	专家水平	具有完全自如的英语运用能力。能恰当、准确、流利地使用英语,并能完全理解语言。
8分	优秀水平	能自如运用英语,偶有不准确和使用不当的情况。在不熟悉的语境下可能出现误解。可将复杂、详细的争论掌握得相当好。
7分	良好水平	能有效运用英语,虽然在某些语境中偶尔出现不准确、不恰当的运用和误解。整体而言对复杂的语言掌握得不错,能够理解详细的推理。
6分	合格水平	大致能有效运用英语,虽然时有不准确、不恰当的运用和误解发生。能够使用并理解比较复杂的语言,特别是在熟悉的语境下。
5分	基础水平	可以部分运用英语,在大多数情况下可明白大致意思,虽然经常出现错误。在自己的领域能够应付基本的沟通。
4分	有限水平	只在熟悉的语境下有基本的运用能力,在理解与表达上常出现问题,无法使用复杂的语言。

续表

分数	语言水平	说明
3分	极有限水平	在极熟悉的语境下也只能表达和理解大致意思,频繁发生沟通障碍。
2分	初学水平	在理解书面英语和口语方面存在很大困难。
1分	不懂英语	除少数几个单词以外,没有能力使用英语。
0分	未参加测试	未能回答问题。

雅思考试口语考官按四项标准分别评等级分:流利性与连贯性、词汇多样性、语法多样性及准确性、发音。具体的评分标准见表3-3。

表3-3 雅思考试口语评分标准

分数	流利性与连贯性	词汇多样性	语法多样性及准确性	发音
9	表达流利,非常偶尔出现重复或自我修正情况 出现犹豫仅为准备后续表达的内容,而非搜寻合适的词汇或语法 表达符合情境,衔接手段完全可以接受 话题阐述非常连贯且延展恰当	在所有情境中灵活准确地使用词汇 持续使用准确的语言和习语	除了英语为母语者也会犯的口误外,语法结构始终精确无误	使用丰富多样的语音特征表达精确及/或微妙的意义 在表达过程中始终灵活使用各种话语连贯特征 表达过程中听者理解毫无障碍;口音不影响理解
8	表达流利,非常偶尔出现重复或自我修正情况 偶尔出现犹豫是为搜寻合适的词汇或语法,但通常是基于思考内容话题 阐述连贯、怡当、贴切	可以使用丰富的词汇自如灵活地谈论任何话题并表达准确信息 熟练使用不常见的词汇及习语,但词汇选择和搭配偶尔欠准确 根据需要有效使用改述	灵活地使用多种语法结构;大部分语句准确无误 偶尔出现使用不当或非系统错误;可能反复出现一些简单错误	使用多样的语音特征表达精确及/或微妙的意义 能够保持合适的节奏;在长句的表达中灵活运用重音和语调,但偶尔出现偏差 表达过程中始终易于听者理解 口音几乎不影响理解

续表

分数	流利性与连贯性	词汇多样性	语法多样性及准确性	发音
7	能进行持续、充分的表达,无明显困难 有时出现犹豫、重复及/或自我修正情况,经常出现在句中,表明搜寻合适语言时存在问题,但不影响连贯性 灵活使用口语语篇标记、连接词和衔接手段	可以灵活地使用词汇讨论一系列话题 有一定能力使用不常见的词汇及习语,对语体及词汇搭配有明确意识,但有时不甚恰当 有效地进行改述	灵活地使用一系列语法结构,语句通常准确无误 有效使用简单与复杂句型,但存在一些错误;可能反复出现一些简单错误	展现出6分水平中的所有积极特征及8分水平中的部分积极特征
6	能进行持续表达,并展现出充分交流的意愿 由于偶尔的重复、自我纠正或犹豫,有时缺乏连贯性 能使用一系列口语语篇标记、连接词和衔接手段,但无法保持一贯恰当	具有足以详尽讨论一些话题的词汇量;用词有时不当但意思表达清晰 基本上能成功地进行改述	混合产出简单及复杂的句式以及一系列句子结构,但灵活性有限 使用复杂结构时经常出现错误,但极少影响沟通	使用多种语音特征,但掌握程度不一 语块使用基本得当,但节奏可能受到重音时长缺失及/或语速过快的影响 有时可以有效使用语调和重音,但这种情况无法持续 个别单词或音素存在发音错误,但仅偶尔导致清晰度下降;听者基本上没有太多理解困难

续表

分数	流利性与连贯性	词汇多样性	语法多样性及准确性	发音
5	通常能够持续表达,但需要依赖重复、自我修正及/或降低语速等方式 出现犹豫情况经常是为了在句中搜寻相对基础的词汇和语法 过度使用某些语篇标记、连接词和其他衔接手段 较复杂的话语通常表达不畅,但较简单的语言能够流利表达	词汇量足以讨论熟悉和不熟悉的话题,但用词灵活性有限 尝试进行改述,但并非总能成功	基本句式的准确性掌握较好 尝试使用复杂句式结构,但范围有限,几乎总会出错且可能需要重新表达	展现出4分水平中的所有积极特征及6分水平中的部分积极特征
4	无法在没有明显停顿的情况下持续表达 语速有时缓慢且频繁重复 经常自我纠正 能连接简单句子,但经常重复使用连接词 有时缺乏连贯性	谈论熟悉的话题时词汇量充分,但对不熟悉的话题仅能表达基本意思 用词频繁出现不恰当和错误情况 很少尝试改述	能使用基本句型并正确说出一些简短话语 极少使用从句,总体上话轮较短,结构重复且错误频繁	使用一些可接受的语音特征,但范围有限 产出的一些语块尚可接受,但整体节奏频繁出现偏差 尝试使用语调和重音,但掌握程度有限 单词或音素经常发音错误,导致清晰度下降 听者理解存在一定困难,且可能存在一些语言片段无法理解

续表

分数	流利性与连贯性	词汇多样性	语法多样性及准确性	发音
3	考生在搜寻词汇时出现频繁的、有时长时间的停顿 连接简单句的能力有限，仅能进行简单作答 经常无法表达基本意思	仅限于使用简单词汇，主要用于表达个人信息讨论不熟悉的话题时词汇匮乏	尝试使用基本句型，但除了预先背诵的几句话外，语法错误很多	展现出2分水平中的部分特征，以及4分水平中的部分积极特征
2	几乎每个单词间都出现了长时间停顿 个别词汇可以辨识，但表达几乎没有交际意义	词汇量非常有限；仅说出零散的单词和预先背诵的几句话 若无肢体语言或手势的辅助，几乎无法进行有效的沟通	无法使用基本的句型	用到少量可接受的语音特征（可能因为样本量不足） 尝试进行连贯表达，但受到整体表述问题的阻碍 单词和音素存在发音错误，传达的意思很少；经常难以理解
1	基本未作答 表达完全不连贯	词汇匮乏，仅说出一些零散的单词无法沟通	除预先背诵的内容外，无可供评分的语言	能偶尔说出个别可识别的单词和音素，但无法表达完整意义 无法理解
0	缺考			

雅思考试写作部分大作文的评分标准见表3-4。

表 3-4　雅思考试写作评分标准

分数	写作任务回应情况	连贯与衔接	词汇丰富程度	语法多样性及准确性
9	恰当地回应并深入讨论了问题 以清晰且充分展开的观点直接回答问题 论点相关、充分扩展且有很好的论据支持 内容或论据支撑上的错误极少	可以毫不费力地理解其信息 衔接手段运用自如，行文连贯 连贯或衔接方面的错误极少；熟练地运用分段	词汇使用体现了充分的灵活性及准确性 能准确和恰当地使用丰富的词汇，能自然使用并掌握复杂的词汇特征 拼写和构词方面的轻微错误极少，对于交流影响极小	使用丰富多样的句子结构，具有完全的灵活性和掌控能力 全文的标点符号和语法运用得当 微小错误极少，对交流影响极小
8	恰当且充分地回应了问题 以清晰且充分展开的观点回应问题 论点相关，适当进行了扩展和论据支持 偶尔会出现内容上的遗漏或错误	可以轻松地理解其信息 符合逻辑地组织信息及论点，衔接处理得当 偶尔会出现连贯或衔接上的错误 充分且合理地分段充分且合理地使用分段	流畅和灵活地使用丰富的词汇，达意准确 熟练地在适当时候使用不常见的词汇或习语，尽管在词语选择及搭配上偶尔出现错误 拼写和构词方面偶尔出现错误，但对交流影响极小	灵活而准确地使用丰富多样的句子结构 大多数句子准确无误，标点符号使用得当 偶尔会出现非系统性的错误和不恰当之处，但对交流影响极小

续表

分数	写作任务回应情况	连贯与衔接	词汇丰富程度	语法多样性及准确性
7	恰当地回应了问题的主要部分 呈现并发展了一个清晰的观点 发展主要论点并对其进行论证，但有时会出现过于一概而论的倾向或者论点缺乏重点，支撑论据/材料缺乏准确性	符合逻辑地组织信息及论点，清晰的行文推进发展贯穿全文（有时会出现一些微小错误） 灵活地使用包括指代替换在内的一系列衔接手段，但有时不准确或过度使用，或使用不足 总的来说，分段有效地支持了全文的连贯性，段内的论点组织符合逻辑	使用词汇足够，具备一定的灵活性及准确性 具备使用不常见及/或习语词汇的一定能力 对语体及搭配有一定认识，但有时使用不当 拼写和构词方面仅有少量错误，不影响整体的清晰度	使用各种复杂的句子结构，具有一定的灵活性和准确性 对语法及标点符号掌握得较好，句子通常都准确无误 有时反复出现少许语法错误，但不影响交流

续表

分数	写作任务回应情况	连贯与衔接	词汇丰富程度	语法多样性及准确性
6	回应了问题的主要部分(尽管有些部分的论证比其他部分更充分);格式恰当 提出了一个切题的观点,尽管结论有时不甚清楚、缺乏证明或重复 多个主要论点与问题相关,但某些论点未能充分进行论证或不甚清晰;同时,有些支撑论点和证据不太相关或不充分	连贯地组织信息及论点;总体来说,行文推进清晰 有效地使用衔接手段,但句内及/或句间的衔接有时可能有误或过于机械,出现误用、过度使用或缺失 指代和替换的使用不够灵活或清晰,出现一些重复或错误 使用段落写作,但未能保持段落间的逻辑,并且/或者中心主题未能保持清晰	词汇总体上足够适当地完成写作任务 词汇选择受限或准确性欠缺,但意义总体上清晰 如果作者尝试冒险,可能会使用更丰富的词汇,但其准确性或恰当性较差 拼写及/或构词方面有一些错误,但不影响交流	综合使用简单句式与复杂句式,但灵活性有限 使用复杂句的准确性不及简单句的准确性 有语法和标点符号错误,但很少会影响交流

续表

分数	写作任务回应情况	连贯与衔接	词汇丰富程度	语法多样性及准确性
5	未能完全回应问题的主要部分；某些地方的写作格式可能不甚恰当 表达了一个观点，但展开论证过程未能保持一贯清晰 提出一些主要论点，但十分有限，且未能充分展开论证；并且/或者有时会出现无关细节 有一些重复	组织结构明显，但并不完全合乎逻辑，总体推进缺乏清晰 尽管如此，作答有其内在的连贯性 论点之间的关系明确，但是句子之间的连结不流畅 衔接手段不足、不准确或过度使用 指代和替换使用不足且/或不准确，作文显得重复 分段不足或缺失	使用词汇范围有限，但能达到进行写作任务的最低限度 能准确使用简单词汇，但表达上变化不多 词汇选择常常不够恰当，缺乏灵活性，常出现简化及/或重复 拼写及/或构词上的错误明显，会给读者造成一定的阅读困难	使用有限的语法结构，且有些重复 尝试使用复杂句，但往往出现错误，简单句的准确性更高 语法错误较多，给读者造成一定阅读困难 标点符号不正确

续表

分数	写作任务回应情况	连贯与衔接	词汇丰富程度	语法多样性及准确性
4	仅最低限度回应了问题,或者所答相关性不大,可能是由于对问题的误解 写作格式不甚恰当;观点不甚清晰,读者需要仔细阅读才可识别 一些主要论点难以在文中确认,且这些论点不相关、不清晰,并且/或者缺乏论据支持 大部分的作答内容都有些重复	信息及论点明确,但其组织不够连贯,且未能清晰地推进行文 论点之间的关系不甚清晰,且/或标记不足;使用了一些基本的衔接手段,但有时出现不准确或重复使用 替换或指代的使用不准确或缺失 没有使用段落写作,并且/或者段落内没有明确的主题	使用词汇范围有限,不足以完成任务或与任务无关;词汇比较基础,且重复 不恰当地使用词块(例如,背诵的短语、公式化表达及/或输入材料中的表达) 不恰当的词汇选择及/或构词及/或拼写方面的错误,影响了理解	仅能使用非常有限的语法结构 从句使用很少,简单句占多数;能准确使用一些语法结构,但通常语法错误较多,且影响理解 标点符号经常出错或缺失

续表

分数	写作任务回应情况	连贯与衔接	词汇丰富程度	语法多样性及准确性
3	未能足以回应问题的任一部分,或者误解了问题 无法确认其相关观点,且/或很少直接回应问题 论点甚少,且不相关,或是未能就其充分论证	行文没有明显的逻辑结构;可以辨识其论点,但难以相互关联;使用极少量的次序词或衔接手段 使用的次序词或衔接手段未能明确表明论点之间的逻辑关系 指代关系的识别很困难;分段写作的尝试对读者没有帮助	词汇不足(可能是由于作答长度明显不足);可能过于依赖输入材料或背诵的内容 对词汇选择及/或拼写的掌握非常有限,且错误占多数;这些错误可能严重影响理解	尝试造句,但语法和标点符号错误占多数(除了背诵的短语或是输入材料中表达),导致大多数意义无法传达 作答长度不足,无法体现其造句掌握的情况
2	内容与问题几乎无关 无法确认任何观点 可能闪现一两个论点,但未能展开论证	相关信息很少,或者整个作答都是离题的 没有表明其掌握语篇组织特点的任何证据	词汇使用极其有限,除了背诵的短语之外,几乎找不到其他词组 未显现其对构词及/或拼写的掌握情况	完全无法造句(除了一些背诵的短语)
1	20 词或更少词数的作答被评为 1 分档;写作内容与问题完全无关;任何对题目指导语的抄袭都不予计分	20 词或更少词数的作答被评为 1 分档;作文未能传达任何信息,似乎是由一个从不写作的人写的	20 词或更少词数的作答被评为 1 分档;仅能孤立地使用少数单词	20 词或更少词数的作答被评为 1 分档;没有可评分的语言表达

续表

分数	写作任务回应情况	连贯与衔接	词汇丰富程度	语法多样性及准确性
0	缺考、未以任何方式尝试写作、写作内容完全是预先背诵的内容			
	只应用于以下情况:缺考或未以任何方式尝试写作,全文使用非英语作答,或者有证据表明考生的作答完全是背诵的内容			

二、托福

(一)托福考试的目的与性质

托福(Test of English as a Foreign Language,TOEFL)是美国教育考试服务处(Educational Testing Service,ETS)主办的一项考试,其主要目的是用来衡量母语不是英语的考试者的英语使用水平和交流能力,尤其偏重在学习和学术方面的交流能力。目前,申请美国、加拿大和新加坡的绝大部分大学(包括本科、研究生,有时包括交换生)时,都必须出示托福考试成绩。欧洲和澳大利亚的很多大学在招生时也会接受托福成绩作为语言能力证明。

(二)托福考试的评分标准

新托福考试通过互联网进行,采取机考形式。考核学生在日常交际及进行高等教育教学背景下的听力理解、阅读理解、写作和口语能力。具体的测试重点、时间、任务、材料、分值、题型及题量比例见表3-5。

表3-5 托福考试内容

测试重点	时间	任务	材料	分值	题型	题量
阅读	35分钟	阅读2篇文章	节选自大学程度的教科书,涉及某个学科或主题	30	单项选择 多项选择	20
听力	36分钟	2篇长对话 每个对话包含5个问题 3个Lecture,每个包含6个问题	包括讲座、课堂讨论以及对话	30	单项选择 多项选择 排序 搭配	28

续表

测试重点	时间	任务	材料	分值	题型	题量
口语	16分钟	第1道题是独立口语任务,题目内容涉及考生熟悉的话题。这道题要求考生依据自己的想法、观点和个人经历作答,也可利用任何与题目有关的想法、观点或经历来回答。另外3道题是综合口语任务。回答这类题时,考生必须综合利用多种语言技能。要求考生首先读,听,然后用口语作答。考生可以记笔记,并利用这些笔记回答问题。	商务体裁,如商务计划、营销计划、新闻发布稿、报告和产品说明书等。	30	多项选择	4
写作	29分钟	通常考生需要用课上学到的知识写论文和作文。这要求考生能够将课堂、讲座内容与阅读教材和其他材料相结合,这种类型的写作被称为综合写作。在这种写作题型中,考生必须:对听到和看到的材料做笔记,在写作前利用笔记组织信息;准确地从原文材料中总结、释义和引用信息;写出听到的信息与读到的信息之间是如何联系的	播放一段与文章有关的课堂演讲,其中列举了一些论据反驳之前所给文章当中的论点、论据	30	作文	1

续表

测试重点	时间	任务	材料	分值	题型	题量
写作	29分钟	考生还必须会在模拟线上课堂讨论中，写表达并支持自己观点的论文，这种类型被称为学术讨论写作（Writing for an Academic Discussion），在这种写作题型中，要求考生针对指定话题阐述观点并提供论据：对题目材料中的内容进行回应，或以此为基础表达观点；明确陈述、阐述立场或论点；在学术环境中，准确而有意义地使用一系列语法结构和词汇		30	作文	1
总计	116分钟			120		54

三、剑桥商务英语考试（高级）

（一）剑桥商务英语考试（高级）的目的与性质

剑桥商务英语考试（Business English Certificate）简称 BEC，是剑桥系列考试中专门为学习者提供的国际商务英语资格证书考试，旨在考察应试者在真实工作环境中的英语交流能力，被欧洲乃至全球众多教育机构、企业认可，并将其作为入学考试或招聘录用的英语语言水平要求，其权威性与含金量使其成为"职场英语""商务英语"的代名词。

（二）剑桥商务英语考试（高级）的评分标准

剑桥商务英语考试分为初级、中级和高级三种，本节以高级为例。剑桥商务英语考试（高级）主要考察考生在一般工作环境下和商务活动中英语的听力理解、阅读理解、写作和口语能力。具体测试的内容、题型及分值比例见表3-6。

表3-6 BEC(高级)考试内容

测试的技能	时间	任务	材料	题型	题量
听力	约40分钟	有限作答(即不超过3个词)	信息性独白	填空题	12
		多项配对	来自于5位说话人的5个相关主题的简短独白	匹配题	10
		多项选择	两人或多人之间的对话/访谈/讨论	选择题(三选一)	8
阅读	60分钟	多项配对	常见的真实商务语篇	匹配题	14
		多项选择	常见的真实商务语篇	选择题	6
		多项选择	常见的真实商务语篇	封闭式完型填空	10
		填写合适单词	常见的真实商务语篇	开放式完型填空	10
		删除多余单词	常见的真实商务语篇	改错题	12
写作	70分钟	书写备忘录或电子邮件(120—140词)	提供指导语和图表	简短报告	1
		报告(备忘录或电子邮件);提议(备忘录或电子邮件);商务通信(信件、传真或电子邮件)(200—250词)	提供指导语并补充一些简短输入语篇,如通知或广告	报告、建议书或商务信函	1

续表

测试的技能	时间	任务	材料	题型	题量
口语	3分钟	提供个人信息	考官就个人信息提问	热身对话	1—2
	6分钟	就某一商务主题进行简短口头陈述：组织较长语篇，提供信息，表达并证实观点	商务话题	口头陈述	1
	7分钟	受试间双向交流，考官随后继续给予提示要求受试者回应：表达并证实观点、推测、比较和对比、同意与不同意等	图片或信息卡	讨论	1
总计	186分钟				87—88

BEC(高级)写作部分的评分标准见表3-7。

表3-7 BEC(高级)写作评分标准

级别	描述语
5	全部完成答题要求 所有内容点都已包括在内。 语言规范、自然；错误极少。 多样化的语言结构和丰富的词汇量。 有效地组织，适当地使用衔接手段。 语域和格式完全适当。 给读者的印象极佳。
4	较好完成答题要求 所有重要内容点已包括进去；可能有较少的遗漏。 语言自然；只有运用复杂语言时出现错误。 多样化的语言结构和丰富的词汇量。 总体组织较好，注意逻辑性。 语域和格式总的说来适当。 给读者的印象良好。

续表

级别	描述语
3	尚能达到题目要求 所有主要内容点已包括进去；可能有较少的遗漏； 比较规范，尽管在答题时更大胆的尝试可能会导致一些不妨碍交流的错误。 语言结构和词汇量适度。 组织和逻辑性令人满意。 语域和格式还好，尽管并不完全成功。 给读者的印象较好。
2	不能完全达到答题要求 遗漏了一些主要的内容点或处理得不适当；可能有些不切题。 错误影响交流并可能错误较多。 语言结构和词汇量掌握范围有限；这个水平的语言太初级。 内容的组织条理不清。 语域和格式运用不适当。 给读者的印象不佳。
1	未能达到任务要求 显著的内容遗漏和/或大量内容不切题。 严重不规范；经常出现基本错误。 语言结构单一，词汇量贫乏。 缺乏组织性。 几乎没有使用适当的语域和格式。 给读者印象极差。
0	什么任务也没有完成。字数少于所需字数的25%，或是完全看不懂，或是完全不切题。

BEC（高级）口语部分评分标准见表3-8。

表3-8 BEC（高级）口语评分标准

	发音（包括声音大小、重音、语调、语气）	准确性（包括语法、用词及说话方式）	流利程度（包括语速、长短句搭配）	交流能力（包括独立性、灵活性以及对谈话方式的把握）
3分	尽管有些读音错误，并且有受母语影响的迹象，但比较容易听懂，且抑扬顿挫，表达较流畅。	尽管有错误，但基本上能把意思表达清楚。所采用的句子结构规范，但处理结构复杂的句子比较困难。对熟悉的话题语汇较充分，但表达有欠缺。	听者感觉不错。尽管有停顿，还算较流利，能组织语言，用较长的句子表达意思，但有些句子不够完整。	基本具有独立性，只是有时需要在其他考生的帮助或提示下表达。在与其他考生的交流中占主导地位，回答其他考生所提问题较迅速。

续表

	发音(包括声音大小、重音、语调、语气)	准确性(包括语法、用词及说话方式)	流利程度(包括语速、长短句搭配)	交流能力(包括独立性、灵活性以及对谈话方式的把握)
2分	由于发音受母语影响,某些词不易听懂,有一些读音错误。	有的意思表达不清。所采用的句子结构多为基本句式且有语法及用词错误,对熟悉的话题有一定描述能力。	听者需要有耐心。尽管有停顿但基本流利,句子比较短。	有时需要依靠别人的帮助完成表达。在交流中有不妥之处。不能很快回答其他考生所提问题。
1分	考生的发音很难听懂。经常出现读音错误,受母语影响明显,语调不对且断断续续,给听者造成麻烦。	表达令人费解,基本句子结构出现错误,缺乏用于交流的词汇。	听者需要非常有耐心,经常中断且间隔较长。	需要经常依靠别人的帮助才能完成表达。掌握了一些句式但使用不当,对其他考生的提问反应慢,甚至没有反应。

四、全国大学英语等级考试(四、六级)

(一)全国大学英语等级考试(四、六级)的目的与性质

全国大学英语等级考试(College English Test,简称 CET)是教育部主管的一项全国性的教学考试。大学英语四、六级考试为推动大学英语教学大纲的贯彻执行,对大学生的英语能力进行客观、准确的测量,为提高我国大学英语课程的教学质量服务。全国大学英语四、六级考试的主要对象分别是高等学校修完大学英语四、六级的本科生以及经过所在学校同意的同等程度的大专生或硕士研究生、夜大或函授大学学生。已取得 CET-4、CET-6 合格证书者和参加过 CET-4、CET-6 考试未及格者,都可以再次报名参加考试。

(二)全国大学英语等级考试(四、六级)的考试内容与评价标准

全国大学英语等级考试主要考核学生运用语言的能力,同时也考核学生对语法结构和词语用法的掌握程度。CET-4、CET-6 的试卷结构、测试内容、测试题型、题目数量、分值比例和考试时间分别见表 3-9、表 3-10。

表3-9 CET-4的考试内容

试卷结构	测试内容	测试题型	题目数量	分值比例	考试时间
写作	写作	短文写作	1	15%	30分钟
听力理解	短篇新闻	选择题(单选题)	7	7%	25分钟
	长对话	选择题(单选题)	8	8%	
	听力篇章	选择题(单选题)	10	20%	
阅读理解	词汇理解	选词填空	10	5%	40分钟
	长篇阅读	匹配	10	10%	
	仔细阅读	选择题(单选题)	10	20%	
翻译	汉译英	段落翻译	1	15%	30分钟
总计			57	100%	125分钟

表3-10 CET-6的考试内容

试卷结构	测试内容	测试题型	题目数量	分值比例	考试时间
写作	写作	短文写作	1	15%	30分钟
听力理解	长对话	选择题(单选题)	8	8%	30分钟
	听力篇章	选择题(单选题)	7	7%	
	讲话/报道/讲座	选择题(单选题)	10	20%	
阅读理解	词汇理解	选词填空	10	5%	40分钟
	长篇阅读	匹配	10	10%	
	仔细阅读	选择题(单选题)	10	20%	
翻译	汉译英	段落翻译	1	15%	30分钟
总计			57	100%	130分钟

大学英语四、六级考试口语考试(CET Spoken English Test,简称CET-SET)作为一项单独的测试出现,与笔试相对独立,其测试内容见表3-11、表3-12。

表 3-11　CET-4 的口试内容

任务	任务名称	考试过程	答题时间
热身	自我介绍	根据考官指令,每位考生作一个简短的自我介绍。考试时间约 1 分钟。	每位考生 20 秒(两位考生依次进行)
任务 1	短文朗读	考生准备 45 秒后朗读一篇 120 词左右的短文。考试时间约 2 分钟。	每位考生朗读 1 分钟(两位考生同步进行)
任务 2	简短回答	考生回答 2 个与短文有关的问题。考试时间约 1 分钟。	每位考生 40 秒(两位考生同步进行)
任务 3	个人陈述	考生准备 45 秒后,根据所给提示作陈述。考试时间约 2 分钟。	每位考生 1 分钟(两位考生同步进行)
任务 4	双人互动	考生准备 1 分钟后,根据设定的情景和任务进行交谈。考试时间约 4 分钟。	两位考生互动 3 分钟

表 3-12　CET-6 的口试内容

部分	内容	考试过程	答题时间
第一部分	自我介绍和问答	先由考生自我介绍,然后回答考官提问。考试时间约 2 分钟。	自我介绍:每位考生 20 秒(两位考生依次进行) 回答问题:每位考生 30 秒(两位考生同步进行)
第二部分	陈述和讨论	考生准备 1 分钟后,根据所给提示作个人陈述;两位考生就指定的话题讨论。考试时间约 8 分钟。	个人陈述:每位考生 1 分 30 秒(两位考生依次进行) 两人讨论:3 分钟
第三部分	问答	考生回答考官的一个问题。考试时间约 1 分钟。	每位考生 45 秒(两位考生同步进行)

　　CET4-CET6 的听力理解部分考核学生获取口头信息的能力,包括理解主旨大意、重要事实和细节、隐含意义,判断话语的交际功能,说话人的观点、态度等。具体的技能为:(1)理解主旨大意,听懂重要信息或特定的细节,理解说话人明确表达的观点、态度等;(2)推论隐含的意义,判断话语的交际功能,推断说话人的观点、态度等;(3)辨别语音特征(如从连续的话语中辨别语音、理解重音和语调等),理解句间关系(如因果、比较、条件等);(4)运用合适的听力策略帮助理解。

CET-SET考核学生就熟悉的话题用英语进行口头表达与交流的能力。考核的技能如下:(1)陈述事实、理由、观点等,描述人物、事件、现象等;(2)交换意见、交流情感和观点等,争辩、解释、比较、论证等;(3)运用合适的口头表达与交流的策略帮助表达。

CET-4、CET-6的阅读理解部分考核学生通过阅读获取书面信息的能力,包括理解主旨大意、重要事实和细节、隐含意义,判断作者的观点、态度等。阅读部分考核的技能是:(1)理解主旨大意,理解细节信息,理解作者明确表达的观点、态度等;(2)概括主旨大意,推论隐含的意义,判断作者的观点、态度等;(3)根据上下文猜测词和短语的意思,理解句间关系(如因果、比较、条件等),运用词汇及语法衔接手段理解篇章各部分之间的关系;(4)运用合适的阅读策略帮助理解。

CET-SET主考在评分时使用以下标准:

(1)准确性和范围:"准确性"指考生的语音、语调以及所使用的语法和词汇的准确程度;"范围"指考生使用的词汇和语法结构的复杂度和丰富度。

(2)话语长度和连贯性:"话语长度"指考生对整个考试中的交际所做的贡献、讲话的多少;"连贯性"指考生能进行较长时间的、语言连贯的发言。

(3)灵活性和适切性:"灵活性"指考生应付不同场景和话题的能力;"适切性"指考生根据不同场合选用适当确切的语言的能力。

CET-4、CET-6的写作部分考核学生就熟悉的话题和情景用英语进行书面表达的能力,要求考生在规定的时间内根据所给提示用英语写出一篇短文。写作部分考核的技能如下:(1)表达中心思想,表达重要或特定的信息,表达观点、态度等;(2)围绕所给的题目叙述、议论或描述,重点突出,连贯地组句成段、组段成篇;(3)运用恰当的词汇,运用正确的语法,运用合适的句子结构,使用正确的标点符号,运用衔接手段表达句间关系(如对比、原因、结果、程度、目的等)。

CET-4、CET-6的翻译部分考核学生运用恰当的翻译策略和语言知识将主题熟悉、内容浅显、意思完整的汉语段落用英语表达出来的能力。翻译部分考核的技能如下:(1)用合适的英语词汇准确表达汉语词汇的意思,用符合英语规范和表达习惯的句型准确表达汉语句子的含义;(2)用英语准确、完整地表达汉语段落的信息,译文结构清晰,语篇连贯,语言通顺;(3)运用合适的翻译策略帮助表达。

第四章 应用语言学基础知识

本章学习目标
1. 掌握一定的应用语言学基础知识
2. 提高语言意识
3. 强化语言对文化和社会关系的建构作用

一、语境

(一) 基本概念

语境作为确定语言表述意义的参照点和基础,其作用是帮助交际参与人确定、理解和分析字、词、句、篇的意义,为实现交际目标奠定基础。因此,对于任何语言学习或者语言研究而言,语境都是至关重要的。

一般认为语言学领域对语境的研究开始于波兰籍社会人类学家马林诺夫斯基(B. Malinowski)提出的文化语境与情景语境。前者指说话人生活于其中的社会文化背景;后者指言语行为发生时的具体情景。马林诺夫斯基的学生弗斯(J. Firth)在此基础上明确了语境的构成要素。他认为任何一种语境都必须包括三方面的要素:与参与者相关的特征(如人物、性格等);相关的话题,包括物体、事件;非语言、非人类的事件以及言语活动产生的结果。

(二) 经典理论

语境研究就是研究说话者如何在实际的交际过程中表达自己的意图以及受话者如何根据语境因素的提示来判断与领会这种意图。语境因素涉及交际过程的方方面面,很难从单一的角度来概括。因此,很多学者从不同的角度研究语境问题,如:

1. 雅各布森的语境研究

俄国语言学家雅各布森(R. Jakobson)根据交际情景构成的因素将语境构成要素区分为说话者(Addresser)、受话者(Addressee)、语境(Context)、信息(Message)、代码(Code)和接触(Contact)六类。与之相应的功能分别是情感功能、意动功能、指代功能、诗学功能、元语言功能和寒暄功能。他从功能的角度出发,强调语境对交际的作用,大大拓展了语境理论的发展空间。

2. 系统功能语言学的语境研究

该学派的代表人物韩礼德(M. A. K. Halliday)是弗斯的学生。他在继承马林诺夫斯基和弗斯的语境思想的基础上,将情景语境归纳为场景、方式和交际者三个组成部分。他认为情景语境与文化语境之间是互补关系,情景语境是文化语境的具体示例,二者不是两种不同的现象,而是同一现象,差别在于观察角度的不同:近距离看到的是具体的情景语境,远距离看到的则是整体的文化语境。

3. 海姆斯的语境模型

在社会语言学领域,对语境的研究以美国学者海姆斯(D. Hymes)提出的SPEAKING语境模型为代表。他把语境定义为"话语的形式和内容",认为语境包括场合(Setting)、参与者(Participant)、目的(End)、行为序列(Act sequence)、基调(Key)、信息发布形式(Instrumentalities)、语用规范(Norms)和体裁(Genre)八个变量。说话人可以根据上述变量对交际内容进行逐一的分析,确定词语或句子在语境中的确切含义。

4. 斯珀泊和威尔逊的语境研究

认知视角语境研究主要代表人物是法国学者斯珀泊(D. Sperber)和威尔逊(D. Wilson)。他们将语境定义为一种心理建构体,是听话者对世界的一系列假设,它们以概念表征的形式存在于人们的大脑中,构成了一个人的"认知环境"。这个认知视角下的语境观,同传统的语境观有很大的区别:潜在的认知环境并不能成为表达和理解话语的语境。话语交际是交际者之间的互动过程,涉及信息意图和交际意图的明示 – 推理。语境是互动过程中交际构成双方相互理解并存在于大脑中的一系列假设。对于信息的发出者而言,交际是一个明示的过程;而对于信息的接收者来说,交际是一个推理的过程。交际互动过程中,交际双方需要选择相关信息从一个假设推出另一个假设,只有认知语境显现了相同的事实或假设时,交际双方才能做出共同的认知和判断,从而实现理解和沟通。例如甲对乙说"某某人就是个葛朗台"时,他希望传递的信息是某某人像巴尔扎克小说中的人物葛朗台一样是个吝啬鬼。但是甲在说这句话之前必须要在心里做出假设:乙读过巴尔扎克的《欧也妮·葛朗台》这部小说,或者知道葛朗台这个人物是吝啬鬼的代表。而当乙听到甲的这句话的时候也会在心里做出相应的假设:有很多个叫葛朗台的人,但是甲说的这句话中很可能指的是巴尔扎克笔下的那个人物。如果乙不清楚葛朗台是谁,他就不会明白甲的意图,也无法对甲的话语做出准确的回应。

5. 维索尔伦的语境研究

比利时学者维索尔伦(J. Verschuren)综合了上述学者的研究成果,对语境思想进行了较完整的归纳。他认为语言使用是在动态过程中经过不断协商和不断顺应完成的,而意义的理解也是在这一过程中实现的。交际参与者在各自的社会心理机制下,根据交际意图,能动地改造或创造新的语境,而语言和语境都处于相互构建的动态过程当中。他的语境是一种多元概念,既有静态的因素,又存在动态的影响。实际上,他的语境研究体现出一种将社会文化和个人认知相融合的趋势,属于一种综观的考察。为便于理解维索尔伦的语境观,请看下面的对话:

甲:昨天我遇见王莹了。
乙:哪个王莹?
甲:就是咱们那个高中同学。
乙:想起来了,就是那个大高个,肖元楠的女朋友。
甲:对对对,就是总喜欢穿情侣装的那一对儿。

在上面的对话中,甲的第一句陈述激活了乙对自己高中同学的认知记忆。在甲的提示下,乙成功地回忆起他们所谈论的对象,并给出了进一步的信息:某人的女朋友。而甲也在乙提供的新信息的基础上提供了有关谈论对象更为详细的描述。就整个对话过程而言,甲乙始终在不断地通过协商的形式对语境进行着建构。在这个微观语境中,甲乙双方通过相互提供新信息的方式将谈论对象从最初的一个符号逐步地丰富为鲜活的形象。

二、体裁

(1) 基本概念

体裁"genre"一词源于拉丁语的"genus",是一种话语的类型。早在古希腊时期,亚里士多德(Aristotle)就对文学领域内的体裁现象进行了论述。直到20世纪50年代苏联学者巴赫金(M. Bakhtin)对体裁的全新阐释才使得人们重新认识了这一重要概念。他认为,"每一单个的表述,无疑是个人的,但使用语言的每一个领域却锤炼出相对稳定的表述类型,我们称之为言语体裁"。他将言语体裁分为两类:一类是日常对话;另一类是事务性和文学性的体裁。两类体裁之间存在着原则性的不同,需要分别进行研究。同时他也指出,"研究表述的本质以及人类活动不同领域中表述体裁的多样性,几乎对语言学和语文学的所有领域来说,都具有重大的意义"。随着语言学领域对体裁研究的不断深入,众多研究者都从自身的视角对体裁进行了诠释。

就一般意义而言,体裁是一种言语交际事件,具有形式和行为的双重特性。就形式层面而言,一种体裁就是一种特定的书面或口头的话语类型,具有结构上的要求,如求职信、报关单或体育比赛解说等。从行为层面上看,一种体裁必须是某种事件,具有过程上的规约,如利用报关单完成进口商品的报关流程。海姆斯就曾经指出,体裁既可以在言语事件中得到体现,也可以作为言语事件被确认。因此,体裁研究始终围绕形式和行为两个维度进行,忽略任何一个方面都不能完整准确地实现体裁的功能。

(2) **经典理论**

在体裁研究的主要流派中,学者们从不同的角度对体裁进行不同的研究。这主要是由于体裁现象较为复杂,涉及语言内部的结构因素和语言外部的社会文化因素。此外,体裁的行为特征也使得我们很难用一种理论来解释它。目前,体裁研究主要分为三个派别:新修辞学派、悉尼学派和特殊目的英语学派。

1. 新修辞学派的体裁研究

新修辞学派是由在北美地区从事修辞、学术写作和职业写作研究的一些学者创立的。他们从言语交际的角度研究交际双方语言表达手段。新修辞学派的代表人物米勒(C. Miller)将体裁看作是一种社会行为的表现形式。他指出体裁不应该关注语篇的内容或形式,而应该强调语篇所肩负的社会功能。新修辞学派注重体裁的动态性和社会功能,认为体裁始终处于不断发展和变化之中,甚至可能会消亡。此外,该学派更加强调对"社会动力"(social dynamics)方面的研究,致力于体裁对某学科的社会文化认知功能方面的影响。例如,有学者通过研究发现学生利用MSN等基于网络的社交软件能有效提高专业知识的学习能力。显然,研究者关注的不是学生们利用这些社交软件交流了哪些内容,他们感兴趣的是这种新兴的"体裁"对知识学习等方面产生的积极作用。

2. 悉尼学派的体裁研究

悉尼学派以系统功能语言学为基础,强调体裁的社会目的,认为体裁是一种有步骤的、以交际目的为导向的社会交往活动。该学派甚至提出"文化中有多少种被承认的社会行为就有多少种体裁"的观点。由此可见该学派对社会目的和社会行为问题的关注。人们的社会交往大多具有重复性和习惯性,体裁也相应地具有目的性、交互性和程序性。因此,该学派认为体裁同语境和意义之间就形成了复杂的联结,对于体裁的研究也就成为对行为和目的的研究。该学派受到功能主义思想的影响,非常注重体裁在社会交往中的作用,强调交际者对各种体裁的识别与运用。实际上,该学派在澳大利亚的中小学和大学开展了大量的调查和研究工作,有效地提高了学生的体裁能力。这些专门针对体裁的研究结果对学生的学习起到了极大的促进作用。

3. 特殊目的英语学派的体裁研究

特殊目的英语学派关注体裁的形式,将体裁看作是一种结构特征鲜明、约定俗成的交际事件。人们在使用体裁时要遵守相应的规约或惯例。该学派的代表人物斯维尔斯(J. Swales)归纳了体裁的五个特征:(1)体裁包括一组交际事件,其成员具有共同的交际目的;(2)体裁是交际行为的形式,具有交际功能;(3)交际目的是确定体裁的重要因素;(4)交际目的和话题制约语篇形式、内容和语言难度;(5)同一体裁的语篇形式具有大体相同的图式结构,而这种图式结构影响语篇的内容和语言风格的选择。同前面两个流派相比,特殊目的英语学派的体裁研究更加关注语言教学。ESP学派的研究者认为基于体裁分析的教学法是一种有效的教学手段,通过体裁教学法对英语非本族语的学生讲授专门用途的英语,能够引导学生掌握语篇的文本特征以及谋篇布局的机制。

三、话语

（1）基本概念

　　语言学领域的话语研究关注的主要是语言的使用问题。如哈里斯（Z. Harris）将话语定义为是由连续的句子排列而成的语言形式的段落组成的特殊整体。2001年，塞弗瑞恩（D. Schiffrin）等人主编的《话语分析手册》将话语的定义分为三类：(1)超越句子的任何成分；(2)语言的使用；(3)广义的社会实践，包括非语言的场景。这些定义表明，话语是一种在交际中使用的大于句子的语言单位，包括语言内部结构关系和语言外部场景特征两个维度。对这一概念的了解将有助于我们更好地研究语言和语言使用等问题，帮助我们树立正确的语言观和语言使用观。

（2）经典理论

　　话语在形式上是一个大于句子的语言单位。它在功能上包括任何有语言参与的社会行为以及相应的社会场景。显然，话语既是一个"大"概念，也是一个"全"概念。话语的"大"足以包括人类社会全部成员所说的全部内容。话语的"全"足以涵盖全部的人类社会，因为语言的使用是伴随人类社会形成和发展的全部过程。语言是人和动物"分道扬镳"的最后标志。当人类开始运用语言进行交流的时候，我们便以话语的形式参与并推动着人类社会的发展。因此，对话语的研究涉及很多方面的内容。限于篇幅的原因，本章仅探讨话语分析和话语共同体两个基本领域。

1. 话语分析

　　一般的话语分析分为会话结构和篇章结构两大类。会话结构主要研究在多人交际过程中会话结构的形成、变化与特点等问题，其主要表现形式是会话模式。篇章结构主要分析篇章内部句子的衔接与连贯，句子成分之间的指称、省略与替换等问题，关注语言的组织结构和使用特征，其表现形式主要是独白模式。作为使用中的语言，话语具有鲜明的"实践"色彩。从实践角度切入话语研究，使我们至少能够得到四点启示：(1)话语是一种社会行为，具有交互性；(2)话语的意义来源于互动中的相互协商，具有动态性；(3)对话语的理解离不开语境要素，具有不确定性；(4)话语参与社会现实的建构，具有建构性。

2. 话语共同体和实践共同体

随着语言研究的逐步深入,"话语共同体"(discourse community)和"实践共同体"(community of practice)等概念逐渐进入我们的视野。目前,斯维尔斯关于话语共同体的研究最为全面。他认为话语共同体具有六个区别性特征:(1)话语共同体具有被广泛认同的常见的公开目的;(2)话语共同体的各成员之间具有相互交流的机制;(3)话语共同体运用这种交流的机制作为成员之间交流信息的基本方式;(4)在交流目的的促进下,话语共同体使用并占有一种或多种体裁;(5)除了拥有体裁外,话语共同体还使用一些特有的词语;(6)话语共同体的新手要了解一定的相关内容和专业话语知识。这些特征已经成为界定不同话语共同体的重要参数。

简单地说,语言学意义上的实践共同体由知识背景、人和人的行为三个主要部分构成。它以人的行为为区别性特征对社会群体进行划分,以便为教学等研究提供合理的分析框架。显然,话语实践关注的不仅仅是参与者使用语言的方式以及生成的语言产品,同时也关注参与者对话语资源的使用所反映出的共同体的情况。我们在关注参与者如何在话语共同体中运用语言、非语言及互动行为等资源生成意义的同时,也注意到他们利用这些资源创造并反映话语实践共同体。话语实践既关注社会行为等宏观语境因素,又关注交际者可以运用的微观语境资源。因此,话语实践共同体必须以话语为基础,通过话语建构并反映社会现实。换言之,对话语实践的研究也就是对人和社会现实的研究。

四、言语行为

(一) 基本概念

言语行为的核心观点是"说话即做事"(To say something is to do something),是英国哲学家奥斯汀(J. Austin)20世纪50年代提出的一个概念。他发现人们的日常语言交流中有很多我们习以为常却又难以解释的问题,如提问、命令、询问、请求和道歉等。遗憾的是,很多人并没有注意到这些问题。奥斯汀经过仔细观察并深入思考后发现,人们不仅用语言来描述世界,同时还通过它来实施行为。

(二) 经典理论

言语行为概念的出现,引发了学者们对语言使用研究的再思考。特别是它对说话人意义的关注,成为语用学发展最初阶段的主要研究范式。这一时期的研究主要包括施为句假说、言语行为三分说、言语行为的分类和间接言语行为等。

1. 施为句和表述句

奥斯汀发现日常语言中有一些句子是对客观现实的描述。如"太阳从东边升起在西边落下"或者"我开了一辆黑色的轿车"。我们只需要通过观察就可以对这些句子的真假做出判断。而语言中的另外一些句子却不能通过这样的方法进行判断。如"我道歉"或"我命令你坐下"。他将前者称为表述句(constative sentence),后者称为施为句(performative sentence)。为此,奥斯汀总结出施为句的相关特征:(1)第一人称;(2)宣告性;(3)陈述句式;(4)主动语态;(5)一般现在时。起初认为,凡是符合上述五个特征的句子就是施为句,就是通过说话在做事情。经过深入分析,他发现有一些不符合上述特征的句子也可以用来做事情。因此,他最终放弃了这种区分。

2. 言语行为三分说

奥斯汀放弃施为句和表述句的区分后转而对言语行为的过程进行研究。他最终将言语行为区分为三个在程序上相互独立,在关系上却又相互关联的层次:言说行为(locutionary act)、意向行为(illocutionary act)和取效行为(perlocutionary act)。

言说行为是言语行为最基本的层次,指发音器官参与的发音过程和按照语法规则将所发语音组成符合语法规范的语言单位的过程。例如,当说话人说"今天天气真不错"的时候,他的发音器官首先协同工作,发出 jīn、tiān、tiān、qì、zhēn、bù 和 cuò 这些语音。同时,说话人要按照合乎语法的顺序依次发出这些音,以保证听话人能够明白自己这句话要表示的意义。

意向行为是言语行为最为重要的层次,指说话人通过言说行为实现特定交际目的或执行某种功能的行为。它可以是显性的表达,也可以是隐性的呈现。听话人必须借助语境和语用推理的方式才能实现对意向行为的理解。例如:

甲:明天能和我去逛街吗?

乙:快要期末考试了,我得复习啊。

甲:那好吧,改天再去。

甲通过显性的方式表达了自己的意向行为,邀请乙同她去逛街。乙的意向行为则是隐性的呈现,通过对自己正在准备期末考试这一情况的说明,委婉地拒绝了甲的邀请。

取效行为是说话人的言说行为对听话人产生的影响或结果。听话人的理解可能符合也可能不符合说话人的心理预期。在上面的例子中,乙理解了甲的意向行为,但是没有做出甲所预期的反应。因此,甲没能取得设想的取效行为。而甲的第二句话则表明她也理解了乙的意向行为,并且做出了符合乙心理预期的回应。乙取得了自己设想的取效行为。

3. 言语行为的分类

奥斯汀对言语行为理论发展的另一贡献是对其进行的分类研究。他将言语行为分为五类,并对每个类别的主要动词进行了总结。但是他的分类缺乏清晰一致的分类标准,很多类别并不是对意向行为的分类,各类别之间还存在重叠的情况。他的学生美国哲学家塞尔(J. Searle)继承并发展了他的分类方法,并在一定程度上对其进行了修正性的研究。塞尔重新将言语行为分为五个类别:表述类(representatives),指说话人用语言描述自己所相信的事件,表明他认为表述的内容是真实的;指令类(directives),指说话人通过指令或意愿使得听话人做出相应反应,听话人通过取效行为去实现说话人的指令;承诺类(commissives),是说话人对将来某种行为做出的承诺,是通过说话人的行为履行自己的承诺;表达类(expressives),是说话人表明自身的心理状态或立场;宣告类(declaratives),是说话人通过言说行为改变某些事物的状态。

4. 间接言语行为

塞尔对言语行为最重要的贡献就是提出了间接言语行为理论。简单地说,间接言语行为就是通过实施一个意向行为来间接地实现另外一个意向行为。前面甲邀请乙去逛街的例子中,乙的回答就是一个典型的间接言语行为。从表面上看,乙的回答是一个陈述性的意向行为,但是她真正的回答却是一个拒绝性的意向行为。她是通过陈述要复习备考的事实委婉地拒绝了对方的请求。间接言语行为的存在主要是出于礼貌目的,是一种非常见的言语行为,对于它的理解需要借助交际双方共享的背景知识和语境线索。

五、特殊目的英语

(一) 基本概念

特殊目的英语也被称作专门用途英语（English for Specific Purposes，以下简称 ESP），通常指为实现一定的实用目的而开展的英语教学行为。20 世纪 60 年代以来，受到经济发展、科技进步和语言研究等因素的推动，这一概念被广泛地应用于语言学的研究领域。在众多的研究中，斯特雷文斯（Strevens）对特殊目的英语根本特征的界定具有一定的代表性。他总结了四个根本特征：(1) ESP 为满足学习者的特定需求而设定；(2) ESP 内容（主题和论题）与特定的学科、职业和实践活动相关联；(3) ESP 立足于研究适用于这些实践活动的语言中的语法、词汇、语篇、语义和话语分析等问题；(4) 与一般用途英语（English for General Purposes）形成对照。这一定义表明，ESP 是为了满足某种职业或某个专业的发展需求而形成的，其教学目的倾向于通过语言学习实现专业知识的获取和专业技能的提高。

达德利-伊文思（Dudley-Evans）认为，ESP 是为了满足学习者的特定需求而设定的一种教学活动。以它所服务的学科的基本教学方法和实践活动为基础，立足于研究适合这些实践活动的语言。与斯特雷文斯的关注焦点不同，达德利-伊文思关注的是教学方法。他认为在具体的 ESP 教学过程中，教师的角色应该更像是一个语言顾问，并和具有专门知识的学习者之间保持一种平等的关系。

(二) 经典理论

ESP 的概念实际包括了作为语言的 ESP 和作为课程的 ESP 两部分。ESP 研究相应地也包括两类：一是关于 ESP 语言自身，从教学角度来看是客体，包括从 ESP 词汇、语句特征到篇章修辞特征的研究；二是 ESP 教学，即如何围绕语言学习主体需求而进行课程设计与开发。显然，关于 ESP 的研究重点始终围绕它的分类来进行。

1. 哈奇逊和沃特斯的分类

哈奇逊（Hutchinson）和沃特斯（Waters）发现进入大学学习的本族语者（native speaker）在开始学习专业知识前基本上没有机会接触这些专业知识，

但是他们依然能够成功地掌握这些专业知识,并成为不同行业的专业人士。这说明学生具有一定程度的理解、记忆和应用新信息的能力后就能够应对未来的专业学习。此外,他们发现即使外国留学生在开始专业学习之前没有掌握必要的专业术语知识,也能借助那些可以熟练运用的普通词语迅速完成对专业术语的理解和记忆。此外,那些专业的从业人员在同非专业人员进行交流时,也经常需要运用普通词汇解释专业术语,以便于非专业人员能够理解和认同这些专业知识。这说明ESP的分类既要同通用目的英语相区别,又要能满足不同专业人士的需求。因此,他们根据学科门类将ESP分为科技应用、商贸应用和社科英语三个大类,大类之下还有次级的分类,具体内容请见下表:

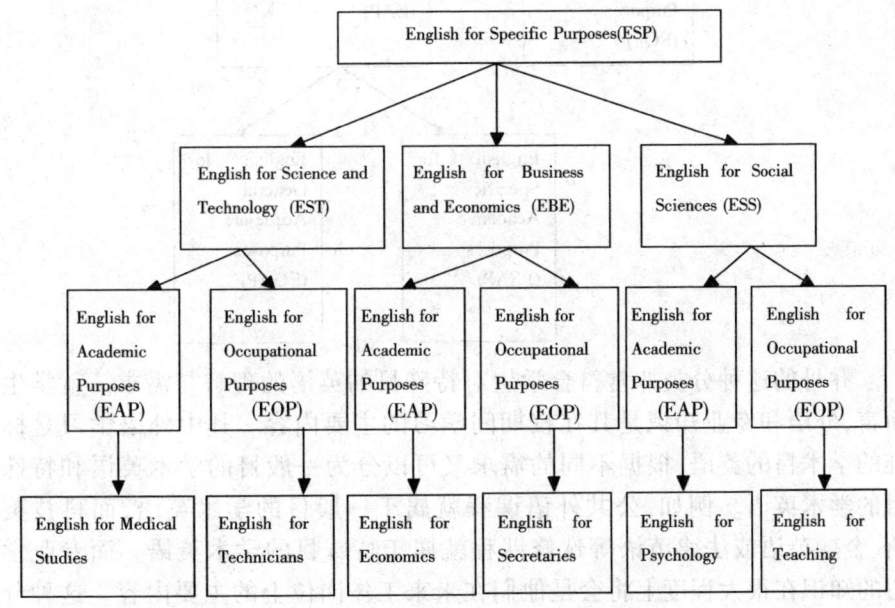

他们的这种分类兼顾了研究者和从业人员的双重需求,既解决了"关于什么"的问题,也回应了"做什么"的问题。

2. 乔丹的分类

乔丹(R. Jordan)以学习者使用语言的目的和环境为依据,将ESP分为职业英语和学术英语两大类,其中学术英语又细分为专门用途学术英语和一般用途学术英语。具体内容请看下图:

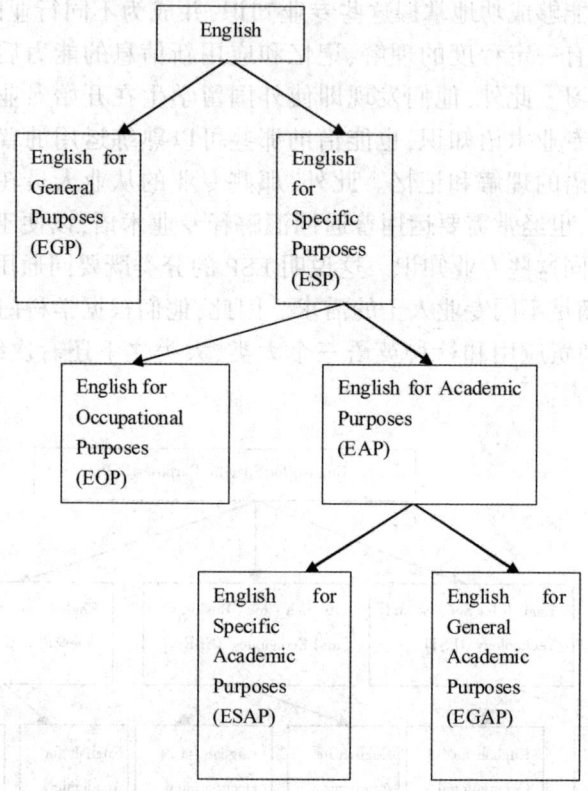

乔丹的这种分类非常符合学生对特殊目的英语的理解与需求。就学生而言，外语和专业知识是其在校期间学习的主要内容。其中外语学习是标准的学术目的英语，根据不同的需求又可以分为一般目的学术英语和特殊目的学术英语。例如，公共外语课程就属于一般目的学术英语，而科技英语、金融英语或法律英语等选修课程就属于特殊目的学术英语。而专业学习的知识在很大程度上将会是他们在未来工作岗位上的主要内容。这种分类的优点是简单清晰，同时兼顾了语言和专业学习的延续性和区别性，能够有效满足人们在学校学习和职场发展的不同需求。

本章学习心得：

_____

_____

第二部分

外语学习策略训练

第五章 词汇学习策略

本章学习目标

1. 了解词汇学习的特点
2. 掌握词汇学习中的主要策略
3. 学会运用词汇学习中的主要策略

词汇学习的本质

  英语单词有四重性,即可听性、可说性、可读性和可写性。英语单词的可听性,指单词的发音可被人们理解和接受,音义相联。听到一个音,就知道它的意思,在极短的时间内完成音义对照过程。如果音与义的对照上存在明显的"时间差",就会造成"聋子英语"。英语单词的可说性,指英语可被人们口头表达,语义相联,发出一个音,就知道它的意思,想表达一个意思,就发出相应的音。如果语义对应有较明显的时间间隔,就会造成"哑巴英语"。英语单词的可读性,指英语单词的拼写形式可被人们理解和接受,即望文而生义,词义相联。在记忆英语单词的时候,要多阅读,增加与单词见面的机会,巩固记忆。英语单词的可写性,指英语单词可被人们正确、规范地书写出来,即知义而写,写则可辨。在记忆英语单词的时候,要勤用笔头,多写多练。英语单词的四重性互相联系,密不可分,不能全面地掌握这四重性,就不能说是真正学会了一个词,掌握了一个词。英语学习者一般都在读和写上面花了很大功夫,因而英语阅读和写作能力都比较强,甚至口头表达能力也不错,而对英语水平测试中的听力部分望而生畏,原因就在于割裂了四重性的有机联系,造成"听"的失衡,使得自己深受其害。因此,英语单词的四重性与使用英语的五种能力(听、说、读、写、译)应有机地结合起来,在单词的记忆过程中,融四重性为一体,达到对单词的完整认识和掌握。

一、词汇学习中的元认知策略

  很多学生花很多时间和精力学习词汇,却不考虑为什么要学习词汇,应该优先学习哪些词语,如何有效地学习和巩固词汇等问题。这些都是词汇学习的元认知问题,对具体的词汇学习有很重要的指导作用,只有端正了词汇学习的态度,才能使词汇学习更有针对性,更有效率。

1. 了解词汇学习的目的

"你学习词汇的目的是什么?"对于这个问题,很多人的回答是"为了学好英语"。这个回答过于笼统。其实,每个英语学习者都有不同的学习目的,同一个学习者在不同的学习阶段也有不同的学习目标。词汇学习也是如此,对于这个问题的回答会直接影响对词汇的选择和词汇学习策略的运用,例如,有的同学要参加英语四、六级考试,那么他们要学习四、六级考试要求的词汇。同时,鉴于当前四、六级考试中听力和阅读占了很大比例,这就决定了对词汇的掌握程度只限于能够在听力和阅读中识别新词。

Task 1
Write down your present reason(s) for learning English vocabulary in the space provided below.

_____
_____

2. 确定优先学习的词汇

英语单词比汉字(包括词组)多得多,大约有一百万个,同学习汉语一样,并不是所有的单词都必须掌握。英语中一般使用的单词不足一万个,日常生活中经常使用的则更少,只有几千个。由于学习材料来源广泛,题材多种多样,学习过程中不可避免地要出现一些不常用的单词。很多同学每当遇到生词,都会不加区分地查字典、记生词,这就加重了学习负担。有些生词比较冷僻,而且使用频率较低,花大量时间记这些单词,显然意义不大。英语学习者尤其是初学者应该把时间和精力用于学习那些使用频率更高的单词。一般来讲,教科书收入的绝大多数属于这类词汇。如果有余力,可以通过课外阅读扩展词汇量。大学生除了掌握基本词汇以外,还可以接触一些与自己专业有关的单词,以利于阅读自己专业的英文文献。

确定词汇学习的方向后,在具体学习过程中还要对单词区别对待。科学的学习方法是,遇到生词要善于判断生词是否重要,是否必须查、必须记。有人会问:我还不认识这个词,怎么判断它是否重要、是否该记呢?以下几

点可供参考:

①看它是否影响对上下文的理解;

②看它在上下文里是否多次出现;

③看它是否"似曾相识";

④看它是否是使用频率高、造句能力强的单词;

⑤看它是否同时有其他派生词;

⑥看它是否是标准语里的词,而不是方言、俚语或仅在某一专业中使用的词;

⑦看它是否是目前常用的词,而不是过时的或生僻的词;

⑧看它是否是你认为有用或感兴趣的词,而不是可有可无或关系不大的词。

Task 2

Read the following passage and select the words you feel important to your everyday English use.

　　It is natural for young people to be critical of their parents at times and to blame them for most of the misunderstandings between them. They have always complained, more or less justly, that their parents are out of touch with modern ways; that they are possessive and dominant; that they do not trust their children to deal with crises; that they talk too much about certain problems and that they have no sense of humor, at least in parent – child relationships.

　　I think it is true that parents often underestimate their teenage children and also forget how they themselves felt when young.

　　Young people often irritate their parents with their choices in clothes and hairstyle, in entertainers and music. This is not their motive. They feel cut off from the adult world into which they have not yet been accepted. So they create a culture and society of their own. Then, if it turns out that their music or entertainers or vocabulary or clothes or hairstyles irritate their parents, this gives them additional enjoyment. They feel they are superior, at least in a small way, and that they are leaders in style and taste.

　　Sometimes you are resistant and proud because you do not want your parents to approve of what you do. If they do approve, it looks as if you are betraying your own age group. But in that case, you are assuming that you are the underdog. You can't win but at least you can keep your honor. This is a passive way of looking at things. It is natural enough after long years of childhood, when you were completely under your parents' control. But it ignores the fact that you are now beginning to be responsible for yourself.

If you plan to control your life, cooperation can be part of that plan. You can charm others, especially your parents, into doing things the way you want. You can impress others with your sense of responsibility and initiative, so that they will give you the authority to do what you want to do.

Important Words:

_____

_____

Task 3
*Based on the result of **Task** 2, discuss with your partner the reasons for your selection and record them in the space provided below.*

_____

_____

3. 确定词汇掌握的程度

对英语学习者来说,确定优先学习的词汇之后,还要考虑词汇应该掌握到什么程度,因此,应当区别主动词汇(active vocabulary)和被动词汇(passive vocabulary)。主动词汇是指能熟练掌握和运用的词汇,也就是可以说出和写出的词汇;而被动词汇是指只需被动了解的词汇,也就是能听懂或读懂,但说不出和写不出的词汇。由此可见,主动词汇的多少关系到英语学习者的语言应用能力。英文程度越好,说明他的主动词汇越多,在实际应用中越能得心应手。我们学习到的大多数词汇首先是被动词汇,其中的一部分经过反复应用可以转变为主动词汇。转变的基本原则就是要经常使用。只了解一个单词的字义是不够的,一定要熟读例句,反复使用。

Task 4
Discuss in groups of 4 or 5 strategies for turning passive vocabulary into active vocabulary and write down the strategies suggested by other students.

另外,所谓的记单词并非仅仅是知道它的汉语意义,而是应该能够根据不同的交流场合适当地使用这些单词,达到交流的目的。所以,毫无联系地死记硬背单词的中文意义是不可取的。

Task 5

Translate the following sentences into Chinese.

① A: Can we meet sometime next week?

　　B: Well, let me check my ***diary***.

② The next morning I found ***a foot of snow*** on the ground.

③ Every vote ***counts***!

要知道,要想牢记某些单词的某些意义是需要时间的。一部分单词记得太牢就意味着没有充足的时间去学习其他单词。把一个单词的某一两种意义记得太牢,就意味着忽略该单词其他的意义。除了那些特别常用的单词以外,一般的词汇学到基本熟悉就可以。如果能在上下文中理解已学过的单词,就不必再特别地加强记忆。除了单词的词义(英语解释和汉语释义),学习者还应该掌握单词的发音、拼写、词性以及用法,忽略以上任何一个方面,都会影响到英语应用能力的提高。

二、词汇学习中的认知策略

Task 6

Step 1: *Try to memorize the following ten words within ten minutes——including spelling, pronunciation and meaning.*

① reinforce (vt.):to make sth. stronger 加强;增援

② considerate (adj.):careful not to hurt others 体谅的;体贴的

③ hiss (vi.):to make a noise which sounds like "ssss" 发出"咝咝"声

④ altitude (n.):the height above sea level 海拔;高度

⑤ distinctive (adj.):serving to make a difference 有区别的;有特色的

83

⑥ transplant（vt.）:move（a plant）from one place and plant it in another 移栽;移植
⑦ carnation（n.）:a small flower with a sweet smell, which is usually white, pink, or red 康乃馨
⑧ deliberate（adj.）:planned; on purpose 故意的;蓄意的
⑨ astonish（vt.）:surprise sb. greatly 使震惊;使惊骇
⑩ approximate（adj.）:almost correct or exact 大概的;近似的

Step 2: *Dictate these words to your partner.*

Some suggestions for dictation:

A. Read the word aloud and ask your partner to write down the word and its Chinese and/or English meaning on a separate piece of paper.

B. Read the Chinese or English meaning of the word aloud and ask your partner to write the word on a separate piece of paper.

Step 3: *Discuss in groups of 4 or 5 the strategies you have used to remember those ten words and write down any different strategies used by other students.*

Strategies used:

_____

_____

_____

_____

1. 在语境中学单词

在语境中学单词就是学习者通过上下文语言环境所提供的信息对出现在语境中的生词进行猜测,进而学习些这单词。语境策略是目前比较流行的词汇学习策略之一,它不仅可以扩大词汇量,而且可以让学生了解相关的文化知识。通过语境加深对单词的理解和记忆已经不是什么新方法,很多人都能这样做。但通过语境学新单词则不那么容易达到理想效果,很多人还是觉得利用上下文猜测生词的意思时无从下手,所以遇到生词时,还是以查字典为主。关于如何利用上下文猜测词义,你可以从下面的任务中得到一些启发。

Task 7

Guess the meanings of the underlined words in the following sentences and write down both the meanings and helpful context clues.

① At first, I was uncertain whether he could do it well or not. However, after two successful weeks, I was much less <u>dubious</u>.

  meaning: _____

  context clue: _____

② The <u>perimeter</u> – the distance around – of the ball is twenty inches.

  meaning: _____

  context clue: _____

③ A logically disconnected sentence is an <u>incoherent</u> sentence.

  meaning: _____

  context clue: _____

④ A good supervisor can recognize instantly the <u>adept</u> from the unskilled.

  meaning: _____

  context clue: _____

⑤ Select a <u>periodical</u> from among the following: Playboy, Fortune, Times or The New Yorker.

  meaning: _____

  context clue: _____

⑥ Driving carelessly will not only <u>endanger</u> your own life but also the life of others.

  meaning: _____

  context clue: _____

2. 根据单词的读音记忆单词

  根据单词的读音记忆单词,也就是根据某些字母或字母组合的读音规则来记忆单词。掌握了单词拼写与读音之间的关系,可以正确地拼写单词。例如,我们知道在元音字母 o 之后,如果是 m,n,v,th 时,o 可以读作[Λ]。根据这条规则,我们不会把 mother、some、come、dove、done 等单词中的 o 写成 u。再如,元音字母组合 ay 读[ei],所以就不难记住 say,day,way,pay,ray,may,lay,play,spray 等词的发音和拼写。虽然英语发音规则很多,又有许多例外情况,但记住一些常用发音规则能够减轻记忆的负担。

3. 根据同音词(Homophone)记忆单词

英语中有许多同音异义词或者发音相近的词,根据同音词记忆单词可以减轻记忆读音的负担。

Task 8

Write down the homophones or the words that have the similar pronunciations of the following words.

Words	Similar pronunciations	Words	Similar pronunciations
quite		affect	
adapt		angel	
dairy		loose	
principal		beam	
dessert		story	
except		sweet	
later		floor	
steal		personnel	
abroad		site	
contact		through	

4. 通过分类加深对单词的理解和记忆

英语中的大多数单词都可以按照某种方式进行归类,而且在一篇文章里,同类词出现的概率较大。用分类法记忆单词能充分发挥大脑的潜力,系统、全面地记忆单词,其优点是:

- 同类单词的语法功能相似,结构相近,便于从整体上进行记忆和掌握,有助于对单词形成完整的类别概念;
- 便于比较,有利于掌握各个单词的异同点;
- 便于集中同类词汇,从而可灵活地进行替换和运用;
- 能使已掌握的杂乱无章的单词条理化、系统化、门类化。

我们可以把学过的英语单词按一定特征分组归类,如名词可分为动物、植物、职业、时间、交通工具、学习用品、生活用品等。同一类词汇中还可以再分几小类。例如:

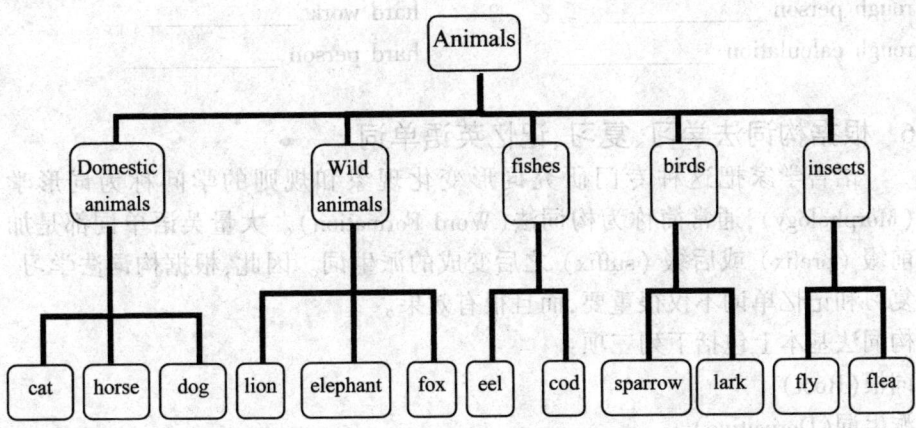

Task 9
Put the following words listed below into the corresponding catalogue listed below.

milk	typist	apple	pig	shirt	Germany	chicken	Japan	shoe	orange	peach
wine	cow	butcher	driver	Greece	sock	Turkey	trouser	baker	dog	sheep
coffee	plum	pear								

country	
job	
fruit	
drink	
animal	
clothes	

5. 利用同义词(Synonym)和反义词(Antonym)进行对比学习

英语中有大量的同义词和反义词。在学习某个词时,如果能用同义词进行解释或利用反义词进行对比,可以加深对单词的理解和记忆。

Task 10
Think of a possible antonym for each different use of the words "rough" and "hard" according to the meaning of the word in each collocation.

rough sea _____   hard exam _____

rough texture _____   hard chair _____

rough area _____   hard journey _____

rough person _____   hard work _____
rough calculation _____   hard person _____

6. 根据构词法学习、复习、记忆英语单词

语言学家把这种专门研究词形变化现象和规则的学问称为词形学（Morphology），通常简称为构词法（Word Formation）。大量英语单词都是加前缀（prefix）或后缀（suffix）之后变成的派生词。因此，根据构词法学习、复习和记忆单词不仅很重要，而且很有效果。

构词法基本上包括下列三项：

词根（Root）
派生词（Derivative）
合成词（Compound Words）

（1）词根

英文单词形成的"根基"部分称为词根（亦称字根）。

现以"like"为例列示如下：

Root: like ·· 像
    a-like ·· 相像
    un-like ·· 不像
    like-ness ··· 相像
    un-like-ness ·· 互不相像

如上例所示，"like"就是"alike, unlikeness"等词的词根。

Task 11

Form a word by putting the following three parts together. Then check each word in the dictionary.

Prefixes	Roots	Suffixes
pre	cord	ed
mis	order	ant
uni	test	er
re	form	ly
con	vent	able
un	eat	ion
dis	lead	ing
①_____	②_____	

③ _____ ④ _____
⑤ _____ ⑥ _____
⑦ _____

(2) 派生词

由词根利用前缀或后缀派生而成的词称为派生词（亦称转成语）。现以词根"friend"为例列示如下：

friend ·· 朋友
friend-ly ·· 友善的
friend-less ·· 没有朋友的
friend-ship ··· 友谊
un-friend-ly ·· 不友善的

前缀和后缀主要都是源自拉丁语，并且都有含义。例如"un-"的含义是"与词根的含义相反"，"-less"的含义是"没有词根的语义"。在记忆单词时应该有意识地进行同根词联想，如："pel-" = drive, push；那么 compel（强迫）；dispel（驱散）；expel（开除，驱逐）；impel（推进，驱动）；propel（推进）；repel（击退，使反感）就容易记忆了。

Task 12

The three words in parentheses before each of the following sentences all belong to the same word family, but only one of them can be filled in the blank. Decide what kind of word belongs there: verb, noun, adjective, or adverb. Then choose the right word to fill in the sentence.

① (depend, dependable, dependably)

  Their new helper is very _____.

② (satisfaction, satisfactory, satisfactorily)

  He has completed the work _____.

③ (beauty, beautiful, beautifully)

  Everyone admires goodness and _____.

④ (collect, collection, collective)

  When do they _____ the mail?

⑤ (artist, artistic, artistically)

  Her niece is very _____.

⑥ (destroy, destruction, destructive)

  The fire produced terrible _____ everywhere.

⑦ (gratitude, grateful, gratefully)
   How can we express our _____?
⑧ (science, scientific, scientifically)
   Your reasons are not very _____.
⑨ (explain, explanation, explanatory)
   What is his _____?
⑩ (repeat, repetition, repetitive)
   Sometimes _____ helps us.

Task 13

Change the following adjectives into their antonyms by adding a prefix to each word.

sufficient _____
loyal _____
possible _____
athletic _____
regular _____
capable _____
willing _____
social _____

(3) 合成词

由两个或两个以上独立且语义不相同的词结合成一个表达新的语义和语词功能的词称为合成词。例如：

class（班级）＋ room（房间）→classroom（教室）
black（黑色的）＋ board（木板）→blackboard（黑板）
note（记录）＋ book（簿, 书）→notebook（笔记簿）
hide（躲藏）＋ and（和）＋ seek（寻找）→hide-and-seek（捉迷藏）
forget（忘记）＋ me（我）＋ not（不）→forget-me-not 勿忘我（草）
Jack（男孩名）＋ in（在……里面）＋ the ＋ box（盒子）→jack-in-the-box（玩偶箱）

合成词的语义有的可以通过结合的原词语义猜测出来，如"class-room"；有的则重点在表达各原词结合的功能，如"jack-in-the-box"。合成词的写法可以如"classroom"拼写成一词，也可以如"hide-and-seek"各词之间用连词符"-"连接成一词。最好是参考词典确定合成词的写法，依照词典的方式拼写。

Task 14

Study the following words and try to work out the patterns by which these compounds are formed, and their word-classes(词性) and meanings.

For example: heartbeat n. (n. + v.) 心跳

  record-breaking _____ chain-smoke _____
  deadline _____ stockholder _____
  have-not _____ dog-tired _____
  lionhearted _____ outgoing _____
  moon walk _____ homemade _____

7. 利用联想（Association）增强学习效果

  遇到生词时同学们应该联想该词和以前学过的词有没有外表类似的，读音类似的，意思类似或相反的。如果有，就赶紧记在这个词的旁边，同时在另外那些词旁边也把这个词加上。这样，以后看见其他词，也会联想起这个词，等于又增加了一次见面机会。

  通过音与形的联想和形与义的联想记忆单词。音与形的联想，即根据读音规则记忆单词；形与义的联想，即根据单词的拼写记忆单词，如：eye 把两个 e 看成两个眼睛；banana 把 a 看成一个个的香蕉；bird 把 b 和 d 看成两个翅膀。

  在日常生活中还可以根据自己学习、工作、娱乐、游览、参观、访问等具体情景和场合，触景生情地联想相关的英语单词。例如：打球时联想到：ball,（play）basketball,（play）football,（play）volleyball, playground, 等等；吃饭时联想到：dining-room,（have）breakfast,（have）lunch,（have）supper, 等等；睡觉时联想到：bed, bedroom, go to bed, sleep, go to sleep, fall asleep, 等等。如果长期坚持对同类词使用联想的方法学习和记忆，效果就会很好。

8. 通过固定搭配(Collocation)扩大词汇量

  在英语中有大量的固定搭配，搭配指的是词和词是如何组合使用的，有些词可以放在一起用，有些则不能。必须固定放在一起出现的，称为固定搭配。对学习者来说，固定搭配非常重要，因为固定搭配会帮助学习者克服中式英语的毛病。英语中的固定搭配一般包括：动词中的固定搭配、介词中的固定搭配、形容词中的固定搭配和名词中的固定搭配。记单词时最好把它们放在固定搭配里一起记忆,这样单词之间有了联系,便于长期记忆,同时让你的大脑"携带方便",也可随时将它们"调"出来使用。因为单一的单词只是原材料,固定搭配已经是半成品,更便于记忆和使用。

Task 15

Write down the verbs or expressions that usually precede the following nouns or noun phrases.

① to _____ a decision
② to _____ a gamble
③ to _____ one's life
④ to _____ one's destination
⑤ to _____ fears
⑥ to _____ an offer
⑦ to _____ a meal
⑧ to _____ a journey
⑨ to _____ a ride
⑩ to _____ money

Task 16

Choose the correct preposition for each of the following sentences.

① In your family, who is usually the first person to *turn to/on* the TV when you get home?
② What programs make you want to *turn off/over* to another channel?
③ When you're watching, do you ever *turn away/up* when something is extremely frightening or exciting?
④ Do you ever *turn* the volume of the TV *up/off* or down? Why?
⑤ If somebody *turns up/on* at your house, do you *turn* the TV *over/off* or do you leave it on?
⑥ If there is a disagreement in your family about which program to watch, who in your family do *you turn up/to* for support?

9. 通过习语(Idioms)扩展词汇量

习语是语言在使用过程中形成的独特的固定的表达方式。习语是广义的,包括成语、谚语、歇后语、典故等。英语历史悠久,包含大量的习语,它们或含蓄、幽默,或严肃、典雅,不仅言简意赅,而且形象生动,给人一种美的享受,例如:Spend money like water(挥金如土),Every dog has his day(凡人皆有得意日),God helps those who help themselves(上帝帮助自助的人),Sphinx's riddle(难解之谜,狮身人面的怪兽提出"什么动物早晨四条腿,中午两条腿,而晚上三条腿"的谜语),等等。由于地理、历史、宗教信仰、生活习俗等方面的差异,英汉习语承载着不同的民族文化特色和文化信息,它们与文化传统紧密相连,不可分割。因此,我们不但可以通过习语扩展词汇量,还可以了解文化差异。

Task 17

Translate the following sentences into English according to the given idioms.

① to ask (someone) for (one's) hand: to ask girl's parents for marriage approval(指男人请求女方家长应允将女儿嫁给他,这里的"someone"是指女方的家长,"one"则是指求婚的对象,hand 只能用单数形式)
　　·他请求她的父母应允他们的婚事。

② to move onward and upward: to be promoted; from good to better situation(情况得以改善,或往更好的方向发展)
　　·他希望能在现在就职的公司里顺利发展,步步高升。

③ to call a spade a spade: to be honest, blunt or frank
　　(直言不讳,有啥说啥)
　　·我妻子对别人谈起她的工作时,总是直言不讳。

④ to play cat and mouse: to play games with aggressive and passive attitude
　　(玩猫戏老鼠的把戏,欲擒故纵)
　　·在商业谈判中,常会有一些猫戏老鼠的把戏。

⑤ to keep (one's) fingers crossed: to hope something good will happen
　　(祝福某人好运或一切顺利。把食指与中指交叉,祈求好运)
　　·他盼望有好运,爸爸能多寄点钱给他。

⑥ to be in the hot seat: to be under lots of pressure or in a difficult position
　　(处于困境,面对很多压力)

- 由于不堪多年的工作压力，他终于辞职了。

⑦ to make waves：to make trouble
（惹是生非，与"rock the boat"意思相近）
- 一些青少年总是会给父母和老师惹麻烦。

⑧ to drive (someone) up the wall：to annoy or upset someone
（惹人生气或者不高兴）
- 这个不听话的孩子让他妈妈大为头痛。

⑨ to have (many) irons in the fire：to have a lot of activities going on at the same time
（同时有许多事，想马上全部做完，但又不知从何开始，似乎忙得不可开交）
- 别打扰他，他事情太多，忙得很！

⑩ to paint the town red：to enjoy oneself；to have a good time
（尽情享受）
- 他今天晚上要玩个痛快。

10. 了解单词的本义（Denotation）和引申义（Connotation）

有的学习者在读一个句子的时候，没有不懂的语法结构，也没有不认识的生词，但却读不懂意思。例如：It is a poem by an unknown pen. 如果理解为"它是一首不详的笔的诗"，读不通。其实这句英语中的 pen 不是"笔"，而是"作家"。这句话的意思是："它是一首作者不详的诗。"Pen 不仅有"笔"的意思，还有"作家"的意思。对大多数学习者来说，一遇到一个单词有多个表面上看似并无关联的意思，就相当头痛。其实，单词的一词多义通常都有逻辑上的内在关联，这同中文颇为相似。

一个词，当它具有两个以上的意义时，其中必有一个是本义，而其他的则是引申义。引申义是从本义"引申"发展出来的，大多数一词多义的英语单词能找出其本义与引申义。例如：bar，本义为"杆、棒"。杆、棒可作障碍用，引申为"障碍物"、"围栏"；又因为法庭上有围栏，引申为"法庭"；餐馆里有"围栏"分开店主与顾客，故又引申为"酒吧"、"柜台"；如此等等。因此，记单词时要格外注意单词的引申义。

Task 18

Discuss in groups of 4 or 5 the denotations and connotations of the following words: **owl**, **liberal** *and* **dog** *in both English and Chinese cultures, and then record your notes in the spaces provided below.*

owl
Chinese culture：
denotation _____
connotation _____
western cultures：
denotation _____
connotation _____

liberal
Chinese culture：
denotation _____
connotation _____
western cultures：
denotation _____
connotation _____

dog
Chinese culture：
denotation _____
connotation _____
western cultures：
denotation _____
connotation _____

三、词汇学习中的社交/情感策略

1. 通过合作学习词汇

　　合作学习是词汇学习过程中的一个重要社交策略。学习者通过合作互教互学，互爱互助，彼此之间交流信息，交流情感。在相互交流与相互评价

95

的过程中,通过相互启发和激励,学习者能体验到一种被他人接受、信任和认同的情感,这为提高交际能力和发展自我意识提供了充分的条件,从而有利于发展认知能力、培养合作能力和团队精神。

Task 19

Dictate any three pairs of the following words and any two sentences to your partners, and have them write down your dictation below.

Words:

- receive/receiving
- believe/belief
- exist/existence/existent
- success/succeed/succession
- lose/losing
- occur/occurred/occurring/occurrence
- write/writing/writer
- perform/performance
- definite/definitely/definition/define
- description/describe
- benefit/benefited/beneficial
- professor/profession
- separate/separation
- necessary/unnecessary

Sentences:

- The problem of staff personnel is a very personal problem.
- The school principal gave the principle speech on the subject.
- My choice is to choose the same thing that I chose before.
- Then I walked farther than he did.
- Those two were too tired to get along too.
- They're getting their books to put there.

2. 通过做游戏学习词汇

通过做游戏来学习词汇既可以增强学习的动机和乐趣,还可以加深记忆,达到事半功倍的效果。例如,"纵横字谜"(Crosswords Puzzles)是世界上广为流行的单词游戏。第一个英文单词"纵横字谜"游戏出现在19世纪的英格兰。如今,在美国"纵横字谜"已经发展为家喻户晓的休闲游戏。游戏要求玩家根据一定的规则在方格中填入单词,构成单词的字母会存在纵横交错连接的情况。"纵横字谜"游戏规则:根据游戏里横向与纵向的提示,将相应的英语单词填入对应的空格内,每空一个英文字母,直到将所有空格填满。

Task 20

According to the clues and the letters offered in the game, guess the meaning of the words, and then write the missing letters in the blank squares.

ACROSS

1. Tuesday is between Monday and _____.

6. I have two ears but only _____ nose.

7. The number after 89 is _____.

9. We hear with each ear, and we see with each _____.

10. This tea is _____ hot to drink.

11. Did she ring that bell? No. He _____ it.

DOWN

1. They were happy when their team _____.

2. What did you eat for _____.

3. You don't like coffee, _____ you?

4. Come back in _____ hour, please.
5. To make green, we mix blue and _____.
8. France is larger _____ England.

本章学习心得：
_____
_____
_____

第六章 听力学习策略

本章学习目标
1. 了解听力学习的本质
2. 掌握听力学习中的主要策略
3. 学会运用听力学习中的主要策略

听力学习的本质

在听、说、读、写、译五项基本语言技能中，听力理解虽然是一项语言输入性技能，但它并不是一个被动地接收信息的过程，而是一个复杂的认知心理过程，不仅受到语音、词汇、语法、修辞等语言知识的制约，同时受到学习者社会背景知识和心理活动的影响。

听者的理解与讲话者的意图之间存在着信息差，听者要真正地理解讲话者的意图，必须在一定的语言知识的基础上，充分调动背景经验，对讲话者的意图进行预测和推断。也就是说，听力不是人脑简单地刻录下所听到的信息的过程，而是新信息与听者原有的知识经验相互作用、建构意义的复杂过程。听者不是一个被动的接受者，而是一个意义的积极建构者。在听的过程中只有充分发挥自己的主动性，才能提高听力能力。

一、听力学习中的元认知策略

1. 计划策略（Planning）

听力学习中的计划策略指听力活动开始之前，学习者本人或他人为学习者对活动的目标、过程、步骤做出规划和安排。例如：确定听力学习目标，分析如何完成任务，安排学习时间，选择学习材料，等。在一项具体的听力任务中，应涵盖预测听力内容的重点、难点及可能提出的问题等多项细则。听力学习中的计划策略主要包括：制订听力学习计划、选择注意对象，以及选择恰当的听力材料。

（1）**制订学习计划**

学习计划一般包含四个因素——目标内容、时间、评价标准和方法措施。目标内容是具体的学习活动和所要达到的目标;时间是指在学习计划中要对完成某项任务的具体时间做出明确规定;评价标准,即在计划中明确一项任务完成到什么程度才算符合要求,例如:我们听一篇文章,理解到什么程度才算完成任务——是听一遍就可以了,还是要听懂每一个词、每一句话;方法措施是指在计划中明确列出完成任务所需要的条件、策略方法和监控措施。

制订学习计划一定要适合自己的语言发展水平,切实可行,而且要具有明确的针对性。这就要求学习者要对自己现有听力水平有一个正确的评价,知道自己的弱项在哪里,不能好高骛远。同时,计划一旦制订就应该按计划执行,除非在对计划执行情况进行监控的过程中发现该计划不适合自己,这时应该找出原因对计划及时做出调整,以免费时低效。

Task 1

Try to identify the factors that may interfere with your listening. Then list them in the blanks below.

① Speaking speed _____
② _____
③ _____
④ _____
⑤ _____

Task 2

Make a one-term study plan for listening.

My study plan for listening:

Aim:
_____
_____
_____
_____

Method:
_____
_____
_____
_____

(2) 选择注意对象

听力理解是一个复杂的心理过程,包括感知、分析和运用三个阶段,与记忆信息三级加工模型——感觉登记、短时记忆和长时记忆相对应。短时记忆是信息加工场所,在这里信息保存的时间在 10—20 秒之间,转瞬即逝,而且容量有限。然而,人的耳朵在同一时刻接收的信息量远远超过短时记忆的容量。也就是说,我们所感知到的听觉信息,绝大多数不会在我们头脑中留下印象,只有经过短时记忆加工的信息才能转化为长时记忆,储存在我们的大脑中,成为我们头脑中知识框架的一部分。因此,当我们面临一项听力任务时,通常应用选择性注意策略,以听的目的为基础,严格地过滤、筛选进入大脑的信息,保证大脑有效地对信息进行编码、储存和加工,减轻记忆负担,提高听力效率。

Task 3

Think about what information you might focus on while listening to a weather forecast.

I will:

① focus on the information that is important to the things I am going to do.

② _____

③ _____

④ _____

(3) 选择恰当的听力材料

"如何选择听力材料"往往被很多听者所忽略。他们认为听作为一项语言输入性技能,是被动的语言接收过程,甚至很多人错误地认为:只要听,无论听什么,都能有效地提高听力水平。实际上,听是一个积极创造的思维过程,更是一个复杂的心理过程。听力理解的程度与学习者积极主动参与的程度有直接的关系。学习者对听力活动的参与程度又直接取决于所采用的听力材料。因此,如何选择恰当的听力材料至关重要,在一定程度上决定着听力水平能否提高。

在选择听力材料方面,所选择的内容一定要适合自己的听力水平。内容过难,不仅会耗费很多时间,而且容易损伤继续学习的信心;内容过于简单,由于缺乏挑战性而使你丧失学习的兴趣。而且,我们要明确听力学习的最终目的不是为做题、通过考试,而是为了和人真正地交往,因此真实的、贴近生活的材料更有利于我们提高听力,实现听力学习的目标。

Task 4

What kind of materials do you usually listen to in your daily study and why do you listen to such kind of materials?

_____

_____

_____

Task 5

Discuss with your partner what kind of materials may be helpful in improving your listening ability, and write down your ideas in the following blanks.

①The material that we are interested in.

②_____

③_____

④_____

2. 监控策略(Monitoring)

　　监控策略指在听力学习的过程中,以学习目标为依据,对学习进程、方法、计划的执行情况等方面进行有意识的监控。监控的先决因素就是在听的过程中,确保注意力指向所要完成的任务。但听力本身的性质决定了听的过程中注意力容易分散,所以在听的过程中如何保持注意的指向性,有效地集中注意力于所听内容,对于有效地实施监控尤为重要。

　　记笔记是监控听力过程的一个重要和常用的手段。通过记笔记,可以使注意力集中于所听内容,加深对所听内容的理解,便于听后总结和分析,使听力成为一种更积极的学习过程。但由于没有掌握恰当合理的方法,很多学习者感到边听边记对他们来说很困难,而且常常会出现为了记录某一内容而漏听其他重要信息的现象,不但没有使注意力有效地指向所听材料,反而分散了注意力,得不偿失。因此,如何简洁有效地记录所听信息,就成为"记笔记"能否发挥其监控作用的关键。

Task 6

Usually, our writing speed can not catch up with that of speaking. Think about the ways we can take notes quickly.

①Only write down the most important information.

② _____
③ _____
④ _____
⑤ _____

记笔记的时候,通常只需要记下最重要的信息,例如:时间、地点、数字等。但有时候即使这样也很难完全记下所有要记的内容,这时可以利用缩写或符号的形式来代替完整的句子和单词,就如同你在网上聊天时用 u 代替 you 一样。通常人们所利用的缩写或符号是因人而异的,没有统一的规定,但对于你个人来说,这套缩写或符号应该具有一贯性,否则一段时间之后,你自己也很难辨认自己所记的内容。另外,笔记的内容并不是在一张纸上你想记在哪儿就记在哪儿,不分主次,而是要有良好的逻辑、条理性。

记笔记既可以是元认知策略,又可以是认知策略,关键在于记的目的是什么。当记笔记被视为元认知策略时,它强调的是对注意力的调控作用;当记笔记被视为认知策略时,则强调其弥补人的记忆的局限性、强化记忆的功能,就像俗话所说的那样——"好记性不如烂笔头。"

笔记的外在形式大致可以分为两种:一是线性笔记;二是结构笔记。第一种可以说是通用笔记,在多数情况下都可以应用;第二种则适合某些特定类型的材料。

(1) **线性笔记**

在这种笔记中通常运用数字或是字母来标示所记内容的先后顺序和重要性,为了体现所记内容的层次性,采用缩进式,如:

Topic: University System in U. S.

I. *Lecture course: Prof. talk. Sts. take notes.*

缩进 1. *Important to take notes because*

缩进 a...

    b...

2. *Sts. listen to lecs. 4-6 hrs/wk. per course*

II. *Discourse section.*

缩进 1. ……

2. ……

(2) **结构笔记**

结构笔记是通过表格、流程图和网图等来表达不同意思之间的关系。

通常在这类笔记中会有圆圈、箭头、线条或方框等图形出现。例如：

a. 在比较两个主题的异同时,可以用圆形交叉图解。

例如:听到一篇关于美国和法国简介中所包含信息异同的文章,就可以用圆形交叉图解来记录所听信息,通常两个圆形交叉的部分为共同点,其余为不同点。

b. 在比较一个主题的两个不同方面时,可以用 T 形图表。

例如:听到一篇关于网络教学的文章,在其中探讨了网络教学的优点和缺点,这时就可以用 T 形图表来记录相关信息。

Advantages	Disadvantages
1. Convenient	1. High requirement of computer skills
2. Less cost	2. Lack of real world friends
…	…

c. 在记录一个特定过程的时候,可以用流程图的形式来表示出每一步骤。

例如:听到一篇关于制作比萨饼过程的文章,其中的每一步骤可以用流程图来体现。制作的第一步为 check the list of ingredients;第二步为 make the dough,在这一步中你要做两件事情:1) Mix everything together, 2) Cover the dough and wait;第三步为 make the dough into a round circle...

d. 在涉及分类叙述时,可以用分类结构来表示各类、各层次间的关系。

例如:听到一篇关于大学生活中社团和俱乐部种类的文章,可以采用分类结构来记录信息。

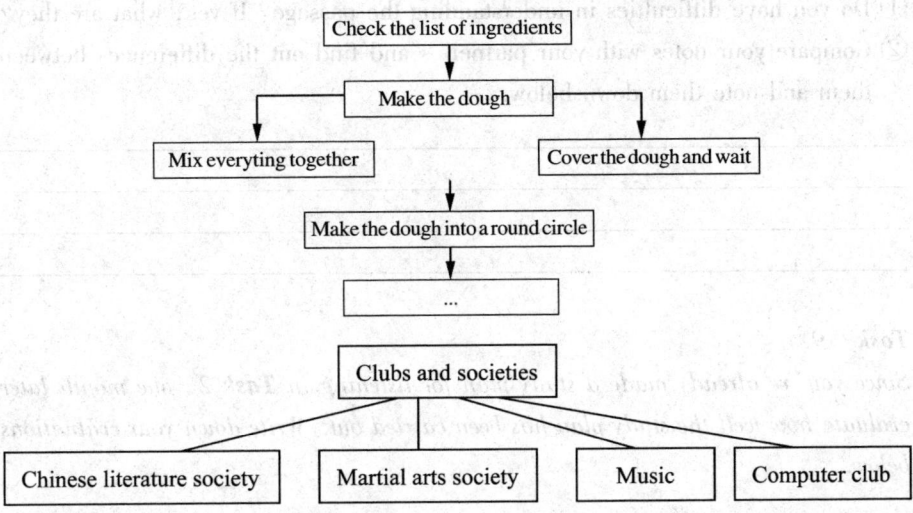

Task 7

In this task, you will hear a passage. The passage will be read twice. For the first time, try to decide what method you will adopt to take notes. For the second time, write down your notes in the way you have chosen.

_____
_____
_____
_____

3. 评估策略(Evaluation)

评估策略是听者自我反思的过程,可以发生在完成一项听力任务之后,也可以是听者对自己一段时间听力状况的反思。在此过程中,听者会对听力材料的难度、计划的完成情况和效果进行客观评价;回顾自己在听力方面的进步,分析听不懂材料的原因并及时调整自己的策略。在听力学习的过程中,听者能否对自己的学习状况做出有效的评价,能否发挥评估策略在听力学习中的导向作用,决定着听者能否切实提高听力能力。

Task 8

Evaluate how well you have done **Task** 7.

① Do you have difficulties in understanding the passage? If yes, what are they?
② Compare your notes with your partner's and find out the differences between them and note them down below.

_____

_____

_____

Task 9

Since you've already made a study plan for listening in **Task** 2, one month later evaluate how well the study plan has been carried out. Write down your evaluations below.

_____

_____

_____

二、听力学习中的认知策略

1. 预测(Prediction)

预测是理解口头语言的重要程序,是积极的参与者在听力过程中必然出现的心理现象。在运用母语进行交际时,交际双方会在无意识的状态下对交际内容进行预测。但在用外语进行交际时,听者面临新的语言系统,往往将注意力集中在语言知识的理解上,而忽视预测这一心理现象对听力理解的积极作用。在听的过程中,听力理解能力强的人总是对将要出现的信息进行预测,减轻大脑处理信息的负担,获得最佳的理解效果。预测贯穿听力活动的始终,听前和听中都有预测,主要包括以下几种:

(1) 听前根据已知文字信息进行预测

对于外语学习者来说,听得最多的就是测试性的材料。这类材料附有检验听者理解程度的问题,并且以文字形式呈现,这时可以根据已呈现的信息预测所要听到的内容。

例如,问题的答案选项为:

a. Because she starts her new business.
b. Because she is a reporter.

c. Because she is nasty.

d. Because she is alike.

这时听者可以根据四个选项——四个由"because"引导的句子,预测出对话可能要谈论的是某事件的原因。

Task 10

The following choices are provided for the questions of six short conversations. Try to predict what topic you will hear for each of the conversations.

① a. At 11 a.m.　b. At 8 a.m.　c. At 8 p.m.　d. At 11 p.m.

② a. Colleagues　b. Staff　c. Classmates　d. Workmates

③ a. She will speak English a lot.　　b. She will keep up with others.
　 c. She will study English very hard.　d. She will do her homework.

④ a. At a bank.　　　　　　b. At a supermarket.
　 c. At a library.　　　　　d. At a restaurant.

⑤ a. Blue shirt without sleeves.　b. Dark blue T-shirt.
　 c. Blue overcoat.　　　　　　　d. A top blue shirt.

⑥ a. Salesman　b. Teacher　c. Student　d. Travel Agent

(2) 根据已有知识和经验进行预测

在完成一项听力任务时,听者的头脑中并不是空的,里面已经存储了各种各样的信息。这些已存储的信息通常会帮助听者完成现有的听力任务。例如,绝大多数人都去过银行,知道在银行通常会说什么、做什么,所以当听到一个发生在银行的对话时,听者会自然地应用他的经验知识预测和理解将要听到的内容。

107

Task 11

Try to predict what might be heard in the following situations.

① barbershop（理发店）

_____

② shopping center（购物中心）

_____

③ restaurant（饭店）

_____

④ library（图书馆）

_____

（3）听中根据已获得的信息线索进行预测

除了听前预测，在听的过程中，听者应该不断地以已听到的信息——主题句、句子结构、连接词、语法关系以及语言环境等为线索，预测下文将要出现的内容和情节。例如，在行文中通常会出现 but, yet, however 之类的转折连词，在这种情况下，即使没有听清其后的内容，根据这些词本身的特点，也能推测出后面的内容应该和前面谈到的是相反的或是不同的。

Task 12

Read the following conversation about what to take for a ski trip between a wife and a husband —— David and Susan, and try to predict what David will say after "but"?

Susan: Come on, David. Let's get ready for the ski trip.

David: Already?

Susan: What do you mean "already"? We're leaving tomorrow morning.

David: Oh. Well. I don't need to get ready. I can just take a few things, you know, a ski jacket, a sweater, my ski boots. I don't need much.

Susan: You need more than that. How about gloves?

David: Oh, yeah. I guess I need a pair of gloves.

Susan: Right. And how about a hat? You've got a great yellow and black ski hat. Take that.

David: Oh, right. Okey. Where is my hat? Great. I found it. And here are my black gloves. Ahhh... here's my blue sweater. I'll take this

too. Susan, where is my yellow and green ski sweater?
Susan: I thought you only needed one sweater.
David: Well, yeah, but...

_____
_____

2. 重读（Stress）

一句话中重读的部分通常是讲话者所要强调的内容，承载着讲话者的意图。句中重读位置不同，往往传达的信息也不同。因此，在听的过程中要注意句子重读位置，利用重读判断讲话者所要表达的真正意思。

Task 13

The boldfaced parts in the following two dialogues are stressed. Pay attention to the stresses and guess what the man means in each dialogue.

① Woman: When does Mary **plan** to finish the homework?
　　Man: I don't know if she **even plans** to do it.
　　The man means _____

② Woman: I missed the plane.
　　Man: **Didn't** I tell you this would happen?
　　The man means _____

Task 14

The boldfaced parts in the following sentences are stressed. The sentences in each pair are the same in structure and words, but with different stressed parts. Try to read them by yourself and write down what each sentence means.

①a. **Jack** did not visit John **either.**
_____

　b. Jack did not visit John either.
_____

②a. **He** may not go **tomorrow**.
_____

　b. He may not go tomorrow.
_____

109

3. 语调（Intonation）

与重读相同,讲话者的语调也是听者判断语义的重要依据。在有些情况下,即使听者理解了讲话者所用词汇的意义,但不能准确把握其语调特征,也不能准确了解讲话者的意图。往往同一句话,用不同的语调来表达,它所传达的信息也是不同的。因此,在听的过程中要善于抓住讲话者的语调信息,通过语调正确判断讲话者的真正意图。

Task 15

The sentence ——"*I got 75 points on the test*" will be spoken in three different ways. Try to circle the speaker's feeling in each case.

① a. sad   b. happy   c. angry
② a. sad   b. happy   c. angry
③ a. sad   b. happy   c. angry

Task 16

Work with your partner to read the following two sentences. One reads it in three different ways—angry, surprised and amused, and the other tries to identify the feeling the reader wants to express.

① You left the groceries at the supermarket.
② You put my car keys in the refrigerator.

4. 推测词义（Inferencing）

在听力的过程中,往往会遇到生词和不熟悉的表达方式,这时很多学习者会产生过度焦虑的心理,导致听力失败。在这种情况下,千万不要受到不良心理状态的影响,应该明确即使是在母语的听力中,也会遇到陌生的表达方式,而绝大多数情况下这些表达并不影响我们对所听内容的理解。这时应该根据已经听到的内容判断它们是否影响对内容的理解。如果不影响,则可以将其忽略;如果对所听内容来说是关键词,那么可以充分利用我们的语言知识、经验及上下文语境来推测其意义。

Task 17

In this task, you will hear 10 short conversations. While listening, try to infer what the following words mean in the corresponding short conversations. Then discuss with your partner how well you have inferred.

① pushy：

② kick back：

③ culprit：

④ go out：

⑤ vacuum：

⑥ print：

⑦ drag：

⑧ cozy：

⑨ sentimental：

⑩ off – the – wall：

5. 略听(Skim listening)

略听时,注意力通常集中在篇章的题目、首句和尾句及关键词上,而不用过分关注细节。它常用于获得所听材料的大概意思,或是判断是否有必要进一步听材料的详细内容。

Task 18

In this task, you will hear a passage. You are required to write down the main idea based on what you've heard.

111

6. 寻听（Scan listening）

寻听是为了寻找特定的信息。在这种情况下，听者必须首先明确所要寻找的特定信息是什么，例如：在下面的任务中要求根据所听内容补全一个申请表中的个人信息，在听的过程中注意寻找空格内需要填写的信息即可，无须关注其他信息。这样就会具有明确的针对性，减轻听的负担，从而提高听的效率。

Task 19

In this task, you will hear a conversation. Try to fill in the missing information based on what you've heard. If you can not get the information about any item, write NA (not available) in the corresponding blank.

```
                        APPLICATION
          NAME: Ted _____
          ADDRESS: _____ Drive
          TELEPHONE: 818 - _____
          WORK: _____
          CREDIT CARD NUMBER: _____
```

7. 精听（Intensive listening）

精听是指"精确听力练习"，侧重于听的质量训练，目的在于训练听的基本功。通常要求在注意力高度集中的情况下尽量把所听到的语言材料完全听懂，准确地理解其中的每个单词、每一句话，并且要准确地把握语音和语调。为了达到精确这一目标，通常需要反复多次地听，甚至是逐词逐句地听。这样听容易使听者感到枯燥无味，所以精听对听者的耐心和毅力有较高的要求。

（1）准确把握每一个单词、每一句话

听力练习和测试中最常见的"听写"是典型的精听，在完成该类听力任务时，要求听者准确把握所听内容，准确理解每一个词、每一句话。

Task 20

① In this task, you will hear a passage three times. You are required to fill in the blanks numbered 1) to 8) with the exact words you have just heard. For blank numbered 9) you are required to fill in the missing information. You can either use the exact words you have just heard or write down the main points in your own words.

    Welcome to the University of Oxford. Oxford is the 1)_____ university in the English-speaking world and lays 2)_____ to nine centuries of 3)_____ existence. As an internationally 4)_____ center for teaching and research, Oxford 5)_____ students and scholars from across the globe, with almost a 6)_____ of our students from overseas. More than 130 nationalities are represented among a student population of over 16,000.

    Oxford is a collegiate university with 39 self-governing colleges 7)_____ to the University in a type of federal system. There are also seven Permanent Private Halls, 8)_____ by different Christian denominations.

9)_____
_____

② *You will hear a short passage three times. While listening, write down all the sentences of the passage. You should write the exact words you hear. Then discuss with your partner how to deal with this kind of task.*

The passage:
_____
_____
_____

How to deal with this kind of task?
_____
_____
_____
_____

(2) **模仿语音、语调**

    精听除了上文提到的听写形式之外,还有语音、语调模仿练习和英文歌曲学唱等其他形式。这类形式,通常以准确把握每一个单词、每一句话,训练听力基本功为基础,目的在于熟悉目的语使用者的语音、语调等音律特征,纠正自己的发音,提高听力能力。

Task 21

In this task, you will hear an English song——Blowing in the wind. Try to imitate it until you can sing it by yourself.

8. 泛听(Extensive listening)

泛听是指广泛地听各种不同类型、风格和来源的声音材料,例如,我们平时听英文广播、收看英文节目、听英文讲座等都是常见的泛听形式。其目的不是听懂每个词、每句话,而是巩固和扩大精听的成果,更多地接触语言现象,提高听觉的反应能力和对所听内容的整体理解能力。因此,在听的过程中,应注重对所听内容整体的把握。对某一听力材料来讲,泛听是一个连贯的过程,不宜中断而过多地关注对个别的生词、短语的理解。另外值得注意的是,泛听虽然与精听相比形式较为轻松,但仍然要求听者必须集中注意力。

如果说精听解决的是"质"的问题,泛听就应该是针对"量"的问题。在听力学习的过程中,不仅要注意到听的"质量",也要关注听的"数量",只有二者有效合理地结合才能保证听力水平的不断提高。

9. 视觉和听觉提示(Visual and aural clues)

无论是在视听材料中,还是在现实的交际中,听都不是孤立地存在的,总是发生在一定的环境中,而且听者经常以语境为依据,判断讲话者的真正意图。通常语境是由丰富的除交际双方话语之外的视觉和听觉信息构成的。例如,我们在看一部恐怖电影时,剧中的人物并没有说话,却能通过背景音和当时的情景让我们万分恐惧。这种感觉完全取决于我们对当时环境的感知,而非对方所说的话语。另外,要意识到交际不单纯只有言语的参与,同时还伴随着非言语的信息,例如手势、面部表情等体态语言。这些都对讲话者意图的推测起着不可忽视的作用,也为听者在语言基本知识缺失的情况下提供了可靠的线索。

在用本族语进行交际时,听者会在无意识的状态下自然利用交际环境中的一些听觉和视觉信息来理解对方的意图。在用外语进行交际时,听者面临一个全新的语言系统,注意力完全集中于言语信息的解码,而且听力本身的特点决定其信息是转瞬即逝的,没有足够的时间和精力去关注非言语信息。因此,外语学习者在关注言语信息的同时,要有意识地调动交际中的听觉、视觉等提示信息。因为,语言是用来交际的,只有在真正的语言环境中才能获得其真正的意义。作为外语学习者,理解交际内容,更加需要大量语境信息的帮助。

Task 22

You will hear an audio clip of the movie King Kong. Write down any information you get below.

_____
_____
_____

Task 23

In *Task* 22 you only heard the voice. In this task, you will see the clip. After seeing it, write down the information you have got. Then try to contrast the information you have got from the 2 tasks.

① The information you get after seeing the clip:
_____
_____
_____

② The differences between the information you have got from the 2 tasks:
_____
_____

Task 24

List some visual and aural clues that have helped you understand the information in the clip.

① Visual clues:
_____

② Aural clues:
_____
_____

三、听力学习中的社交/情感策略

1. 合作策略(Cooperation)

听力学习中的合作策略是指通过小组活动最大限度地促进自己以及他人的学习,以达到共同的目标。小组成员互相帮助、互相依赖、沟通,共同参与到明确的集体任务中。这样不仅可以使学习者更全面地认识事物,而且能够通过组内成员之间的相互依赖,形成相互的心理支撑,减少压力,降低心理焦虑,使学习者处在较佳的学习状态。

Task 25

Do you have any experiences of cooperation in listening? If yes, share it with your partner. If not, discuss with your partner how to cooperate in listening. Record any experiences in the space provided below.

_____
_____
_____
_____

2. 求解和澄清策略(Asking for clarification and verification)

求解和澄清策略作为询问策略的一部分广泛地应用于听力中。当听者是交际的一部分时,这类策略体现在听者请求语言水平较高的讲话者放慢语速、释义、重复、解释或者通过其他方式澄清自己的意图等,或是听者向讲话者确认自己的理解是否正确。在这种情况下,听者能否运用恰当的方式求解、澄清是交际能否成功的关键。

Task 26

What are the appropriate ways of asking for clarification and verification when you are carrying out a face-to-face communication?

①   Would you repeat that, please?_____
② _____
③ _____
④ _____
⑤ _____

⑥ _____
⑦ _____

以上是求解和澄清策略在面对面交际中的运用,对于一个语言学习者来说,还存在着另外一种情况——非真实交际性的听力练习。这时该策略旨在对课内外听力中存在的问题主动提问,大胆发言,同学间互相请教,交流听力学习经验。在学习的过程中每个人都会遇到各种各样的问题,仅依靠自己的力量有时会导致费时低效。但是有的人害怕他人知道自己对某一个问题不理解,害怕因此被人笑话,所以宁愿自己单独解决问题,也不愿和他人沟通。如果自己解决不了,则干脆将问题搁置。其实听力学习并不是无法求助的,而是你愿不愿意求助。在听力学习的过程中要尽量大胆地和其他人沟通,交流学习经验,在交流中你和他人一定是互助的,你可以从他们的经验中找到解决自己问题的捷径,别人也可以从你的经验中得到启发。

3. 明确动机、消除焦虑、自我鼓励

作为引起学习活动的一种学习者内在驱动力,动机不仅能够维持学习,而且能够推动学习。在听力学习中如果学习者具有强烈的听的动机和愿望,在听的过程中就能充分调动自身已有的语言及背景知识,运用各种元认知策略掌控自己的听力学习,运用各种认知策略积极获取信息。动机的性质决定学习者本身才是绝对的调控者,这就要求学习者不仅要努力培养自己对听力学习的兴趣,更要树立正确的学习目标,具有完成目标的坚定信念。

焦虑是外语学习者在听力中普遍存在的一种心理状态。在听的过程中,听者无法控制所听内容的难度和速度,对于多数听力练习和测试材料来说都缺乏多感官协同作用,而只能靠听觉感知。除了练习性的非真实的语言材料,在听的过程中几乎没有再次听的机会,所听的内容转瞬即逝。一旦遇到障碍,听者的自尊心和面子就会受到极大的威胁,因而产生紧张恐惧的心理状态。这种状态容易导致听者不是把注意力集中在听力材料上,而是把注意力分散在各种各样的担忧或多余的动作上,这样势必会影响正常的听力理解过程,对听力能力的提高极其不利。而且人在紧张的状态下,思维通常处于混乱的状态,比较、分析、综合、抽象、概括等具体思维能力无法正常工作,从而阻碍听力活动的正常进行。所以在听的过程中,听者要尽量通过诸如深呼吸、沉思等方式降低自己的焦虑程度,调整自己的心态,正确地认识所面临的听力任务,使自己的注意力集中于所听内容,保证"听"的有效

进行。

　　学习者通常希望从他人那里得到认可和赞许,而忽视了自我肯定和鼓励。在听力学习的过程中,要善于发现自己的点滴进步和优势,充分肯定自己的语言能力,要相信自己有能力完成学习任务,对自己持积极肯定的态度,勇于表扬和奖励自己。不要有自卑的心理,过度地夸大自己在听力学习中的劣势。要认清自己的弱点,但目的不是用自己的弱点和别人的强项去比,使自己丧失信心,而是要想办法解决听力中存在的问题,扬长补短,切实地提高自己的听力能力。

Task 27

Most people have the experience of being anxious when doing listening tasks. Work in groups of 3 or 4 to find some effective ways to relieve anxiety. Write down your ideas below.

_____

_____

_____

Task 28

Do you have any experiences of encouraging yourself in listening? If yes, describe it; if not, try to find some ways to encourage yourself, then write them down below.

_____

_____

_____

本章学习心得:

第七章 口语学习策略

本章学习目标
1. 了解口语学习的特点
2. 掌握口语学习中的主要策略
3. 学会运用口语学习中的主要策略

口语学习的本质

　　口语交际能力的发展大致分成两大阶段:(1)技能学习(skills-getting);(2)技能运用(skills-using)。第一阶段是第二阶段的基础。只有经过这两个阶段的训练,才能在真实的交际情景中自如地运用学到的知识。

　　技能的学习和运用这两个阶段并非截然分开的,而是相互联系的。首先,技能的学习是为了掌握技能而进行的知识方面的积累和准备。只有在了解了语言系统的基本知识后,才可能进行交流;同样,如果不知道为什么使用这些语言,则这些语言就是毫无用处的。因此,可以概括地说,好的口语交际能力应该同时具有准确性(有赖于对语言系统的掌握)和流利性(源于个人尝试语言的经验)两种特性。这两种特性分属于语言学习的操练阶段和产出阶段。学习者应该做到能清醒地意识到自己在这两方面的需求和不足。准确性和流利性之间的关系可以以下面的示意图来显示:

初级阶段　　　　　　　　高级阶段

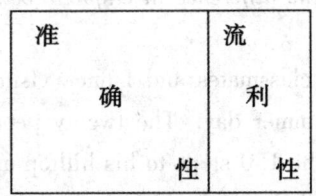
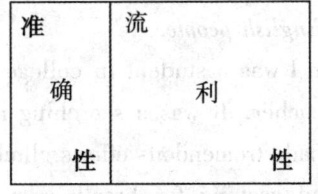

　　口头交际并不是单方面的说的过程,而是指在听者和说者之间进行的双向的交流过程,听、说双方都在交流中起积极作用。简言之,说者必须以正确的语言形式把他想传达的语言信息编码,而听者也要同样积极地破译(或解释)这个信息。因此,口语学习的本质就是以交流为目的,从听与说两方面着手,培养语言输入与输出的能力,应付真实生活中的语言环境。那

119

么,如何才能最大限度地实现这一目标呢?首先,学习者必须掌握所能掌握的语言系统,即语法、词汇和语音体系。同时必须牢记:语言系统的学习并非学习的终点,而只是通往终点的手段。其次,学习者还要清楚地认识到他们需要机会去实践所学到的知识。只有将技能的学习与应用充分结合,才有望在真实的交际情景中自如地运用外语。

  Oxford(1990)根据与所学语言材料的关系将英语学习策略分为直接策略和间接策略。他认为凡与所学语言有直接关系的策略为直接策略,包括记忆策略(建立内在连接、运用影像和声音、系统复习和运用相关动作等)、认知策略(各种练习、信息的接收与传达、分析与归纳、组织和整理等)和补偿策略(运用线索来猜想、克服说写的困难);而与所学语言没有直接关系的策略为间接策略,包括元认知策略(集中学习、计划安排学习和评价学习等)、情感策略(缓减焦虑、自我鼓励和注意学习情绪调整等)和社会策略(澄清疑问、同伴合作、移情作用与文化了解)。

一、口语学习中的间接策略

1. 注意对目的语国家文化习俗的了解

  要学好一个国家的语言,了解这个国家的文化背景常识是必不可少的。文化常渗透在日常交流的方方面面中。了解文化方面的各种差异,可以使我们与外国人沟通起来更自然,口语表达更恰当得体。因此,学习者在平时应通过书刊、电视或网络等多种渠道来拓宽自己的视野,增加文化方面的知识。

Task 1

Read the following case and then point out the difference in etiquette between Chinese and English people.

  When I was a student in college, my classmates and I once visited our American teacher. It was a scorching hot summer day. The twenty people including me made tremendous efforts climbing the 150 steps to his hilltop apartment. Sweaty and gasping for breath, we sprawled on the sofa, chairs and floor. "Would you like some tea?" our teacher asked. "Oh, no!" came the chorus from us. "We don't want to trouble you!" "Are you sure?", he asked again. "No, too much trouble," we repeated hesitantly this time, for we were actually dying of thirst. As he stayed in China for a while, knowing a little bit of Chinese custom of this kind and his common sense and our facial expressions also told him that we were desperate for something to drink, just standing on ceremony, he offered a third time. "Are you sure you don't want tea? Raise your hands if you do." Then hands shot up everywhere. Some even raised two hands, as if they were being robbed. "Help yourself!" he said. We unceremoniously raced for the teapot.

Task 2
Look at the following situations and discuss why misunderstanding arises.
①Herr Heiko Grosshoff from Germany gets upset when Peter Jackson from the USA keeps calling him Heiko. He is so angry that he finishes the negotiation early.
②Jose Garcia from Spain got to know his Korean counterpart Kim Lee very well. When he meets her again for a negotiation, he gives her a hug and kisses her on the cheek. She is terribly embarrassed.
③Jack Nicholson from the UK is in a negotiation with Mr. Tanaka in Japan. There are long silences during the negotiation, so Jack keeps finding things to say. Mr. Tanaka thinks he is a rather unintelligent person.
④When Mike Smith first meets Chang Lee from mainland China, he is embarrassed to be asked "Are you married?", "How much money do you make every month?" and "How old are you?".

2. 创造机会,营造口语环境

学习者想要熟练掌握一项外语口语技能,仅仅将口语练习局限在课堂上是不够的,一定要在平时学习与生活中抓住和创造各种机会去操练外语。例如,可以通过听英文流行音乐或广播来培养自己的语感,纠正发音;可以在英语沙龙或俱乐部结交一些外国朋友,从而直接接触最纯正的英语;可以与一些同样热爱英语的同学一起在课余时间编排英语短剧;等等。

很多学习者抱怨学不好外语是因为没有语言环境,还有些人认为只有和外国人或英语水平比自己高的人练习口语才能有所进步,这些都是误区。诚然,每个人都不会否认在英美国家学习英语的好处,但这并不意味着中国人在国内无法完成英语口语的学习。大量成功的事例证明,只要掌握了正确的方法并持之以恒地练习,在中国学习一样可以说出一口流利的英语。此外,与语言水平比自己高的人交谈固然能够提高得更快,但并不是人人都有这样好的条件。事实上,和与自己在年龄、经历、背景、兴趣、爱好等方面都比较相似的人进行交谈,既可以共享谈话内容,又有较好的理解基础,从而可以避免文化背景与知识水平差异过大带来的交际困难。

Task 3

Have you ever been to an English salon (or English corner) or any other activities like that in your school? If yes, share your experience with your partner. If not, think about what you can do to create chances to speak English.

3. 缓解紧张感(Lower Your Anxiety)

在语言的各项技能中,口语技能受到紧张感的影响最为显著。很多学习者往往读也能读懂,听也能听懂,但就是张嘴说话的时候感到有异常大的压力,紧张得满头大汗,支支吾吾,甚至头脑一片空白,一个词也说不出来。

如何缓解这种紧张感呢? 在说话之前可以深呼吸几次,让浑身的肌肉都得到放松,这是缓解紧张感最简单有效的方法。在完成一项紧张的语言任务之前,学习者听上五到十分钟舒缓的音乐,可以让原本绷紧的神经松弛下来,进而转变为一种积极的情绪。俗话说得好,微笑是最好的良药。根据科学家的研究,大笑能够使人体内产生重要的生化反应,从而提高机体的免疫能力,所以现今很多医院都在采用"微笑治疗法"来帮助病人放松神经,缓解痛苦。这种方法也完全可以移植到语言学习中来。比如在口语课上或参加英语沙龙时可以先给大家讲一个小笑话,欢声笑语过后,大家也就不再局促不安了。

除了以上提及的一些技巧,积极的自我鼓励也是行之有效的一种缓解紧张感的方法。很多学习者在与人交流时,第一句总是说"My English is very poor"(我的英语非常糟糕)。这说明他在张嘴说英语前,已经给了自己一个非常消极的暗示,这种暗示会使学习者笼罩在自卑与胆怯中,难以完成语言任务,如在遇到生词难以表达时,消极的学习者会完全放弃,而不是采取迂回的表达方法继续完成语言任务。相反,如果学习者在完成一项语言任务之前,先默默地给自己一个积极的心理暗示,如"I can make myself understood even though my vocabulary is limited"(即使我的词汇量有限,我也能表达清楚我的意思),在这种心理暗示下,学习者会非常放松,即使遇到生僻的单词,也会积极在脑海里搜寻有限的词汇去表达所要表达的东西,从而完成语言任务。

Task 4

List more positive statements that one can make privately to themselves before a potentially difficult language activity.

4. 勇于"开口"(Being Bold Enough to "Open the Mouth")

口语学习中有两种常见的情况：一是由于怕说不好而羞于开口，二是口若悬河不管别人的反应。这两种情况都是我们在英语口语学习中要避免的。

在前一种情况中，学习者总是要求自己要么不张口，只要张口就应说出漂亮的、没有任何语法错误的句子来，因而当对自己的表述没有十足的自信时，宁可放弃交流的机会。初练口语的学习者或多或少都有这样的心理障碍，其根本原因在于他们对犯错误非常恐惧。要克服"张不开口"的问题，学习者要牢记：真正的交际是意义的传递。语法的作用是监控句子的规范程度，它是为有效地表达意义而服务的，所以不能因噎废食，舍本逐末。认识到这一点后，在练习过程中应适当提高自己对语法错误的容忍程度，养成勇于开口的好习惯。

在后一种情况中，学习者则认为流畅至上。在与人交流的过程中，他们总是滔滔不绝，气势逼人，至于对方是否听懂或接受则完全置之不理。究其原因主要是他们对口语好坏的标准存在一些误解：有人认为能不停地说就表示口语水平高，有人认为说得快就是水平高，也有人认为语音语调动听就是口语好，更有人认为所说的英语听起来有美国味或英国味就是口语好，诸如此类的认识都有一些偏颇。当然，能够滔滔不绝地说英语自然是那些找不着门道的初学者可望而不可即的事情。但是，对于口语已经入门并希望得到进一步提高的学习者来说，成功的语言交际应该以语用恰当为标准，即所说的话语既符合语法要求，又符合说话人的身份和说话的场合。语言交流是双向的，一个人口若悬河而不顾对方的反应，或所答非所问、讲话离题万里，即便讲话人的英语再流利，也不能算作成功的交际。所以，只会开口还不够，还要学会如何倾听。

Task 5

Do you think you are brave enough to speak English? If yes, give a few examples to show it. If not, discuss with your partner how you can improve.

Task 6

Find a person who you never talk with before as your partner and tell him/her the differences between what you expected from college study and what's actually happening in real situation.

二、口语学习中的直接策略

1. 朗读(Reading-aloud)、复述(Retelling)与背诵(Recitation)
(1)朗读

朗读是进行自由口语表达的一种有效准备。可挑选一些难度适宜、自己又很感兴趣的文章进行阅读。由于这些材料不需要自己组织语言,因此精神上会比较放松,可以细细体味文章的意境,体味抑扬顿挫的语音语调,又可以提高自己的外语语感。每天抽出一小段时间,找一个宁静的地方朗读自己喜欢的文章,一方面可以聆听自己的发音,另一方面也可以当作对学习的一种适当调节。通过朗读可以训练发音,同时还可以帮助记忆。

Task 7

Practice reading the following passages loudly. One is a story; the other is the lyrics of an English song. Choose one to read in front of the class. After that, discuss in groups of 3 or 4 what aspects you should pay close attention to when doing reading aloud.

There was a kindly nobleman whose wife had died of illness leaving the nobleman and his three daughters in despair. After losing all his money in useless and bad inventions, the family had to move into a peasant's cottage, where the daughters did their own cooking, sewing and cleaning. When the time came for the daughters to marry, the father became even more depressed as his daughters could not marry without dowries, money and property given to the new husbands' families. One night, after the daughters had washed out their clothes, they hung their stockings over the fireplace to dry. That night Saint Nicholas, knowing the despair of the father, stopped by the nobleman's house. Looking in the window, Saint Nicholas saw that the family had gone to bed. He also noticed the daughters' stockings. Inspiration struck Saint Nicholas and he took three small bags of gold from his pouch and threw them one by one down the chimney, and they fell into the stockings. The next morning, when the daughters awoke, they found their stockings contained enough gold for them to get married. The nobleman was able to see his three daughters marry and he lived a long and happy life.

Key Words:
nobleman 贵族　despair 绝望　cottage 小屋;村舍
dowry 嫁妆　pouch 小钱袋

Perfect
By Simple Plan

Hey, dad look at me
Think back and talk to me
Did I grow up according to plan?
Do you think I'm wasting my time...
Doing things I wanna do?
But it hurts when you disapprove all along

And now I try hard to make it
I just want to make you proud
I'm never gonna be good enough for you
I can't pretend that I'm alright
And you can't change me

Cuz we lost it all
Nothing lasts forever
I'm sorry I can't be perfect

I try not to think
About the pain I feel inside
Did you know you used to be my hero?
All the days you spend with me
Now seem so far away
And it feels like you don't care anymore

Nothing's gonna change the things that you said
Nothing's gonna make this right again
Please don't turn your back
I can't believe it's hard just to talk to you
But you don't understand

Key Words：
perfect 完美的　　disapprove 不赞成

(2) 复述

　　复述是提高语言组织能力的一个很好的练习方式。在练习过程中，学习者可以先通读一下所选的材料，了解了主要内容之后试着用自己的语言把主要的故事情节重新讲述一遍。如果没有学习伙伴听自己复述，可以用录音机把自己复述的故事录下来，然后对照原文检查复述的准确性和完整性。

Task 8

Read the following stories first, and then try to retell one of them in the class. After that, discuss with your partner what problems you've had in retelling and how to solve those problems.

Story One

   I recently heard a story about two bricklayers and a news reporter. The reporter asked the first worker, "What are you doing?" His reply was a complaint. He said that he spent his days wasting his time, placing bricks on top of one another. The reporter asked the second worker the same question. His response, however, was quite different. "I'm the luckiest person in the world," he said, "I help turn simple pieces of brick into beautiful houses." Both of these workers are right, but the difference is in their visions. We see in life what we want to see. If you want to find fault with other people, your job, or the world in general, you'll certainly be able to do so. However, the opposite is true as well. If you look for the extraordinary in the ordinary, you can train yourself to see it. The second bricklayer sees a beautiful house within the pieces of brick. Indeed, there is so much to be grateful for, so much to think about. If you put your attention on this fact, seemingly ordinary things will take on a whole new meaning.

Key words：
complaint 抱怨   vision 构想,念头   extraordinary 不平常的

Story Two

   Two friends were walking through the desert. During their journey, they had an argument, and one friend slapped the other. Without saying anything, the injured friend wrote in the sand, "Today my best friend slapped me in the face." They kept on walking, until they found a place with water and trees. They decided to take a bath. The one who had been slapped ventured too far into the water and became stuck in the deep mud and was drowning, but his friend saved him. After he recovered from the incident, he carved into a stone, "Today my best friend saved my life." The friend, who had both slapped and saved his best friend, asked him, "After I hurt you, you wrote in the sand, and now, you write on a stone. Why?" The friend replied, "When someone hurts us, we should write it down in sand, where the wind can wipe it away, but when someone does something good for us, we must carve it in stone where no wind can ever erase it."

Key words：
argument 争吵   slap 掴、拍   venture 冒险前进
drown 淹没   incident 发生的事

(3) 背诵

许多学习者都是从背诵优秀短文开始走上英语学习成功之路的。背诵不仅可以锻炼发音和语调,更有助于学习者在反复练习中仔细品味语言的用法和修辞的特点,在记忆和模仿中培养语感。在选材的时候应着重考虑简单短小的散文、诗歌、歌词等。

Task 9

Translate the following proverbs, and try to recite them in five minutes.

- A merry company is music on a journey.
- Practice makes perfect.
- Time and tide wait for no man.
- One can not set back the clock.
- Every bean has its black.
- Self do, self have.
- Grasp all, lose all.
- As said, so done.
- He who loses credit can lose nothing further.
- Wit and will strive for the victory.

Task 10

Translate the following poem, and try to recite it in five minutes.

- Thank you for comforting me when I'm sad
- Loving me when I'm mad
- Picking me up when I'm down
- Thank you for being my friend and being around
- Teaching me the meaning of love
- Encouraging me when I need a shove
- But most of all thank you for
- Loving me for who I am

2. 收集和整理习语(Idioms)

有些英语学习者在学习的过程中往往会遇到这样的问题:听到或看到的句子中每个单词都认识,但把它们组合在一起后,就不知道是什么意思了。这主要是因为他们对英语习语缺乏了解。所谓习语,就是经过长时间的使用而提炼出来的固定短语或短句,即习惯用语。习语大都具有鲜明的形象,适宜用来比喻事物,因而往往带有浓厚的民族色彩和地方色彩,比如北京人说盖了帽儿了,外国人就很难理解,这就是习语。所以在和外国人交流时,如果能适当地运用他们民族的习语,他马上就会觉得很亲切,也很愿意和你交流。

  英语习语就其广义而言,包括成语、谚语、俚语等。成语是在语言使用过程中形成的一种独特的、约定俗成的、具有完整独特意义的语言。其语义并非等同于组成成分意义的简单相加,人们很难从个别词义猜出整个成语的含义。例如,rain cats and dogs (meaning: rain heavily) 倾盆大雨; wear one's heart upon one's sleeve (meaning: show one's feeling plainly) 心直口快。

  谚语是民间流传的至理名言,措辞简练,便于记忆。谚语内容精辟,寓意深邃,因而有广泛的感染力。谚语往往能反映一个民族的地理、历史、社会制度、社会观点和态度。比如,有些民族住在沿海一带,靠海为生,他们的谚语往往涉及海上航行、经受风雨、捕鱼捉蟹等内容。像阿拉伯人这样的游牧民族的谚语则多涉及沙漠、草原、羊、马、骆驼和豺狼。尊敬老人的社会就会有颂扬老人足智多谋的谚语。妇女地位不高的社会就会有许多轻视、贬低妇女的谚语。人们的经历和对世界的认识在不少方面是相似的。因此,尽管中国人和讲英语的人文化背景不同,但在英语和汉语中相同或相似的谚语却很多,例如:

  Strike while the iron is hot. 趁热打铁。
  Many hands make light work. 人多好办事。
  Haste makes waste. 欲速则不达。
  Out of sight, out of mind. 眼不见,心不烦。
  Birds of a feather fleck together. 物以类聚,人以群分。
  Look before you leap. 三思而后行。
  Where there's smoke there's fire. 无风不起浪。
  Where there's a will there's a way. 有志者事竟成。
  Give a person a dose of his own medicine. 以其人之道还治其人之身。
  All good things must come to an end. 天下没有不散的宴席。

  最贴近人们生活和最能反映平民要求与社会生活特征的是俚语(slang)。俚语是一种非常特殊的语言形式。它历史悠久,处在不断更新变化之中,具有独特的语言表现力和拟人力,是一种非正式的语言,通常用在非正式的场合。简言之,俚语就是一些比较流行的说法,即使是美英本土的人,都不一定能听得懂。就像现在的年轻人说的很多非常时尚的词语,比如说"达人",表示在某方面比较厉害的那些人,这个就是俚语。俚语的风格新颖时髦,不落俗套,生动诙谐,表达多样。如严厉批判某人,用 to criticize 过于平淡,为了别具一格而造出 badmouth;消防队员被形象地喻为 smoker eater;对男友失约,说 stand him up 自然要比 keep him waiting 新颖;解雇某人,用 dismiss 太过陈旧,不如用 give him the air。为了赶时髦,俚语经常更新,从而有大量的同义词语出现。如俚语中"电视"的表达方式就有很多,有 telly, the box, idiot box, goggle box, the one eyed monster,个个生动形象。不同的社会群体往往有自己特定的生活圈,因此不同的阶层和地区有各自不同的俚语,如大学生俚语(college slang)中的 He is just a booker 意为 He studies too much; You are out of your tree 是说 You are out of mind; Watch it! You might rattle the troops 是想告诉你 Don't upset your parents。

成语、谚语和俚语等是一个社会的语言及文化的重要组成部分。这部分语言不仅难以理解,更难以运用得当。然而能否正确使用成语、谚语、俚语,往往是一个人的语言水平高低的标志。不论说话还是写文章,如果完全不使用成语、谚语或俚语,就会显得语言文字枯燥无味,缺乏文采;当然用得过多或使用不当,也会使语言文字显得矫揉造作,不大自然。因此,为了能够自如地表达,有必要对习语(如俚语、成语及英美人生活中常用的一些固定表达)进行收集和整理。事实上,做这些工作并不需要特意花费很多时间,平时可以准备一个小本子,专门用来搜集在阅读报纸、书籍或与别人交流时遇到的一些地道表达,随时随地记在小本子上。这样日积月累一定会使自己的语言越来越成熟,可以大大提高口语表达的自如度和自信度。

Task 11
Try to guess the meaning of the following expressions.
①Drop me a line!
②Get yourself together!
③I am so fed up.
④Don't get on my nerve!
⑤Give me a break!
⑥Don't give me a hard time!
⑦I don't get the picture.
⑧It's on me.

⑨Don't get uptight! Take it easy.

⑩Keep your study (work) on track.

Task 12

Read the following dialogue and try to guess the meaning of the underlined expressions.

Ruth: Do you want to go with me to Ellen Robertson's house?

Jim: <u>Not on your life</u>! After her behavior at my party, I don't even want to see her again!

Ruth: Why not? What did she do that has you so <u>up in arms</u>?

Jim: Well, it was very late and my neighbors complained several times about the noise.

Ruth: Why didn't you ask everyone to <u>quiet down</u>?

Jim: I did! But every time I turn the music down, Ellen walked over to the stereo and turned the music up! When I asked people not to dance, she even said I was a terrible host. I was so <u>fed up with</u> her that I finally <u>showed her to the door</u>.

Ruth: Really? I never heard about all this. When did it happen?

Jim: Last year, at my birthday party.

Ruth: A year ago?! I think you should <u>let bygones be bygones</u>.

Jim: Oh, I suppose you're right.

3. 自然主动地与人交流(Starting a Conversation Naturally)

很多学习者不愿意主动开口与陌生人进行交流,因为他们对自己的口语不自信,总是担心遭到冷遇,于是便寄希望于对方主动与自己搭讪。由于太在意自己的"面子",很多机会就在等待与胆怯中白白溜走了。如果已经克服了这种心理障碍,则还需要找到合适、自然的开口方式。

Task 13

Discuss with your partner how you can start a conversation with a stranger. Add to the list below.

① <u>Greet someone actively.</u>

② _____

③ _____

④ _____

Task 14

Work with 2 or 3 students to make a list of the most important points you feel you need to bear in mind for communicating naturally.

_____

_____

_____

4. 迂回策略(Speaking in a Roundabout Way)

迂回,顾名思义就是当交际遇到障碍的时候,比如突然某个单词想不起来了、不知道该如何表达了或对某个句型不太确定时,想方设法拐弯抹角地把自己的想法表达出来的一种灵活应对手段。采用迂回策略虽然是一种迫不得已的选择,但是总比保持沉默或回避某一话题要积极得多。我们提倡学习者在交际过程中遇到困难的时候不要知难而退,而要头脑冷静,采取各种手段积极应对,只有这样才能不断锤炼自己的语言,取得进步。

迂回表达有以下几种方式:

(1)解释词的意思,即释义法。当你不知道英语中与某个意思相对应的单词时,可以用一句话来解释同样的意思。比如,当你不知道"岛屿"这个词怎样表达时,就可以用描述法说成"周围有水包围的陆地"来解释。又如,在表达"我看到他们从车库出来"的时候,若突然想不起 garage 这个词,则可以换种说法"We saw them get out of the... the room where you keep the car"来解释。

(2)使用核心词汇或广义词。如用"动物"代替"鹿",用"工具"代替"锤子"。在相同的类别上使用与所要表达的单词同义的词,如"lake"代替"pond","stone"代替"rock"。

在采用迂回策略时,经常用到的句式有 It's a kind of...;It's a sort of...;Well, I can explain it like this...;等。

Task 15

Situation: You are talking with your foreign friend about your future plan. You want to be a policeman (solider, lifeguard, tailor, journalist, doctor, shop assistant, etc.), but the word "policeman" (solider, lifeguard, tailor, journalist, doctor, shop assistant, etc.) escaped you for the moment. How can you make yourself understood?

Task 16

Describe a famous film to your partner to see whether he or she can figure out the name of the film. You should only focus on the main plot of the movie. Do not provide self-evident clues, such as the real names of the leading actors or actresses, the director of the film, the country in which the film is produced, etc.

Task 17

Work in a group of 3 to act out the following situation.
Situation: Student A acts as an American tourist who comes to China for the first time. Student B acts as a tour guide. Student C acts as a Chinese shop assistant. Before going back home A wants to buy some presents for his wife, so B accompanies A to a shop and meets C. They begin a conversation...

Task 18

Work with 2 or 3 students, discuss what strategy (strategies) you have used when doing task 7 to 9 and if (that) those strategies are used successfully.

5. 适当使用补白词(Using Hesitation Fillers)

适当使用补白词是日常对话中常见的交际策略之一。说话人为了延长思考的时间,往往会很自然地在话语间插入诸如"嗯"、"这个"、"就是说"、"那么"等口头语。这个策略同样适用于英语会话。许多初学者都会在对话中使用一些补白词,如"um"、"well"、"you know"、"let's see"等等。但是能够恰当自如地使用这些补白词是需要一个过程的。而且补白词的使用也需要有个限度。有些人在表达时,一句话之中会穿插若干个补白词。事实上,过多的补白词会让人感到说话人缺乏自信,尤其是在做报告或演讲时,频繁地补白会使人感到讲话人的准备不够充分。当发现这个问题时,一定要有意识地控制自己的语速,尽量避免过多地使用补白词。

Task 19

Hesitation fillers help you overcome communication difficulty. But too many hesitation fillers will produce the opposite effect. Why? Add more to the list below.

① Too many hesitation fillers make others believe you are not confident.
② _____
③ _____

6. 积极回应对方(Responding Actively)

在与别人交谈的过程中,要不断地对对方所说的内容做出积极反应。各种各样的停顿词、答语和感叹词会向对方传达一个信息,那就是,我在认真地倾听你的话、我对你所说的内容很感兴趣。这是交谈的礼貌也是策略。有效地回应不仅能使交谈显得十分自然,而且能使交谈双方得到进一步沟通,进而实现交际意图。

Task 20

The following is a table listing the feelings and attitudes you want to express. Think of English words or expressions you can use to fill in the corresponding blanks.

Functions	To show approval	To show surprise
Expressions		
Functions	To ask for repetition	To check if you understand him/her
Expressions		

Task 21

Read the conversation below and underline the expressions which are used to show approval, disapproval, to ask for repetition and to check understanding.

Richard: In my view, poverty is the major cause of crime. If we got rid of economic problem, most crime would disappear.

Alan: I agree that poverty is one of the major causes of crime, but is your argument that if we got rid of poverty, we would get rid of crime?

Linda: Just a minute, can I just get clear what you two are saying? First of all, is your point that crime is caused by poverty?

Richard: Yes.

Alan: Yes.

Linda: In other words, because someone is poor, this inevitably means they will become involved in crime?

Richard: No, not exactly. My point is that those who become criminals in a society do so because they feel deprived of what they see others having in the same society. They see they are not getting their fair share, so they do the only thing they can do to deal with the problem—turn to crime.

Linda: So let me see, if I've got this straight—you feel that although not all poor people become criminals, those that do so because they are poor?

Richard: Yes.

Alan: I'd agree with that too.

Linda: So just to take this a little further, if you don't mind. Would you go so for as to say, then, that everybody who has ever been a criminal became one because they were poor?

Richard: No, no, that's not what I'm saying at all.

Alan: No, I wouldn't go along with that either.

Linda: So could you tell me exactly what your point is then?

Richard: Well. I think you're taking the argument further than we intended. We didn't really mean to say that everyone who is poor becomes a criminal or that the cause of all crime is poverty.

Linda: No, maybe not, but what we really meant to say was that if you're poor it makes it very difficult for you to avoid crime in one way or another.

Richard: Yes, so a poor person will not necessarily become a criminal, and sure, obviously not all criminals are poor. But what we would argue is that a major cause of crime is poverty.

Linda: Well, OK, I think I could go along with that. But I'm still rather worried about another aspect of your argument. What exactly do you mean by "crime"?...

7. 提出问题(Raising Questions)

在交谈过程中提出恰当的问题是一个很重要的能力。恰当的问题不仅能够帮助提问者获得所需的信息,而且能够使对方很快融入到对话中去。提问大致分两种,一种是封闭式,一种是开放式。所谓封闭式问题,就是能够用"Yes"或"No"回答的问题,例如:"Do you like living in China?"。封闭式问题主要用来询问一些特定信息。而开放式问题则能够鼓励对方提供更多的信息,例如你可以向对方询问:"Why do you enjoy living in China?"或者"How do you feel about studying in this university?"。开放式问题更能够充分调动对话者的积极性,使对话自然而顺畅地进行下去。

Task 22

Read the following conversation and try to fill in the possible questions.

A:_____?
B:I'm an engineer.
A:_____?
B:At IBM in New York City.
A:_____?
B:Two years.
A:_____?
B:Yes, I do.

Task 23

Ask some questions to find out your partner's information as much as possible. Note down the information you get. Then check if both of you have noted the details down correctly.

8. 使用肢体语言(Using Body Language)

  研究表明,人们在日常交流中,言语只传达了7%的信息,语调及音色传达了38%的信息,而非语言的暗示竟传递了55%的信息。这就表示人们从非语言沟通中领悟到的信息比从说出的话语中得到的信息要多得多。所以,在交际时,注意人们如何使用非语言暗示是非常重要的。

  口语交流是面对面进行的,不仅讲话者的语言可以传递信息,讲话者的面部表情和形体动作也同样可以传递大量丰富的信息。因此,要想成为一个口头交际的高手,还需要注意借助形体语言传递情感、表达想法、帮助交流。几个非常重要的技巧包括:微笑(Smile);开放式的站立姿势(Open Posture);身体微微前倾(Forward Lean);接触(Touch);目光交流(Eye-contact);点头(Nod)。把这几个技巧的首字母连起来,就是唐·加博尔(Don·Gabor)所归纳的善用体态语言的六字技巧:S-O-F-T-E-N。以美国人为例,他们在谈话时特别期望别人对其所讲的话有所反应。对他们来说,有礼貌的谈话者应该用惊喜、讨厌、吃惊或悲哀的表情来与别人心领神会。在谈话中,他们会以扬眉、点头、有礼貌的微笑以及保持适度的目光接触来表示他们的注意,并可能使用一些肢体语言。比如,食指与中指交叉代表祝你好运;而食指与中指交叉放在背后则表示"我在说谎!";要是你听不懂他在说什么,可以一脸茫然或者把手举过头顶向后甩,表示"我不懂"。

总之,流利的口语再加上"身"情并茂的肢体语言会使我们的口语表达上升到一个全新的境界。在交流时运用肢体语言和眼神,能够使我们更准确地表情达意,而不只是一个讲英语的"机器人"。

Task 24

Study the two pictures below carefully and finish the following two tasks.

The woman—Mrs. Jane Lee
The man—Mr. Stephen Smith

① Role play.

You and your partner act as Mrs. Jane Lee and Mr. Stephen Smith separately. You two meet at a party. Now, talk with each other according to what has happened in the two pictures.

② Discuss the reasons for the differences with your partner.

9. 寻求帮助(Appealing for Help)

当交际遇到障碍时,有几种选择,要么迂回表达,要么避而不谈。当自己无法表达而又非说不可时,还可以向对方求助。这是一个较为积极的手段,但往往有一个前提,即对方是操本族语者或者英语水平比自己高的人。向操本族语者求助时,可以用实物、图画、手势、提问等方式请求对方帮你补充不会的词或表达方式。向英语水平比自己高的本国人求助时,则可以直接用母语。对于许多学习者来说,从对话者那里得到直接的帮助是一个基本的学习策略。以下是一些可以获得帮助的表达方式:

I'm sorry. I didn't understand. Could you repeat that, please?
Could you say that again, please — more slowly?
Could you explain this to me?

Could you help with my pronunciation, please? How should I pronounce this word?

What's the word for...?

What's the name of...?

I can't remember the word for....

Task 25

Think of useful ways to appeal for help when you have difficulty in expressing yourself in speaking and complete the following list.

We can appeal for help by

① Using gestures.

② _____

③ _____

④ _____

本章学习心得：

_____

_____

第八章 阅读学习策略

本章学习目标

1. 了解阅读学习的特点
2. 掌握阅读学习中的主要策略
3. 学会运用阅读学习中的主要策略

阅读的本质

　　阅读是一个复杂的、对书面信息进行认知构建的心理语言过程。阅读在今天被认为是一种具有四方面意义的复杂脑力活动,即:认字、释文、思索和融会贯通。人们通过阅读学习,获得外来信息。在阅读的过程中,阅读者既需要掌握词和句子等语言知识以理解文字符号的表层结构,又要理解语义的深层结构转化,要能对读物所传递的信息进行分析加工、联想和预测。因此,阅读理解是作者、语言信息和读者等几方面相互作用的过程。

　　随着语言学家、心理学家和教育专家对阅读过程的深入研究,出现了不少关于阅读的新解释。一些学者提出了两种不同的阅读模式:一种为"自下至上"(bottom-up)模式。这是一个对字母、单词、词组、短语、句子等语言单位的详细而精确的辨认过程,得到的意思就是这些语言意思相加的总和。另一种为"自上至下"(top-down)模式,是选择最少的必要语言提示来进行猜测,所以这种方式可以被称为"心理语言学猜测游戏"。然而现在越来越多的人认为阅读理解不是以上述其中一种模式自始至终单独进行的。阅读过程是"自下至上"和"自上至下"这两种过程的相互作用,称为"交互阅读模式"。当我们在阅读一篇文章时,我们至少有两个活动同时在进行:一个活动是从词、句、短语等语言形式上进行字面理解;另一个活动是在理解字面内容的基础上利用自己原有的世界知识和背景知识重建信息。而这两个活动又是紧密结合并相互作用的。

　　阅读是对文字符号做一种有意义的解释,并获取信息的过程。20世纪80年代初,有人提出了"现代图式理论",它分为内容图式与形式图式。内容图式指读者对一篇文章的熟悉程度,即狭义的背景知识;形式图式指读者对文章结构排列的熟悉程度,即通常所说的篇章知识。该理论充分揭示了阅读的本质,强调阅读的实质是读者及其背景知识与阅读材料所输入的文字信息交互作用的过程。

一、阅读学习中的元认知策略

阅读学习中的元认知策略是指学习者作为一个主动的个体,有意识地使用元认知对阅读学习任务进行合理的安排、计划、监控、调节和评价,通过不断调整与完善,使自己的阅读学习方法和过程更趋合理、高效。

1. 确定阅读目的

当代外语教学理论认为,阅读的目的有三个:(1)为获取信息而阅读(Reading for Information);(2)为学习语言知识而阅读(Reading for Linguistic Knowledge);(3)为掌握阅读技能而阅读(Reading for Reading Skills)。因此,阅读能力的培养不仅仅是为了学习阅读材料中的语言知识,更重要的是为了获取其中的语言信息,并通过阅读过程学习和掌握一定的阅读策略。

阅读的最终目的是要培养独立的阅读者。一个独立的阅读者应当具有下列阅读技能:

(1) 能快速阅读;
(2) 能掌握文章的中心思想和基本事实;
(3) 能把握主要逻辑线索;
(4) 能把握故事发展的时间和空间顺序;
(5) 能根据语境和构词法猜测生词;
(6) 能独立使用工具书;
(7) 能根据上下文理解作者的态度和观点;
(8) 能根据已知的事实推断出未直接写出的意思;
(9) 能阅读不同题材的文章(如人物传记、故事、广告、记叙文、社会文化、文史知识、科普小品等);
(10) 能阅读不同的实用文体(如小说、信件、请柬、通知、便条、图表、常见标志等)。

Task 1

Discuss your English reading purposes with your partner.

2. 选择阅读材料

阅读材料的选择取决于阅读目的,目的不同,选材就不同。

Task 2

Match the reading materials in the right column with the reading purposes in the left column and then compare your choices with those of your group members. Please Note: some of your choices may be overlapping.

	a. novels and short novels
	b. plays
(1) reading for information	c. poems
	d. newspapers and magazines
	e. course books
(2) reading for pleasure	f. advertisements, catalogues
	g. letters, postcards, telegrams
	h. e-mails, website pages
(3) reading for language	i. dictionaries, telephone directories
	j. instructions, directions, notices, signs, menus, tickets

大多数的外语学习者最初都是通过其所学习的课本来接触阅读材料的,而这样的阅读材料通常都是经过非本族语编者简化或改写的,其目的是帮助学习者学习特定的语法和词汇知识。要提高阅读水平,阅读者除了阅读课本之外,还要尝试阅读原文阅读材料。

所谓"原文阅读材料",是指由本族语者所写的,以帮助本族语者获得更多的信息或进行娱乐,而并非进行语言教学的文字材料。一般而言,要依据难度、熟悉度和兴趣对材料进行选择。

(1) **难度**

阅读过程中,如果阅读者太过频繁地使用字典辅助阅读,就会在接下来理解文章词句和全文的过程中很快变得疲惫甚至疑惑。值得庆幸的是,原文阅读材料的难易程度不一,有较为简单的(如车票、时间表、菜单等),有难度适中的(如通知、报道、小故事等),也有较为复杂的(如文学作品、评论、科普文章等)。阅读者应选择适合自身阅读水平的阅读材料。

(2) **熟悉度**

对于阅读材料主题的熟悉程度会影响阅读者对文中生词意义的猜测和

对语言能力不足的补偿。初学者或中等程度的阅读者应该选择自己了解的材料。例如,阅读者如想练习阅读英文报纸或杂志,则可以先选择关于某一主题的汉语文章,再阅读同一主题的英语文章。

(3) **兴趣**

兴趣能使阅读者更容易继续阅读下去。例如,阅读者如果想要旅行,就可以阅读用英语书写的旅游手册;如果想要提高外语的使用水平,可以多读相关国家的报纸和杂志等。

3. 制订阅读计划

常言道:"凡事预则立,不预则废。"英语阅读更是如此,阅读没有计划,不仅造成时间上的浪费,也使得阅读过程缺乏系统性,进而导致阅读效果不佳。阅读者为阅读过程制订计划就好比是足球教练在比赛前针对对方球队的特点提出对策。制订了阅读计划就意味着自己掌握了阅读的主动权,可以保证把课内和课外时间有意识地利用起来,自主监督阅读活动,有目的地增强自己的阅读能力,并最终形成自主阅读的学习能力。

通常来讲,制订阅读计划是指阅读者依据阅读任务的性质和特点,确定阅读过程中需要实施的步骤,考虑选择何种阅读策略,预计阅读结果等。这一策略具体包括设置阅读目标、浏览阅读材料、提出问题以及分析如何完成阅读任务。

Task 3

Read a passage. Before reading, consider the following questions. After reading, reflect on what your reading process involved.

① What famous fast food brands do you know about?
② How would you like to comment on fast food?
③ What information can you get from the title?
④ What procedures would you like to take in order to understand the passage?
⑤ How will you plan to control your speed and the time spent on the passage?

Fast Food Invasion

American fast food restaurants have invaded the island of Jamaica. It's a peaceful invasion, but local restaurant owners don't think it's a friendly one. Kentucky Fried Chicken (KFC), Burger King, Pizza Hut, and TCBY (The Country's Best Yogurt) have all opened restaurants around Jamaica. There is no sign this craze will slow down. Fast food restaurant owners don't want to say how well their businesses are doing. They will say hungry consumers are spending millions of dollars.

Recently, Subway, a popular American sandwich shop, opened a fifth restaurant in Kingston, the capital city of Jamaica. McDonald's has three restaurants there, as well.

Jamaicans have always liked fast food. The patty, a local meat-filled pie, has been a favorite for decades. Other spicy local treats like jerked chicken and jerked pork are still very popular.

However, the popularity of Burger King and Pizza Hut have influenced business. Smaller restaurants that sell local dishes have to try hard to stay in business. They don't have the money to advertise like the big American chain restaurants do.

One of those local stores is Tastee's, makers of the patty. Tastee's has been in business for 25 years. But now, it is trying to keep its popularity. Because the patty is cheaper than American fast food, it still sells well at Tastee's.

However, Tastee's has had to add different kinds of food to their menu to compete with American restaurants.

"The patty is not as expensive as the pizza or the burger. So, we still sell a lot of them," says a manager at Tastee's. A patty is smaller than a hamburger, but very filling. It sells for 46 cents. A hamburger costs $4.6 and a pizza costs from between $5.80 and $15.

Jamaicans have difficult work schedules. This is the main reason for their interest in fast food. "It's very convenient," says one diner. "People are busy and don't have time to make a meal at home. They eat fast food when they're going to work and coming home from work."

The result is that Jamaicans are not eating healthy food. Fast food is cheaper than healthy food. Healthy food takes more time to shop for and prepare. Of course, Jamaicans would like to eat food that is both healthy and fast. To help with this problem, the yogurt shop TCBY has been creative. They have four stores in Jamaica that sell yogurt as well as low-fat ice cream.

Many fast food restaurants are starting to offer more healthy foods. It seems that the fast food restaurants will do anything to keep their customers happy. Their success will probably last a long time in Jamaica, and in other parts of the world.

4. 监控阅读过程

监控是指在阅读活动中,阅读者依照一定的评价标准对阅读进行及时评价,发现不足,并及时修正、调整策略,以达到预定目标。监控策略主要包括:

(1) 方向监控

即确定应该采用何种阅读的方式。例如,采用略读策略来扫描文章,从而迅速掌握主旨大意;采用寻读策略来搜索、确定具体信息,从而达到找出答案、解决问题的目的;采用泛读策略来处理较长材料,从而达到整体理解文章的目的;采用精读策略来处理关于细节的阅读,运用 what, who, when, where, why 和 how 提问法,对主体及其情节发展脉络进行有效的监控。

(2) 进程监控

即边阅读边进行思考、观察、识别阅读材料提示的重要信息;理解中断后,识别难点并应用有效方法理解难句;通过上下文猜测词义;根据有关线索判断重要信息,完成相关的阅读要求。

(3) 策略监控

即采用自我提问的方式,检验自己的答案正确与否;从多角度分析问题,进行推理;懂得运用有效策略处理综合性问题。

Task 4

Read the following passage, and then try to:

① *find out what kind of reading methods you have adopted in order to understand the passage.*

_____

② *find out important inferential information.*

_____

③ *underline unfamiliar words and phrases and guess their meanings from context clues.*

_____

There are three kinds of goals: short-term, medium-range and long-term goals. Short-term goals are those that usually deal with current activities, which we can apply on a daily basis. Such goals can be achieved in a week or less, or two weeks, or possible months. It should be remembered that just as a building is no stronger than its foundation, our long-term goals cannot amount to very much without the achievement of solid short-term goals. Upon completing our short-term goals, we should date the occasion and then add new short-term goals that will build on those that have been completed.

The intermediate goals are built on the foundation of the short-term goals. They might deal with just one term of school or the entire school year, or they could even extend for several years. Any time you move a step at a time, you should never allow yourself to become discouraged or overwhelmed. As you complete each step, you will enforce the belief in your ability to grow and succeed. And as your list of completion dates grow, your motivation and desire will increase. Long-term goals may be related to our dreams of the future. They might cover five years or more. Life is not a static thing. We should never allow a long-term goal to limit us or our course of action.

5. 自我评价阅读过程

自我评价是指阅读者按照阅读计划,在阅读活动结束时,自我检查阅读效果如何,总结得失,包括纠正阅读过程中的错误,排除阅读障碍和调整阅读思路。事实上,这一过程既是阅读活动的结束,又是使用调节阅读策略、采取相应的补救措施的新一轮阅读活动的开始。

成功的阅读者往往能对是否达到他们阅读前所设置的目标以及阅读理解的效果做出评价。如果未能达到预期目标和理想效果,他们就会寻找原因以便在下次阅读过程中做出相应的调整,达到阅读的预期目标。例如,他们会评价自己在阅读过程中做出的预测和利用上下文猜测的词义是否恰当和正确,如果失败,他们会思考如何在下次阅读过程中做出调整。

Task 5

After finishing Task 4, answer the following questions:
① *What is the main idea of the passage?*

_____

② *How long does it take you to finish reading and understanding the passage?*

③ What are the new words and phrases you have learned during your comprehension process? And how did you try to figure out their meanings?
_____
_____
_____

④ Have you tried to make inferences and judgments?
_____
_____
_____

⑤ Have you had any difficulties during the comprehension process? If yes, what are they? How did you overcome them?
_____
_____
_____

6. 记笔记

在阅读过程中,阅读者往往可以记录一些重要的信息,以帮助进一步理解阅读材料的全文和细节。好的阅读笔记应该尽可能简短、精确,但不遗漏任何重要信息。

在记笔记的过程中,阅读者首先应明确材料的写作目的以及自己的阅读目的,有选择地进行记录。其次,要明确信息的组织方式。一般来讲,阅读材料中的信息都是按照逻辑顺序进行组织的。因此,记录阅读笔记时,阅读者也应该遵循一定的逻辑顺序,具有一定的逻辑性。一般应遵循以下顺序:

- 篇章的主题思想;
- 事件的主要阶段或过程的主要步骤;
- 从最重要的信息点到最次要的信息点;
- 从简单的思想到复杂的思想;
- 从主旨思想到具体思想;
- 从某一事物的最大部分到最小部分;
- 提出问题及解决方法;
- 事件的起因及结果。

Task 6

Read the following passage. While reading, take notes to enhance your comprehension.

_____
_____
_____
_____

Like many lovers of books, Mary and her husband, Richard Goldman, seldom walked past a bookstore without stopping to look inside. They often talked of opening their own store one day.

When Mary was hospitalized with heart trouble in 1989, they decided it was time to get serious. Richard, who worked for a business company, was eager to work for himself, and Mary needed to slow down from her demanding job.

They started by talking to bookstore owners and researching the industry. "We knew it had to be a specialty store because we couldn't match the big chains dollar for dollar," says Mary. One figure caught her attention: She'd read somewhere that roughly 20 percent of books sold were mysteries (推理小说), and many buyers spent more than $300 a year on books. She and Richard were themselves mystery readers.

On Halloween 1992, they opened the Mystery Lovers Bookshop and Cafe near their home. With three children in college, the couple could not spend all the family's money to start a shop. To cover the $100,000 cost, they drew some of their savings, borrowed from relatives and from an bank.

The store merely broke even in its first year, with only $120,000 in sales. But Mary was always coming up with new ways to attract customers. The shop had a coffee bar and it offered gifts to mystery lovers and served dinners for book clubs that met in the store. She also invited dozens of writers to discuss their stories.

Today Mystery Lovers makes sales of about $420,000 a year. After paying taxes, business costs and the six part-time sales clerks, Richard and Mary together earn about $34,000.

"The job you love may not go hand in hand with a million-dollar income," says Richard. "This has always been about an enjoyable life for ourselves, not about making a lot of money."

二、阅读学习中的认知策略

阅读认知策略是指阅读过程中,阅读者处理阅读材料的方法,或针对某一具体阅读任务所采取的具体阅读方法。事实上,阅读是一个积极思考、主动理解的过程,而不是一个简单的消极、被动接收信息的过程。阅读时,文字本身并不会产生任何意义,只有当读者与阅读材料进行积极的交流时,才会产生意义。因此,好的阅读者在阅读文章的同时,会结合有效的策略来处理阅读材料,以求最大程度理解文章。

1. 预测(Prediction)

预测是指在理解已知信息的基础上,对随之可能出现的信息(即下文)做出大致的推测。预测是阅读者理解文章意义、进行推理的第一步。阅读时人们往往都自觉或不自觉地进行或多或少的预测。在实际阅读过程中,预测的时间非常短暂。对于熟练掌握了这一技巧的人或有经验的读者而言,阅读时的预测阶段往往融于理解阶段中,与其几乎是同步进行的。通常阅读者可通过以下线索对未知信息进行预测:

(1) **通过标题和主题句来进行预测**

通常情况下,阅读者往往可以根据意义指向较为明显的标题和阅读材料的主题句来预测下文的内容。这一策略有助于阅读者在阅读文章之前进行初步的自我提问,并在阅读过程中怀有找到问题答案的期望,这在很大程度上会促进阅读理解的进程与效果。

Task 7

Now, you are given the title of an article — Shopping Online. Try to predict what this article is about and how it may develop. Note you can try to make predictions by asking such questions as "What is shopping online? What is shopping online for? Why do many people love shopping online? Are there problems with shopping online?"

_____

_____

Task 8

In this part, you are given the topic sentence of a paragraph. Try to predict what this paragraph is about and how it may develop. Then complete the paragraph by yourself.

In the 21st century, net surfing will continue to be a new trend. _____
_____
_____

（2）结合背景知识进行预测

在有些情况下，与文章主题相关的背景知识也可以帮助阅读者预测文章内容，加深对文章的理解。例如，当读到一篇以 *Only One Earth* 为题的文章时，阅读者往往可以猜测出这篇文章的主题应该是关于环境污染或者环境保护的，接着就可以回想自己这方面的已有知识，为更好地阅读文章做准备。例如，阅读者可以自行设问：What are the damages people bring to the environment? What should we do with our garbage? What is an endangered species? Should people hunt or fish? 如果在接下来的阅读过程中，阅读者发现这些问题与文章的主题相关，那么对文章的理解程度会大大加深，阅读速度也会大大加快。

Task 9

Brainstorm as much information as possible based on your previous knowledge concerning the topic — Trends of Teenagers in the 21st Century.

（3）通过信号词（**Signal Words**）和连接上下文的承接手段（**Transitional Devices**）进行预测

信号词是指连接文中上下句的词。这些词往往表示句子间的关系（例如：apart from, in the same way, owing to 等），有助于阅读者把握各细节间的相互关系。因此，可以利用信号词和一些承接手段，根据前文内容，结合篇章知识来预测下文的内容。

Task 10

Read the following (segmented) paragraph, and then try to:
① *identify the signal words*
_____

② *make as many predictions as possible based on the information already given and write them down in the blanks.*

Robert Hooke's work in science was varied and important through the 1700s in

England. In first place he served as the head of the Royal Society

He was also a well-known architect

Of all Hooke's gifts to human being, however, the most important was his own research in science

(4) 利用已知线索,预测下文内容

阅读是阅读者频繁做出猜测,并不断肯定或否定已有猜测的过程,这意味着阅读者并非以一成不变的方式阅读文章中所有的句子,而是利用文字和逻辑线索去预测下文的内容。

Task 11

After reading each of the sentences in column 1, look at column 2 and choose the sentence which you think is most likely to follow (the first column could be covered by a strip of paper while you are considering the possibilities in the second column). Go on in the same way until you reach the end of the text.

Column 1	Column 2
The average person in the world now uses approximately 43,000 calories people per day.	a. However, there are few "average" in the world. b. However, calories are essential to live. c. Some people may use more.
However, there are few "average" people in the world.	a. Most people should use far less calories. b. The Egyptians, for instance, consume 9,200 calories a day. c. Some people use far more energy.
Some people use far more energy than that, while most use far less.	a. An average citizen of the so-called "developed" countries uses 136,000 calories each day. b. The number should be much higher. c. But on the whole, everyone consumes far too many calories.

续表

Column 1	Column 2
An average citizen of the so-called "developed" countries uses 136,000 figure calories each day.	a. In Japan, for instance, the average is 74,000 calories per day. b. However, more than two-thirds of the world's people live in the "developing" areas, where the average person uses only 8,200 calories of non-metabolic energy daily.
However, more than two-thirds of the world's people live in the "developing", where the average person uses only 8,200 calories of non-metabolic energy daily.	a. This is why it is so difficult to be an average person. b. This explains why one part of the world is much poorer than the other. c. Such vast differences are hard to comprehend.

2. 略读(Skimming)

略读,又称跳读(reading and skipping)或浏览(glancing),是指以尽可能快的速度进行阅读,迅速获取文章大意或中心思想。事实上,略读要求阅读者进行选择性阅读,获取一些主要信息,略过一些次要信息和细节,同时,阅读者应该确定文章的结构和作者的语气。

在运用这一策略时,阅读者应该注意如下几点:

· 判断文章属于何种题材,涉及了什么内容。

· 阅读文章第一段,抓住主要情节或论点,以便为下文的略读做一定的准备和铺垫。

· 在阅读下文的过程中,读每段的头两句话和最后两句话,以便了解文章的大意和线索。

· 快速阅读文章,寻找字面上或事实上的主要信息和少量的阐述信息。

· 根据文章的难易程度和所要达到的目的,不断灵活地调整阅读速度。

· 如果文章的最后一段是总结或结论,应稍微细致地对该段进行阅读。

Task 12

Read the following passage as quickly as possible and try to answer the following questions.

Statistics reflect recent changes in the U.S. college population. One change these days is that there are fewer foreign students than several years ago but that more U. S. students are studying abroad. There are over half a million foreign students in colleges and universities in the United States (down 5-6 percent). The leading country of origin is India, followed by China, Korea, Japan, Canada, Mexico, Turkey, and Thailand. Meanwhile, there are 175,000 U. S. students who are studying abroad (up 8.5 percent). American students typically spend much less time abroad than foreign students do in the United States. In fact, 92 percent of all U. S. students who go abroad spend only one semester there.

① What is the main idea of the paragraph?
___

② How do you try to grasp the main idea?
___

③ Have you read every detail in the passage?
___

3. 寻读(Scanning)

寻读是一种快速寻找某些特殊信息的阅读方法,即要求阅读者带着问题去寻找答案。熟练的读者善于运用寻读获得具体信息,以提高阅读效率。这种方法要求阅读者把需要回答的问题记在心中,带着问题,有目的地从材料中迅速查找某一项具体事实或特定信息。

寻读的目的非常明确,即找到所需要的信息。信息一旦被找到,寻读即宣告结束。寻读时,应该首先浏览文章后的各个问题及其选项,避免在与问题无关的词语和细节上浪费时间及精力。

Task 13

Read the following advertisements and answer the questions within 2 minutes. Then consider how you managed to locate the exact place of each question.

A

Restaurant

Supervisor

Waiting staff

Telephonist

The ideal candidates must have relevant experience gained in a high quality hotel. Please call personnel on 071 – 722 – 7733 or send your CV to: Regents Park Hilton, Lodge Road, London. NW8 7JT

B

USE YOUR LANGUAGES

AND EARN 450 – 1200 P. W.

We are one of the largest business publishers in Europe and have limited vacancies for intelligent young people in our London advertisement sales office. Enquiries from German, Spanish and eastern European speakers especially welcome. Phone Andrew Warburton on 071 – 753 – 4300.

C

SECRETARY

Busy chartered

Accountants require experienced /efficient secretary, accounts, typing experience and an excellent telephone manner essential, shorthand useful.

Please send CV to: box No. 9246 c/o evening standard classified, 2 Derry Street, Kensington W8 5EE. 071 – 228 – 8546

D

TRAVEL COMPANY

Vacancy for self-confident person to look after bookings for our Caribbean hotels. Salary based on applicant's experience & suitability. Please send CV to Ian Taplin, MRI LTD, 9 Galena Road, London, WG OLX

071 – 223 – 8563

```
E
NANNY WANTED

For 9 month old handful. Artistle /Prof household Notting Hill, 3 days per week. Some hours flexibility required. Knowledge German/Hungarian advantage not essential.

071 - 221 - 7375
```

```
F
JOIN THE STARS!
FOOD SERVERS

The biggest and busiest restaurant in London is seeking additional stars for its team of dedicated professionals. If you have experience in high volume restaurants and are looking for a challenge, then come on down for an audition.

Interview day is on Friday, 6th MAY from 12 noon to 7 p.m. . Planet Hollywood is located at 13 Coventry Street, London. W1.

071 - 225 - 7852
```

① If you want to look after a child, you should dial _____.
    a. 071 - 722 - 7733   b. 071 - 221 - 7375
    c. 071 - 225 - 7852   d. 071 - 223 - 8563

② If you want to be a waiter, you should write to _____.
    a. box No. 9246 c/o evening standard classified, 2 Derry Street, Kensington W8 5EE
    b. Regents Park Hilton, Lodge Road , London
    c. Ian Taplin, MRI LTD, 9 Galena Road, London , WG OLX
    d. 13 Coventry Street, London. W1.

③ Which jobs would particularly like a German speaker?
    a. Advertisement salesman.   b. Travel agent.
    c. Advisement salesman.   d. Babysitter.

4. 关键词阅读(Key Words Reading)

关键词阅读是指略过非实质词语而只阅读句子的核心部分及某些修饰

核心部分的形容词和副词的阅读技巧。它通常用于快速了解文章大意和主要细节,由于省去了很多非关键词,阅读速度快了许多,但同时理解的准确度也受到了影响(通常在50%至70%)。

一般来讲,确定关键词应遵循如下原则:

关键词的词性	关键词的确定依据	关键词的例外原则	关键词的优先原则
• 名词或名词性短语 • 形容(副)词或形容(副)词性短语 • 专有名词 • 数字或年代	• 在文章中出现频率较低 • 醒目好找,有利于及时确定答案	• 文章标题中的单词一般不宜作为关键词 • 在文章中出现频率较高的词一般不宜作为关键词 • 动词一般不宜作为关键词	• 短语优先于单词作为关键词 • 形容(副)词的比较级、最高级优先于原级作为关键词

在利用关键词回答阅读理解的相关问题时,可以使用以下方法:
- 先在文中找到问句中的关键词及短语的相应位置。
- 在很多情况下,仔细读关键词语所在的句子,即可找到相关问题的答案。
- 如果根据关键词语所在的句子无法确定问题的答案,那么阅读者也可接着读随后的一至两个句子,这样就可以基本确定问题的答案了。

Task 14

Read the following paragraph and try to underline the key words. After that, compare the key words you found with those of your partner, and then state your reasons why you choose those words.

Please NOTE: during this process, pay attention to the principles of identifying key words mentioned above.

A reading habit thus formed will prove valuable to you. Whenever you have spare time, you will resort not to places of pleasure, but to the bookshelves, you will not feel lonesome when you are alone, because you can see all kinds of characters moving and acting on the pages, and you can hear all kinds of good counsel. In the long run, your imaginative power will be increased, your esthetic sensibility heightened, your vocabulary enlarged, and finally your ability of writing tremendously improved.

5. 意群阅读(Sense Groups)

　　意群是指有意义的语法结构。在阅读过程中,孤立的单个词本身是不会产生任何意义的,只有与其他词联系起来,才能构成一定的意义。构成一定意义的这一组词,就是意群。"意群阅读法"也就是按词组、短语在文中的组合意义整体阅读,而不是单个词的阅读。

　　意群的划分一般以语法单位为标准,即主语部分、谓语部分、状语部分和补语部分,若各部分较长,则可进一步分为中心词与修饰语,以及修饰语中更小的意义单元(如介词短语)等。

Task 15

Please read the following paragraph containing 75 words TWICE. For the first time, read the paragraph word for word, and for the second time, read the paragraph in sense groups. (During the second time, mark where you make pauses)

　　Like many small cultural groups, most of the Inuit tribes chose to explore and find a new home planet where they could more easily preserve their way of life. The planet they chose and named Sedna was a small ocean planet where most of the land was near the poles. Because the average temperature of Sedna was quite a bit lower than earth, there was very little forest-type land, which the Inuit generally left alone, and the rest of the land was tundra, like the land of their origin on Earth. While education was still very important to growing up, so was learning the traditional way of life. The settlers are very careful to make sure there is a balance between the humans and the natural wild life, which they hunt.

6. 猜测词义(Guessing Word Meaning)

　　猜测词义是指在阅读过程中,阅读者根据对语篇的信息、逻辑、背景知识及语言结构等的综合理解去猜测或推断某一生词、难词、关键词的词义。阅读者在阅读过程中能很快通过上下文的线索或生词本身的结构特点推断出词义,提高阅读速度和阅读能力,增强学习英语的兴趣和信心。

　　猜测词义的策略大体可分为两大类:一类是通过上下文推测词义,另一类是根据生词本身的特点推测词义。通过上下文推测词义是根据一个词所处的具体的语言环境,运用有关线索,如同义词、反义词、举例、重述或定义等推测词义,或运用逻辑推理和其他知识,如生活经验、普通常识等推测词义。根据生词本身的特点推测词义是指根据构词法知识,如词根和词缀等推测词义。

Task 16
Have you ever tried to guess the meanings of unfamiliar words and phrases in your English reading? If yes, what kinds of methods have you used?

_____
_____
_____
_____

(1) 利用定义或解释说明猜测词义

很多句子中,在生词的附近,往往会出现该词的定义或对该词的解释和说明。这种定义或解释说明类的线索可以帮助我们较为迅速、直接地猜测出句中生词的含义。

Task 17
Read the following sentences, and try to figure out the meanings of the underlined words from the context and write them down in the blanks. At the same time, tell what context clues you have used to identify the meanings.

① There is a drawback, a disadvantage, to that idea.
　　drawback = _____
　　context clues used _____

② In a number of countries, education is both compulsory—required—and universal, available to everyone, at least in primary school (elementary school).
　　compulsory = _____
　　context clues used _____
　　universal = _____
　　context clues used _____
　　primary school = _____
　　context clues used _____

③ A veteran means a person who served in the Armed Forces of the United States on active duty, for reasons other than training, and has been discharged under other than dishonorable conditions.

 veteran = _____

 context clues used _____

④ A person or thing beyond comparison, a model of excellence, is called a <u>paragon</u>.

 paragon = _____

 context clues used _____

⑤ A <u>light sleeper</u> is a person whose sleep is easily ended as by a soft noise.

 a light sleeper = _____

 context clues used _____

(2) 利用同义词和反义词猜测词义

有时,阅读者可以利用句中的同义词和反义词来对生词进行词义猜测。

1) 利用同义词猜测词义

在猜测词义的过程中,阅读者往往可以根据语言环境,利用已知词义的同义词或近义词来解释另一个比较难的词,这就为阅读者猜测生词的词义提供了线索。除了已知词义的同义词,有时为了更好地猜测生词的词义,阅读者还可以利用文中的一些信号词,例如:or, and, also, moreover, further, likewise, in addition, besides, similarly, as well as, the same as 等。

2) 利用反义词猜测词义

在进行对比的过程中,作者一般会用一些互为对应、互为反义的词语,使不同事物的特点更为突出。通过上下文的逻辑关系,从对两种事物或现象进行对比的描述中,阅读者可以根据其中一个熟悉的词推断出另一个生词的词义来。另外,在表示这种对比关系时,作者通常会用一些信号词来表明另一个词与前面的词语互为反义。

常用来表示对应关系和提供相反信息的信号词有:but, however, while, whereas, on the other hand, on the contrary, as apposed to, to the opposite, otherwise, compared to, in spite of, despite, even though 等。

Task 18

Read the following sentences, and try to figure out the meanings of the underlined words from the context with the help of their synonyms or antonyms and write them down in the blanks. At the same time, tell what context clues you have used to identify the meanings.

① The man appeared very vigorous despite his 80 years. In fact he was so strong that he could still lift heavy objects.

  vigorous = _____

  context clues used _____

② A school system in one country is not identical to the system in any other country. It cannot be exactly the same to that of another because each culture is different.

  identical = _____

  context clues used _____

③ Doctors believe that smoking cigarettes is detrimental to your health. Similarly, they also regard drinking as harmful.

  detrimental = _____

  context clues used _____

④ In the past the world seemed to run in an orderly way. Now, however, everything seems to be in a state of turmoil.

  turmoil = _____

  context clues used _____

⑤ The main point of the plan is clear to me, but the details are still hazy.

  hazy = _____

  context clues used _____

⑥ He always seemed to be engaged in some constructive/helpful activities rather than destructive ones.

  destructive = _____

  context clues used _____

⑦ Some human actions are learned, but other actions are innate.

  innate = _____

  context clues used _____

(3) 利用列举猜测词义

  为了阐明某一种重要观念或者讲清楚某一个抽象概念，作者往往采取举例的方式对这一观点或概念进行具体的说明和解释，从而使阅读者理解得更具体，那么文中的例子自然也就成了阅读者理解文章生词的线索。

  表示列举关系的信号词有：like, for example, for instance, such as, especially, include, consist of, specially 等。

(4) 利用重述(Restatement)猜测词义

有时作者在阐述某个概念或某一事情时,为了把它讲述得更清楚,可能采取另一种方式重述一下前面的内容。这种重述往往采用比前面的词更为简单易懂的词语,它们为前面较难的词语提供了猜测的线索。因此,阅读者在阅读的过程中遇到生词时,不要停下来不知所措,不妨看一下该生词后面是否有另一种阐述或解释。

表达重述,作者也经常使用一些信号词,这些信号词有:in other words, to put it another way, that is to say, or, that is, i.e., to be precise 等。

(5) 利用因果关系猜测词义

因果关系(cause and effect)是一种常见的、行之有效的能提供生词词义信息的逻辑关系。作者在叙述原因的过程中,一般会把词或句子置于一种因果关系的逻辑之中,这为阅读者推断生词词义提供了很好的线索。

作者通常会用一些信号词表示句子之间的因果关系,这些信号词有:since, as, because, for, so, thus, consequently, therefore, hence, due to, result in, result from, as a result, for this reason, accordingly, so that, so...that, such...that 等。

(6) 利用生词所在的前后文提供的解释或说明猜测词义

有时作者在阐述某人、某物或某一现象的特点时,先一般性或概括性地表述一下,然后再做具体的说明或解释;或者先做具体的阐述,然后再进行归纳总结。阅读者如果能抓住作者的思路,就能从具体说明、解释或归纳中找出猜词的线索来。

(7) 利用普通常识、生活经验和逻辑推理推测生词词义

1) 利用普通常识和生活经验推测词义

阅读者有时可以根据自身的直接或间接的经验,或运用已有的常识将生词的意义推测出来。比如了解一些英美国家的天文地理、风俗习惯、宗教信仰、政治结构、社会制度等,可以帮助我们加深对文章的理解,遇到生词时,猜测词义的能力自然就增强了。

2) 利用逻辑推理推测词义

作者在写作时,要把一些分散的、复杂的信息组织在一起,使它们之间形成密切的内在联系,成为结构严谨、层次分明、形式与内容一致的语言整体。阅读者如果按照上下文,顺着作者的思路,通过询问关系、语境对生词进行合乎逻辑的推断,就可以推测出生词的大概意思。

Task 19

Read the following sentences, and try to figure out the meanings of the underlined word using the strategies you have learned above and write it down in the blank. At the same time, tell what context clues you have used to identify the meaning.

① Defined most broadly, <u>folklore</u> includes all the customs, belief and tradition that people have handed down from generation to generation.

    folklore = _____

    context clues used _____

② Before the main business of a conference begins the chairman usually makes a short <u>preliminary</u> (i.e. introductory) speech, or make a few preliminary remarks. In other words, he says a few things by way of introduction.

    preliminary = _____

    context clues used _____

③ Since I could not afford to purchase the original painting, I bought a <u>replica</u>. An inexperienced eye could not tell the difference.

    replica = _____

    context clues used _____

④ Another habit which can slow your reading is called "<u>subvocalization</u>". In this case your lips do not move, but you still "hear" each word in your head as you read silently.

    subvocalization = _____

    context clues used _____

⑤ When a doctor performs an operation on a patient, he usually gives an <u>anesthetic</u> to make him unconscious, because he does not want his patient to feel pain or to know what is happening to him.

    anesthetic = _____

    context clues used _____

⑥ If you are capable of working twelve hours a day without a rest, and if you can engage in physical exercise for hours without seeming to get tired, then you are <u>indefatigable</u>.

    indefatigable = _____

    context clues used _____

(8) 用构词法猜测词义

英语中特定的词缀往往表示特定的含义。另外,句子中有时会出现一些合成词,这些词看似不为阅读者所了解,但经过仔细观察,不难发现它们是由我们熟知的一些词组衍生而来的。例如,break out—outbreak,set out—outset,come in—income。

Task 20

Read the following sentences, and try to figure out the meanings of the underlined words using your knowledge of word formation and write them down in the blanks. At the same time, tell what affixes you have used to identify the meanings.

① He had been overworking and fell ill at last.

   overworking = _____

   word formation knowledge _____

② You must stop dreaming and face reality.

   reality = _____

   word formation knowledge _____

③ The country is trying to popularize education.

   popularize = _____

   word formation knowledge _____

④ Family members take turns choosing a special activity for the evening, and everyone partakes in for fun.

   partake in = _____

   word formation knowledge _____

7. 了解文章的组织结构

(1) 归纳和确定主题思想(Main Idea)

主题思想是作者在材料中要表达的核心内容、主要观点或贯穿材料始终要说明的问题,它往往反映了作者的写作意图。对阅读材料的理解首先是对材料主题思想的理解,确定阅读材料的主题思想是正确理解材料的关键。在阅读理解的过程中,问题设计者主要会针对文章的主题、中心思想、适用标题或写作目的进行提问,这就要求阅读者具有总结、概括和归纳的能力。

文章的主题思想通常出现在文章的开头,有时也会出现在文章的中间或结尾,有时文章的大意不会直接出现在文章中,阅读者必须自己进行总结和归纳。

Task 21

Read the following paragraphs. While reading, try to identify the main idea of each paragraph, and then write it down. You can copy the main idea directly from the paragraph, or use your own words to restate the main idea.

Paragraph A

A good understanding of human weakness is essential if a company wants to sell a product. One way that advertisers persuade us to buy a product is by targeting our dissatisfaction with ourselves, our fears. Consider for a moment a typical fear — fear of being offensive to other people. Advertisers persuade us, for example, that if we don't buy their mouthwash, we'll have bad breath and offend other people. Dentists tell us that mouthwash is actually unnecessary; they explain that we need only simple dental hygiene—regular, correct use of a soft toothbrush and of dental floss. But we continue to spend money on mouthwash, breath freshener, and breath mints. Our fear of offending people outweighs our dentists' logic.

Main idea: _____

Paragraph B

The 19th-century American philosopher Henry David Thoreau was famous for saying, "Simplify, simplify." Unfortunately, the trend these days seems to be "complicate, complicate" instead. Many people are working longer hours, spending more money, and getting in more debt than ever before. They are also relaxing less and spending less time with family and friends. However, there is also a countertrend—a trend toward voluntary simplicity. People in the voluntary simplicity movement take various steps to make their lives both simpler and more enjoyable. Some people work few hours each week. Some move close to their workplace to avoid a long daily commute; they walk or ride a bike, instead. Some plant a vegetable garden; this gives them fresh air, exercise, and time with their families — not to mention organic produce. But all people in the voluntary simplicity movement try to cut back — to buy less; they cut up their credit cards and stop buying unnecessary items. In short, the priority in the voluntary movement is to follow Thoreau's suggestion: simplify.

Main idea: _____

Paragraph C

So how does this work? A job seeker can reply to a "Help Wanted" notice on a company's website. This person can also post his or her resume (page with information about education and work experience) on one—or many—of the online job boards. If a company is interested, the person still has to take the next step, the old-fashioned way—actually go to the job interview and perhaps take a skills test. However, even this might soon change. In the near future, companies will be able to give the person a skills test and check his or her background (job history and education) online. But what about the interview? Companies will soon be able to interview the person by videolink, so people can interview for jobs in other cities—or even other countries—without leaving home. Clearly, job hunting is not what it used to be.
Main idea:_____

Paragraph D

People have worried about smog for many years, and the government has spent billions of dollars to try to clean up the air of big cities. But now we find that there is no escape from unhealthy air. Recent studies have shown that air inside many homes, office buildings, and schools is full of pollutants: chemicals, mold, bacteria, smoke, and gases. These pollutants are causing a group of unpleasant and dangerous symptoms that experts call "sick-building syndrome". First discovered in 1982, sick-building syndrome most often includes symptoms similar to those of the flu (watering eyes, headaches, and so on) and respiratory infections such as tonsillitis, bronchitis, and pneumonia.
Main idea:_____

(2) 辨别与理解指示代词

在阅读过程中,对于阅读者来说,把结构上彼此独立的句子连接起来,以理解文章的意义尤为重要。这需要阅读者利用到一些指代上文曾经出现过的或者即将在下文中出现的指示代词。事实上,在所有的语言中,无论是书面语言还是口语,都存在利用指示代词指代人物和事物的现象,不能正确地理解指示可能会导致对于文章的误解。

Task 22

In the following passage all the underlined words refer to something mentioned before, or after, in the text. Read the passage carefully and complete the table underneath. An example has already been given.

It is quite another thing to produce a proof of the correctness of that idea. Darwin thought he had that proof in his notebooks. He saw that all animals had a struggle to survive. Those which were best at surviving their environment passed on the good qualities which had helped them to their descendants. This was called "the survival of the fittest". For example, in a cold climate, those who have the warmest fur will live. Darwin believed that this necessity for an animal to deal with its environment explained the immense variety of creatures.

Underlined words	refers to something		What it refers to
	before	after	
It		√	to produce a proof of the correctness of that idea
that	√		
his	√		
He	√		
Those	√		
their	√		
them	√		
their	√		
This	√		
those		√	
this	√		
its	√		

(3) 区分概括性话语和具体细节

在阅读过程中,学会区分概括性话语和具体细节也很重要。

Task 23

Here are a number of statements. Decide which ones are generalizations and which ones are more specific statements. Then match the generalizations with the examples.

a) When I was young I could think of nothing but becoming a policeman.

b) Do you know the name of the product for which Scotch Tape is but a brand name?

c) The aim of advertisers is to create consumer wants.

d) The youths who attacked X in Chicago last week had all seen the ABC movie three nights before.

e) All children cherish a dream.

f) If the people who originally built many of our Eastern cities had been able to predict the automobile, there would certainly be less traffic problems nowadays.

g) Violence on TV is probably more harmful than we think.

h) Many of the problems one finds in city and suburban life result from a lack of proper learning.

i) So effective has brand advertising become that, for some products, the most familiar brand name is used to cover all similar items.

j) A producer of paper handkerchiefs recently launched a campaign to convince people they needed one box of tissues in each room of their house.

Generalizations						
Specific statements	↓	↓	↓	↓	↓	↓

(4) 进行推理

进行推理要求阅读者利用背景信息推测作者隐含的意思。这是一个连接阅读者已知知识和文章信息的过程。例如,通过"The king of France is bold"这句话,我们可以推测出"There is a king in France"。

Task 24

What can you infer from the following sentences?

① Blandida is a country which has every climatic condition known to man.

② When she came into the room the large crowd grew silent.

③ The painting had been in the family for years, but sadly Bill realized he would have to sell it.

三、阅读学习中的社交/情感策略

阅读学习中的社交/情感策略是指阅读者利用他人的帮助来辅助阅读以及运用自我情感控制来帮助完成阅读的策略。

阅读过程中,影响阅读效果的一个重要因素就是阅读者的情感状态。影响阅读者情感状态的因素主要涉及以下几个方面:

- 阅读者对阅读材料的语言本身所持的态度和兴趣。这决定了阅读者对所学内容是否具有积极的态度和情感状态。
- 阅读者的阅读欲望。它决定了阅读者对外语阅读的态度,也会影响阅读过程中的策略选择。
- 阅读者在阅读过程中的焦虑程度。它是指阅读者由于不能达到预期的阅读目标或不能克服阅读过程中的障碍,使自尊心与自信心受挫,或使失败感和内疚感增加而形成的紧张不安、带有恐惧感的情绪状态。

一般情况下,阅读者的焦虑程度在很大程度上决定了他们在面对阅读障碍时的心理状态。许多学生习惯于阅读短篇材料,而面对篇幅稍长的材料时则缺乏耐心,常表现出烦躁不安、无信心和缺乏毅力等现象,尤其当文章内容涉及自然科学和文化历史等题材时,他们的不耐烦情绪就更为显著。

因此,在阅读过程中,阅读者应尽力克服自己的焦虑情绪,保持良好的心理状态,做到:

- 避免阅读期望值过高,希望一次阅读就掌握所读材料

这种急于求成的心理状态,不仅影响阅读时的心境,也使得视觉器官和大脑都不能集中于阅读过程本身,阅读的效果自然不好。

- 避免过度重视阅读方法和技巧

如果阅读过程中过多思考阅读的方法、技巧等因素,而忽视了阅读材料

及阅读本身,从某种程度上讲,就会使阅读者注意力分散,阅读兴趣大大减弱。

· 保持注意力集中,避免思想开小差

有些阅读者对文字视而不见,翻了许多页,但脑子里仍一片空白。这样就降低了注意力,影响了正常思维。

本章学习心得:
___
___
___

第九章 写作学习策略

本章学习目标

1. 了解写作学习的本质和特点
2. 掌握写作学习中的常用策略
3. 学会运用写作学习中的主要策略

写作学习的本质

　　长期以来,无论是从事语言研究的语言学家,还是在教育第一线工作的语言教师,都认为:语言首先是口语,口语是第一性的;文字是记录语言的,是第二性的。人们习惯把能说一口流利的口语作为衡量一个人语言学习好坏的首要标准。因此,听说训练在外语学习中一直被放在首要地位,听先于说,读写为辅,读先于写。可见,人们对写作技能的训练是有所忽略的。然而,写作是一个可以巩固知识,特别是巩固听说的重要技能。

　　首先,写作并不仅仅是口语的记录,写作和口语是有区别的。从语言的严谨性来看,写作者所用的语言是经过反复推敲的,比说话人所用的语言准确,从拼写、语法、标点符号到修辞、逻辑性等都要仔细推敲。所以,文字不能模棱两可,含糊不清,以免误导读者。从传递信息的角度来看,写作可以穿越时空的限制,不受人脑记忆力的限制。有了书面文字,我们才能追溯历史,才能与异地的人展开交流,才能把口语不能储存的信息保留下来。

　　其次,写作作为信息传递的重要手段,可以帮助操不同方言的人顺利交流。一个国家尽管有多种不同的方言,人们之间仍然可以相互沟通,相互理解。比如,我国有五十六个民族,各民族大都有自己的语言或方言,通过口语大家可能是无法交流的,但我们有历史形成的统一的汉字系统,使得我们能顺利地交流。

　　最后,写作能力是用书面语传递信息的一种交际能力。很多学习者在写作这一环节上是相当薄弱的,因为在听说读写四项技能中,写作是最难培养的。因此,加强写作的训练是提高外语水平的必然要求。只有具备较强的写作能力,才能成为真正意义上的外语人才。

　　写作学习从根本上说是学习运用自己喜欢的方式自由表达自己的思

想。"自由"是每一个学习者都想要达到的目标,但要想真正做到"自由"并不容易。对于中国的英语学习者来说,从接触写作那天起就不习惯"自由表达",在写作课堂上老师经常会提供一些优秀的范文供学生欣赏和模仿,不可否认在这个过程中学生汲取了别人文章的优点,但却忽略了自己的感受,认为只有写成范文那样的文章才算是好文章。这样的指导思想落实到行动上就是"模仿",模仿"好文章"的格式、句式、行文以及思路。这种方法对于应付某些考试会奏效,但并不能从根本上提高英文写作能力。写作能力的提高并不是一蹴而就的事情,要靠平时点滴的积累,并要时刻练笔,因为没有千万字的写作练习,是谈不上对写作有体会的。学习者平时应该经常把自己的想法用文字呈现出来,逐渐培养自由表达思想的写作习惯。

一、过程写作论

顾名思义,过程写作就是重过程(process-oriented approach)的写作教学方法,与之相对应的是重结果(product-oriented approach)的写作教学方法。大部分英语学习者对后者并不陌生,这种方法是教师让学生模仿或改写教师提供的范文,目的是让学生写出语法正确、行文连贯的所谓"完美"的文章。学生按照固定的模式进行写作,很少考虑表达自己的想法。而前者则强调写作的过程,因为写作是一项复杂而系统的工程,并不是单词加正确的语法等于文章那样简单。在这种方法的框架下,不期望写出"完美"的文章,要在反复推敲、小组讨论、修订润色的过程中使文章接近完美。

在学写文章的最初阶段,模仿是重要的写作技巧,正所谓"熟读唐诗三百首,不会作诗也会吟",现成的范文会提供一些有价值的思考。但到了一定阶段,仅仅依靠模仿是不够的。因为,写作的最终目的是运用自己喜欢的方式自由表达思想。过程写作鼓励学习者开动脑筋,独立思考,按照自己的方式自由表达思想,在写作过程中形成一整套写作策略,包括动笔前的酝酿(选题、构思、搜集资料、确定中心思想、反复讨论确定方案)、写作过程中的反复推敲(字斟句酌、组织成文)、写作后的校订(注意修辞、句子结构和语法)等。在经历这样一个系统的工程后,学习者才能写出自己的文章,而不是整齐划一的八股文。

当然,重过程写作和重结果写作这两种写作教学方法并不是绝对对立的,二者应该你中有我,我中有你。如果想提高写作水平,就一定要掌握过程写作中重要的策略,这些策略并不是可以迅速提高写作水平的灵丹妙药,学习者在平时的写作中要注意积累,在适当时候正确使用这些策略,来写出好文章。因为有了好"过程",才能产出好"结果"。

二、准备写作:开动脑筋,挖掘思路

"One can not make bricks without straw!"(巧妇难为无米之炊),这是人们熟知的一句谚语。写作是一种典型的语言输出形式,在输出之前一定要有大量的语言储备,因此写作之前的准备工作显得尤为重要,比如、构思、确定中心思想、搜集与题目相关的背景资料、进行头脑风暴、自由写作等。这一过程我们称为:"开动脑筋,挖掘思路!"

1. 图片(Pictures)

通过图片在头脑中产生联想。这种策略特别适合视觉型的学习者,利用图片的刺激在头脑中产生联想,拓展写作思路。

Task 1

Work with your group and have a discussion on the topic of "Love". Look at the following pictures first and then answer the corresponding questions.

① Does each picture describe the same kind of love? How do you define "love"?

② What does love mean to human beings?
_____

③ Give some examples to illustrate the power of love.
_____

2. 访谈(Interview)

访谈是一种互动性极强的方式。通过访谈你可以了解别人的想法,同时还能拓展自己的写作思路。访谈的形式很多,可以自由交谈(free talk),也可以按事先设计的问题进行。

Task 2

Interview a classmate about his or her "Favorite Cities". Use the following questionnaire and add your own questions if you wish.

Questionnaire

(1) Where are you from? _____
(2) What is your major? _____
(3) Which cities have you ever traveled? How much do you like those cities?
   City A:
   (circle the appropriate number)   1   2   3   4   5
                                   dislike   like best
   City B:
   (circle the appropriate number)   1   2   3   4   5
                                   dislike   like best
   City C:
   (circle the appropriate number)   1   2   3   4   5
                                   dislike   like best
(4) What impressed you most when you traveled there?
   City A:_____
   City B:_____
   City C:_____
(5) In which city would you like to work when you graduate from university? Why?
   City A:_____
   City B:_____
   City C:_____

---

3. 谚语(Idioms)

动笔之前,在头脑中迅速搜集与题目相关的名人名言、谚语或俗语,必要的时候可以写在纸上。但在使用谚语时一定要符合文章的主题和风格,否则会弄巧成拙。恰当地使用谚语可以增加文章的可信度,起到锦上添花的功效。

Task 3

Below are some idioms about "Success". Match the explanations in the right column with the idioms in the left one. Write the corresponding letters in the blanks. Add your own idioms concerning success if you wish.

(1) _____ One is never too old to learn.	a. You always need help from others.
(2) _____ Success is the reward of hard work.	b. You have to make full preparation for the success.
(3) _____ Many hands make light work.	c. Believe in yourself no matter what you may face.
(4) _____ Time is money.	d. Never give up.
(5) _____ Failure is the mother of success.	e. As you live, you learn.
(6) _____ Opportunities belong to the person who is prepared.	f. Good luck can assist you on the way to success.
(7) _____ Self-trust is the first of success.	g. Try until you succeed in spite of failures.
(8) _____ Perseverance can carve mind and gold.	h. Work hard.
(9) _____ The secret of success is having a definite aim.	i. You have to bear a determined object in your mind.
(10) _____ I am a lucky dog.	j. Don't waste time.
(11) _____	k. _____
(12) _____	l. _____
(13) _____	m. _____
(14) _____	n. _____

4. 图表(Graphic Organizer)

图表可以帮助我们直观地整理思路,我们的想法和一些细节的问题都可以通过图表表示。图表还可以呈现出不同观点之间的关系,帮助作者在头脑中对所陈述的想法建立联系。

Task 4

Complete the following graphic organizer concerning the title "To Be a Good English Learner".

Considerations

(1) Motive: why do people need to learn English?

(2) Importance: why is English so important to us?

(3) Strategies: what are some ways to enhance English learning?

(4)

Details

People learn it out of interest.

English is a world language.

I read English every day.

5. 阅读材料(Reading Materials)

阅读是实现语言输入的最重要的形式。与写作相比,大多数学习者感觉阅读的难度要小得多。之所以有这样的观点,是因为他们只是泛泛而读,并没有带着任务去读。当阅读为写作服务,即通过阅读相关的文章并从文章中捕捉相关信息的时候,阅读的难度就增加了。因此,必须进行有目的的阅读,从中提炼出精华,增加对背景知识的了解,进而加深对题目的理解。

Task 5

Imagine you are required to write a paragraph entitled "A Good Book to Me" in 80-100 words. The following are three passages concerning "Book". Go through these passages and try to find important information that might be helpful for you to finish your writing.

Essay One

   Books are our good friends. When we began elementary school, we started our friendship with them. They never leave us unless we throw them away. When we are alone, they help us to get rid of lonely feelings. When we are in low spirits, they encourage us to stand up again. Whenever we are in trouble, they always offer help to us. However not all books are worth reading. Certain ones can be harmful to our young people who have committed crimes(犯罪) and finally are sent to prison. This is the negative influence(负面影响) that these books bring to their young reader. So it is important to make wise use of books. Our aim is not only to read them, but also to use them. How can we use them more wisely? The answer is to practice what we have read. Only by practicing and using the knowledge we have acquired from books can we achieve more in our life.

Essay Two

   We may say with certainty that the more one reads, the better one understands; and that the better one understands, the more one is inclined to(喜欢) read. In other words, from reading comes understanding, and from understanding comes more reading. The reading habit is actually cultivated(培养) by reading itself.

Essay Three

   A man may usually be known by the books he reads as well as by the company(朋友,交往的人) he keeps, for there is a companionship of books as well as of men; and one should always live in the best company, whether it be of books or of men.

A good book may be among the best of friends. It is the same today as it always was, and it will never change. It is the most patient and cheerful of companions. It does not turn its back upon(背弃) us in times of adversity(逆境) or distress(不幸). It always receives us with the same kindness; amusing(使快乐) and instructing us in youth, and comforting and consoling(安慰) us in age.

6. 自由写作(Free-writing)

所谓的自由写作,并不是真正地开始写作,而是集中精力把头脑中闪现的所有与题目有关的念头都记录下来,直到写不出来为止。在写的过程中,不管拼写、标点、语法的正误,也不需要回头阅读和修改写过的文字。它是克服思路滞塞的一个好办法,同时也是解除对写作恐惧的有效手段。自由写作最好有个时间限制,十分钟或十五分钟比较适宜。此外,自由写作时偏离了题目也不要紧,因为这不是正式的写作,而是为了归纳思路(brainstorm,"头脑风暴")和放松。自由写作一旦结束,回过头来读一下所写的内容,找到值得在文章中去用的东西。下面的图片是一位学生自由写作的样本。

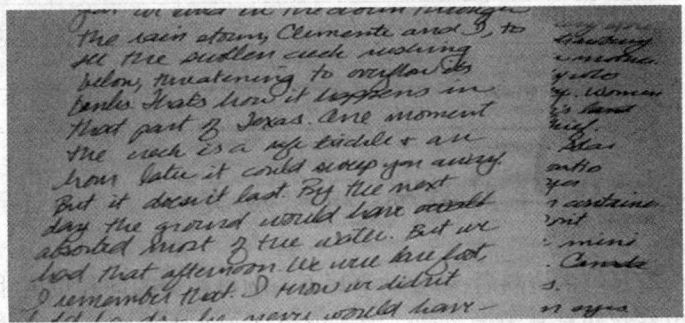

Task 6

Write down anything related to the following topic for ten minutes without stopping. Give specific examples from your own experience to support your point of view.

In your opinion, what are the best ways to make friends and build up good relationship with others?

7. 口头陈述(Oral Presentation)

当通过以上各种途径搜集完信息后,就要将信息进行汇总,即将所搜集的信息整理、加工并理出头绪。口头陈述就是最有效的一种方式。在这一过程中,既可以通过讨论与同伴分享信息、开拓思路,又可以锻炼自己的总结能力,可谓一举两得。

Task 7

Work with your partner and present the information you have gathered in task 6. In your presentation, you should include:
①The importance of friends and friendship;
②The ways to make friends and build up good relationship with others.

三、开始写作:字斟句酌,组织成文

当手头有足够的资料后,就要动笔写下与题目相关的词和短语,因为词是构成句子以至文章最基本的单位。它不仅包括文章中用到的实词,还有对文章的连贯起主要作用的连接词等。最后,将正确的句子组织起来,形成段落。

1. 构建词汇库(Vocabulary Chart)

词是构成文章的最基本的元素,看到一个题目,要首先想想与其有关的词汇,并要根据词的属性对其加以分类。下面的 *Task 8* 就是用图表的方法对与"看病"相关的词汇进行的总结和分类。

Task 8

Read the following short conversation about "Seeing the Doctor". Write the underlined words and phrases in the chart according to the classification. Add your own *classification if you wish.*

Seeing the Doctor

Doctor: What's the matter with you, young man?
Robert: I don't feel well, doctor. My head aches. My arms and legs feel weak. And I have a sore throat.
Doctor: How long have you been like this?
Robert: Since three or four days ago.
Doctor: Put this thermometer under your tongue.
Robert: All right.
Doctor: Yes, you do have a temperature. I want to take a look at your throat. Open your mouth. Please say "Ah".
Robert: Ah-ah. Is it very serious, doctor?
Doctor: Take it easy. You have got a case of the flu. I'll give you an injection and some medicine for it.
Robert: I hate injections. Is only medicine OK?
Doctor: Well, aspirin is a very safe pain reliever. Sometimes tea with lemon and honey will relieve the pain effectively.
Robert: Is it effective?
Doctor: Yes, sometimes it works very well. Some people are completely cured by it.
Robert: All right. I'll try it.
Doctor: Besides, you'd better take more water and lie on bed for two days.
Robert: Thank you very much. I'll follow your advice.

Nouns	Verbs	Adjectives	Adverbs	Phrases
thermometer	feel	weak	effectively	take a look at

Task 9

The following words and phrases are those that you can use to talk about "Good Manners". Complete the paragraph by using them.

polite	offer to
patience	helpful
behave	smile
in return	respectfully
respect	full of

Good Manners

Be (1) _____ to everyone, no matter who he is. Greet people pleasantly, and remember to (2) _____. A smile on your face will make your appearance more welcome, and people will probably smile (3) _____, too. Don't be rude or insulting or demanding. Even if you are angry or upset, (4) _____ and politeness will usually get you further than threats and insults.

Show (5) _____ for everyone, male and female, young and old, and especially your elders. Speak to them (6) _____, and do not interrupt them. Listen to their advice. When you (7) _____ this way, you will most likely have earned the same respect. Be (8) _____ whenever you can. Hold the door for one whose arms are (9) _____ packages. (10) _____ help an old lady across the street. If someone asks you for directions, take the time to help him if you can. This will brighten both his day and yours.

以上活动都是针对写作过程中对实词的使用和积累的,而一篇好的文章还要注重上下文的逻辑性和连贯性,仅仅靠实词的堆砌是远远不够的,还需要在恰当的时候使用一些虚词和连接词。现在来了解一些连接词的意义及使用。下表是在写作时经常会用到的连接词及其所代表的逻辑关系。

逻辑关系	连接词
并列	and, also, too, as well as, nor, and … not, not… neither, neither, or, or else
转折	but, however, yet
递进	furthermore, moreover, additionally, besides that, add to this, in addition, also, what's more
比较	likewise, similarly, in the same way, in this way, in comparison
对比	in contrast, on the contrary, on one hand… on the other hand, although, even though, yet, but, still, however, nevertheless, nonetheless, conversely, regardless, despite, in spite of
说明	that is, I mean, in other words, to put it another way
举例	for instance, for example, such as, specifically, to illustrate, as an illustration, namely
因果	thus, consequently, therefore, as a result, hence, accordingly, so that, in order to, if… then, so, since
时间	meanwhile, afterwards, by this time, from now on, first, in the first place, second, third(firstly, secondly, thirdly), next, before then, soon after, as soon as, later, during, while, subsequently, immediately, eventually
地点	next to, above, behind, beyond, near, nearby, across, from, to the right, here, opposite to, at the side, in the distance
总结	to sum up, in short, briefly, to get back to the point, anyway, in summary, to summarize, in a word, to put it briefly, finally, on the whole, as I have demonstrated, as the data show
替代	instead, rather than, on the contrary

Task 10

Complete the following ten sentences by using the conjunctions in the box below.

otherwise	indeed
for instance	on the other hand
moreover	however
consequently	instead
therefore	in short

① I did not understand the teacher's point; _____, I ask her to repeat it.

② They decided not to go to the movie; _____, they went to play badminton.

③ I decided to skip lunch; _____, I would be late for class.

④ Conflicts almost always exist within the family; _____, it is still the most enduring social issue.

⑤ Ants can help human beings in many ways; _____, they can cure a kind of disease called arthritis.

⑥ _____, this book reflects the great changes after Reform in 1979.

⑦ In earlier days, only unusual highly intelligent men chose science as a career; _____, scientific work was carried on in a dedicated spirit.

⑧ John had great difficulties playing cricket. But _____, he was an awfully good football player.

⑨ The storm knocked out the electricity; _____, we could not read or watch television.

⑩ A bomb exploded very close; _____, the medical team in which Dr. Bethune was continued to work at great tension.

2. 写出正确的句子

要写出正确的句子,首先要避免以下几种常见的句子错误:

(1) **句段或片语**(Sentence Fragments)

句子是具有独立的主语和谓语并能表达完整思想的独立单位,句子的末尾以句号结束。而有些结构虽然以句号结尾,但却不是句子,它们可能是一个单词、词组或是一个从句,这些成分被称为句段或片语。例如:

Sentence fragments: I thought she could undertake this task. But soon changed my mind.

Revised version: I thought she could undertake this task, but I soon changed my mind.

有些句段虽然结构上也不完整,但由于其特殊的功能而被认为是合法的句段,也就是说它们可以被看作是正确的。例如:祈使句、感叹句等。

(2) 串句(Run-on Sentences)

串句是指两个完整的句子融合在一起,而中间并没有必要的符号将两者分开,这样会导致句子结构含糊不清。例如:

Run-on sentence: I bought a used car from a friend last summer it needed several repairs.

Revised version: I bought a used car from a friend last summer. It needed several repairs.

(3) 错位修饰(Misplaced Modifier)

错位修饰是指修饰语被放在了句子中不恰当的位置。例如:

Misplaced modifier: The monkey attracts the visitors with funny actions.

Revised version: The monkey with funny actions attracts the visitors.

(4) 代词与先行词的不一致(Faulty Agreement Between Pronoun and Antecedent)

例如:

Faulty agreement between pronoun and antecedent: They put the blame on the president, not on himself.

Revised version: They put the blame on the president, not on themselves.

(5) 连排句或不连贯短句(Choppy Sentences)

连排句是指在作文中连续出现而又太短的句子。短句或简单的句子会使文章显得言简意赅,然而书面语毕竟有别于口语,过多地使用短句会使文章显得不连贯、不正式。例如:

Choppy sentences: There was a knock at the door. I asked. Nobody answered.

Revised version: There was a knock at the door. I asked who it was, but got no answer.

(6) 冗长句(Stringy Sentences)

冗长句指一个句子中有太多的小句,使用太多的诸如 and, but, so, because 这样的连接词,给读者的感觉是一眼望不到边。例如:

Stringy sentences: Many students attend classes all morning and work all afternoon and then they have to study at night so they are usually exhausted by the weekend.

Revised version: Many students attend classes all morning and work all afternoon. Then they have to study at night. As a result, they are usually exhausted by the weekend.

（7）悬垂（Dangling Modifier）

所谓悬垂主要是指逻辑上的错位。例如：

Dangling modifier: Swimming in the river, a rock cut my foot.

Revised version: Swimming in the river, I had my foot cut on a rock.

（8）赘言（Wordiness）

当作者使用过多的、不必要的词来表达思想的时候，他实际是在说废话或制造赘言。赘言一般表现为不必要的重复、无用的扩展以及绕弯的表述等等。例如：

Wordiness: The problem of cheating in exams is a serious problem.

Revised version: Cheating in exams is a serious problem.

Task 11

There are some errors in the following sentences. Correct the errors and then write down the right ones in the blanks.

① The next afternoon we came to the valley. The most beautiful sight on our journey.

② I took lots of Vitamin C however, I still came down with the flu.

③ When only five years old, my father took me to a concert.

④ Xiao Hong visited her aunt when she was in Beijing.

⑤ As for her family we know nothing about them.

⑥ Seeing from the mountain, the city looks very beautiful and attractive.

⑦ He nearly lost ten dollars last night.

⑧ He found the kitchen window open. He put a ladder against the window. He climbed in.

⑨ I have never met Alan but I have heard a great deal about his adventures so I am eager to see him.

⑩ He gave a reason for not attending the meeting, which nobody believed.

3. 段落的写法
段落写作要注意以下要点：
- 每个段落通常由主题句(topic sentence)、拓展句(supporting sentences)和结尾句(concluding sentence)组成。
- 主题句是段落的核心，它表明作者的态度、观点、意图等，同时反映了段落的中心思想；主题句所表述的观点不能太极端，应该统领全文；此外，主题句除了位于段首，还可以出现在段中和段末。
- 拓展句主要围绕主题句进行叙述、说明或论述等，每一个拓展句都传递着一定的信息，以支持主题句。
- 结尾句是指用一句话将段落的内容进行概括性的归纳和总结。

(1) 主题句

主题句通常位于段落的开始，即段首句，起到提纲挈领的作用，它可以清楚地点明段落的中心思想，使读者可以很快地了解作者的意图及观点。有时主题句也可以放在段落中间或者末尾。当主题句在段落中间时，它可以起到突出重点和过渡的作用；当主题句在段落末尾时，它带有一定的结论性，明确了作者的态度。

Task 12

Write a topic sentence for the following paragraphs. Pay attention to the position of the topic sentence.

①Topic sentence at the beginning of the paragraph

Topic sentence: _____

They have language and the power of speech, which enable them to connect the present with the past, plan joint activities, make arrangements, and share their experiences. Some animals can communicate by means of signs, but they can not use symbols and concepts to give order and continuity to their experiences.

②Topic sentence in the middle of the paragraph

John and Henry are twin brothers. They share similarities in most parts. They have almost the same appearance. They are both tall and handsome. They both have blond hair and blue eyes. Every day they go to the same school in the same clothes. Most people can not distinguish them from one another.

Topic sentence:

John is quite extroverted. He always spends most of his time with others. He is ready to make new friends as well. After class, he never stays at home. Instead, he attends all kinds of activities outside home. Henry is quite different. He is quite silent. Most of time, he tends to stay alone and read some books by himself. After class, he usually goes back home directly and does something that he likes.

③Topic sentence at the end of the paragraph

Computers are very useful in modern society. They can do simple computation with lightning speed and perfect accuracy. Once given a "program", they can gather and store a wide range of information. Besides, they can also solve complicated problems that once took months for people to do.

Topic sentence: _____

(2) 拓展句

通常情况下,一个段落有若干个拓展句,每个拓展句都有一定的信息,以支持主题句。

Task 13

For number ①—⑤, *choose the sentence that best develops the topic sentence.*

①Fire safety techniques should be taught to children.

   A. Hundreds of children are killed each year, and hundreds more are injured because of firework displays.

   B. If a child's clothes are on fire, the child should stop where he is, drop to the ground, and roll over and over to smother the fire.

   C. Since child seat-belt laws have been in effect, thousands of lives have been saved.

②Effective study habits include regular review.
   A. Good note taking includes the use of outlines and colored highlighters to mark important points.
   B. One should study at the same time and in the same place every day. One should also take good notes.
   C. The reason cumulative exams are difficult is because it is easy to forget those things which we do not use. To stay sharp in those areas will only require about half an hour of review each week for each subject of study.

③Reading to young children requires certain skills.
   A. You should be sure to choose the book for them, or they might not choose the book that is best suited for themselves.
   B. Learn to express enthusiasm. Making eye contact with the children and getting them involved in the story is much easier if you are enthusiastic about the story.
   C. You should be sure to have them sit quietly in rows in front of you so that you can see them. Otherwise, they might get into things.

④The horse is one of the most useful animals.
   A. For a long time, horse have been considered as good friend and faithful servant of human being.
   B. The qualities which have made the horse so valuable are its speed and strength.
   C. The horse can bring more convenience to us than other animals.

⑤Some people seem to have a knack(窍门) for learning languages.
   A. They do not depend on the book or the teacher; they discover their own way to learn the language.
   B. They consider language learning as an active process.
   C. They can pick up new vocabulary, master rules or grammar, and learn to write in the new language or quickly than other.

(3) **结尾句**
   结尾句需要与主题句相呼应,总结段落要点,引发读者对段落的进一步认识。

Task 14
For number ①—⑤, choose the sentence that best concludes the paragraph.

①My hometown is famous for several amazing natural features. First, it is noted for the Wheaton River, which is very wide and beautiful. Also, on the other side of the town is Wheaton Hill, which is unusual because it is very steep. The third amazing feature is the Big Old Tree. This tree stands two hundred feet tall and is probably about six hundred years old _____.

 A. These features often make me miss my hometown.

 B. Do you want to visit my hometown?

 C. These three landmarks are truly amazing and make my hometown a famous place.

②In the past, hurricanes(飓风) were always given women's names. In 1979, a group of people decided that it was not fair to name these dangerous storms only after women. _____

 A. Likewise, the custom was changed, and today hurricanes are given names of both sexes, men and women.

 B. Therefore, the custom was changed, and today hurricanes are given names of both sexes, men and women.

 C. Furthermore, the custom was changed, and today hurricanes are given names of both sexes, men and women.

③The reason for education to enter the market is obvious. Many countries are not likely to invest a huge amount of money in education in the near future. Education has to turn to the market to find its own way. It is important to note that teachers' way of production is to teach and train students. The students' knowledge is an invisible product. In addition, their services to students and society are valuable.

 A. So education has to be run in accordance with the law of value to realize the aim that students pay for their education and find jobs for themselves.

 B. As a part of the society, education cannot be separated from the market.

 C. Therefore, it is generally believed that education serves the market, and in turn, receive benefit from it.

4. 列提纲(Outlining)

  在成文之前要有充分的准备。写作犹如建房子,在建房子之前要有图纸,施工人员要根据图纸来添砖加瓦。对于要动笔写文章的人来说也是一样,写之前

在头脑中也要有一个基本的蓝图,甚至还要落实到纸上,这就涉及列提纲。提纲的基本格式为:

Title: _____

  I. Introduction

    A. The background

    B. Thesis statement: _____

  II. Body

    A. First Supporting Idea (Topic Sentence): _____

      1. _____

      2. _____

      3. _____

    B. Second Supporting Idea (Topic Sentence): _____

      1. _____

      2. _____

      3. _____

    C. Third Supporting Idea (Topic Sentence): _____

      1. _____

      2. _____

      3. _____

  III. Conclusion

    A. Closing statement

    B. Restate thesis: _____

需注意:

(1)提纲中序号的层次:一级题目使用罗马数字,然后依次是大写的英文字母、阿拉伯数字和小写的英文字母。

（2）提纲中的陈述要一致、统一，要么使用主题短语，要么使用完整的句子。

Task 15

Make an outline according to the topic and thesis provided.

Title：The Benefit of Running

I. Introduction

　　A. Running is becoming an extremely popular sport for all ages.

　　B. Running is a great form of exercise because it helps people control their weight, develop muscles, and improve mental performance.

II. Body

　　A. weight control

　　　　1. _____

　　　　2. _____

　　　　3. _____

　　B. _____

　　C. _____

III. Conclusion

　　A. _____

　　B. _____

5. 组织成文

（1）文章开头的方法

　　俗话说，"万事开头难"。开头段是文章最重要的一段，它起着统领全文的作用。好的开头段应该开门见山，并能引起读者的兴趣，使读者自然、顺利地进入正文。

Task 16

There are many ways that you can begin a paragraph or a composition. Look at the following paragraphs and summarize how each of them begins. The first has been given.

a. Can a black lawyer, a Chinese fashion designer, and a white school teacher live happily side by side as neighbors? Can a racially integrated community achieve the dream of brotherhood and understanding? An experiment in a small town in Connecticut is providing some extraordinary answers.

b. A ship is a vessel(容器) that moves on the water; the Titanic, the ship that couldn't, yet did, sink, suggests man's struggle against the forces of nature. It suggests cold and the agony of men drowning.

c. "The proper study of mankind is Man," said Alexander Pope. Most psychologists have carried this idea further than Pope would have imagined.

d. The fact that less than 5 percent of the British population graduate from universities may seem surprising, especially when viewed beside the American percentage of over 30 percent. To understand this contrast, one needs to consider social differences between the two countries, as well as differences in their theories of education.

e. A traditional story describes a foolish man lifting a rock too heavy for him and having his own feet squashed(压碎). Hitler was like that foolish man, but he was different in that, before he destroyed himself, he destroyed millions of other people.

f. Salt is one of the most useful and most amazing minerals on earth. For thousands of years, it has seasoned our history, our language and our food. In ancient Greece it was common to exchange salt for slaves, which resulted in the phrase "not worth his salt".

g. My purse strap(皮带) suddenly left my hand, I turned, and saw the man's back just before he vanished(消失) behind a six-foot-high pile of earth across the street. I chased him, screaming, "Stop thief!"

We can begin a paragraph or a composition with:

  a. a question or several questions _____

  b. _____

c. _____
d. _____
e. _____
f. _____
g. _____

（2）段落展开的方法

段落展开的方法有很多，具体使用哪一种方法是由写作的内容和目的决定的。常用的段落展开的方法有定义法（Definition）、分类法（Classification）、因果法（Cause and Effect）、比较与对比法（Comparison and Contrast）、举例法（Exemplification）、时间法（Time）、空间法（Space）、过程法（Process）等。

① 定义法

定义法是通过用简单易懂而且准确的语言阐明某事物的性质和特征来发展段落，使读者对某事物比较抽象的或难以把握的一些特征有一个较清晰的认识。定义法常用于说明、描写和论证，以提供更多的具体解释来说明某一概念或术语。例如：

Love is a very general term. It refers to a strong feeling of fondness for another person. It can happen between people of the opposite sex or between members of a family. No matter where it happens, love can always bring happiness to people.

② 分类法

分类法是按一定标准对事物进行归类的一种段落发展方法。分类可以使文章的脉络一目了然。例如：

There are two kinds of sports: "amateur" and "professional". Amateur athletes do not receive money for competing in sports. Olympic athletes, for example, are amateurs. They do not receive money. Professional athletes, on the other hand, do earn money. Some professional athletes earn a million dollars or more a year. They need this money to support themselves and they can save some for their future.

③ 因果法

因果法用来说明事态发展的原因和结果之间的联系，常用在说明文或议论文中。可以先讲原因，后给结果；也可以先给结果，后讲原因。这要视实际需要而定。有一些段落结果是显而易见的，就集中说明原因；有的段落正好相反，就集中说明结果，因为原因不言自明。例如：

It is difficult for workers to find employment this year. One reason is that many industries are not hiring new workers. In addition, industries are reducing their current staff levels because of a decline in national economic conditions. Another reason is that workers who once might have considered early retirement are now staying at their jobs. Finally, other workers who used to view their jobs as optional now must keep their positions in order to meet their minimum financial responsibilities.

④ 对比法

对比法是指通过叙述或描述两种或两种以上的相关事物之间的相同（相似）的地方或不同之处来表达主题。采用对比法展开段落主要通过两种途径：一个途径是先叙述对比双方的一个方面的全部细节，然后再叙述另一个方面的全部细节；另一个途径是对逐个问题进行双方面的比较。例如：

Why do so many graduates gravitate (被吸引) into business instead of into teaching? Part of the reason is the ever-widening pay gap between these two professions. A bank employee can earn monthly income as high as RMB 8,000, and when one is promoted to the position of a business executive or manager, the salary is even higher. But a college graduate with a bachelor's degree can only get a salary of RMB 5,000 per month for his teaching job. No wonder, college graduates are attracted into more lucrative fields.

⑤ 举例法

举例法是一种常见的展开段落的方法，它是用典型、具体而生动的事例来证明、阐述一个观点，支持主题句，使段落主题句的抽象意思具体化，使文章通俗易懂并具有说服力。但是，在写提供实例的段落时，必须精选例子，要做到恰如其分、准确地说明问题。例如：

It is very difficult to evaluate another person's performance objectively. For example, Linda recently wrote irresponsible remarks about her instructor because she was failing the course. Her friend Jack wrote a marvelous description of the same instructor because he was receiving an A in the course. Both Linda and Jack were not fairly evaluating the instructor. They were influenced by the grades they were earning and were biased in their judgment.

⑥ 时间法

在叙述一个故事或者一系列事件时，通常按事件发生的先后顺序排列句子。在说明文中叙述一件事应该遵循一定的程序或步骤时，也常用时间法。例如：

About 4,000 million years ago, the Earth formed from a cloud of dust and gas orbiting the sun. After some years the oldest rocks surviving today were formed. Following their formation, the first plants appeared and produced oxygen. Now that they had something to eat and could breathe, the first animals appeared many years later, the dinosaurs(恐龙) began to dominate the Earth and then they died out. And finally, the earliest men appeared.

⑦ 空间法

空间法指按物体的空间位置(自左至右、由近到远、由上至下、由下到上、由里到外、由外到里、由中间到两边等顺序)来展开段落。例如：

Great Britain is an island that lies off the northwest coast of Europe. The nearest country is France which is 20 miles away from which Great Britain is separated by the English Channel. The island is surrounded by the Atlantic Ocean to the west, and the North Sea to the east. It comprises the mainland of England, Wales and Scotland. Scotland is in the North, while Wales is in the west. Ireland, which is also an island, lies off the west coast of Great Britain. It consists of Northern Ireland and the Irish Republic. Great Britain together with Northern Ireland constitutes the United Kingdom. Thus, the United Kingdom is composed of four parts. The largest of these is England which is divided into 43 administrative counties. The capital city is London which is situated in southeast England.

⑧ 过程法

这种方法主要用于叙述做一件事应该遵循的程序或步骤，目的是使读者能清楚地跟随描述了解全过程，多见于科技文章和操作说明书。例如：

How to make a telephone call? First, you lift the telephone receiver. Then, you listen for the dial tone. Next, you dial the number you want. After that, you carry on a conversation. Finally, when finished, you put the receiver back on the telephone base.

学会以上这些方法，并把它们有效地运用到不同文体、不同内容的段落写作中去，可以使文章严密并具有逻辑性。

Task 17

Write your own paragraph based on the topic sentence provided below. The method you are supposed to use is given in the parenthesis. Just choose one to practice.

1) Life in a college is quite different from life at a high school. (comparison and

contrast)
2) A good teacher has two important qualities. (classification)
3) Every English learner should have some knowledge of English history. (cause and effect)
4) A "liberated woman" is simply a woman who controls her own life, rather than allowing it to be controlled by other people, traditions, or expectations. (definition)

(3) 文章结尾的方法

俗话说,"编筐编篓,全在收口"。文章的结尾段对于深化文章的主题起着至关重要的作用,其重要性并不亚于开头段。一般来说,结尾段不是简单地重复主题句,或总结已在中间段写过的句子,而是应该对全文的内容进行概括和强调,从而得出合乎逻辑的结论。文章结尾的方式通常有以下几种:

- 总结全文,深化主题(a summary or a conclusion)
- 建议(some suggestions)
- 引语(a quotation)
- 预见未来(a prediction)
- 反问(a question)

Task 18

Read the paragraphs below and try to identify how each paragraph is ended and match them with the ways suggested above and write the corresponding letters in the blanks.

- summary or conclusion ＿＿＿＿
- suggestion ＿＿＿＿
- quotation ＿＿＿＿
- prediction ＿＿＿＿
- question ＿＿＿＿

　　a. "No pains, no gains." Without hard work and perseverance one can hardly realize his dreams.

　　b. All in all, the American family of today is different from the family of fifty years ago. In the modern family, the roles of the father, mother, and children have changed as more and more women work outside the home. The next century may bring more important changes to the American fam-

193

ily structure. It should be interesting to see.

c. Therefore, to make our world a better place in which to live, we must make the best use of every drop of water and work hand in hand to protect water resources.

d. The big question today is, how can an expanding world population find food and space without destroying the land it lives on?

e. If we want to improve the quality of our lives; if we want everyone to be healthy, wealthy and happy; and if we want to see a prosperous, powerful nation in the world, the high-quality sustainable development is quite essential.

四、结束写作：修订润色，最终定稿

在最后定稿之前，要至少仔细检查两遍。第一遍，修改内容；第二遍，修改格式。

1. 修改内容

修改内容时要注意以下几点：
- 首先看文章有没有偏离主题思想。
- 反复确认是否将所要表达的内容都写到了文章中，不要有遗漏的地方；同时，还要避免不必要的细节，该删减的绝不能手软。
- 最后看文章的连贯性和逻辑性。

Task 19

Read the paragraph below, and focus only on the content— the writer's ideas and organization. Think about the following questions:

(1) Does the paragraph have a good topic sentence?
(2) Are all the sentences centered on one subject?
(3) Is all the information coherent?

Don't worry about misspelled words and other errors for now.

A New Class Member

This is about Wang Hong. is a new member of the English composition class at Amarin Community College. There many classes at ACC. he generally likes life in China. He likes the school. He doesn't like his dormitory. He is 18 years old. He is from a village in the north. He studying business administration, English and accounting. In his free time, he play basketball. He goes to movies. He plans to visit the United States next summer, so he needs to learn English.

2. 修改格式

格式的修改包括语法、拼写和标点符号三个方面。

下面是格式修改的基本原则：

- 文章的标题应该写在第一行的中间位置。
- 标题中除了介词、冠词、连词和动词不定式，其他的词一律大写。但介词等位于开头时例外，需要大写。
- 标题与正文之间空一行，每段的开头要缩进4—5个字母。
- 文章的左右留有空白。
- 以句号或问号结束每一个完整的句子。
- 句号之后留有空格。
- 每个句子的首字母必须大写。
- 需要大写的词还有专有名词、人名、地理名词、星期、节日、方向等。
- 逗号、句号、问号等标点符号不能出现在句首。
- 一个完整的自然段至少由四个句子组成，不能只写一两个句子。

Task 20

Now edit the paragraph in **Task** 19 again. This time, focus on form. While editing, check the following:

①The writer's use of third-person singular verbs in the present tense;
②The writer's use of negative forms, capitalization, and punctuation;
③The writer's use of sentence and paragraph form;
④Any other mistakes in form(use the guidelines above to help you).

本章学习心得：

_____

_____

第十章 文化学习策略

本章学习目标
1. 明确文化学习在外语学习中的重要性
2. 了解文化学习的内容
3. 掌握和运用文化学习的策略

一、文化的定义

关于文化的定义,历来有多种解释,这是因为文化是一个包罗万象的概念。根据《现代汉语词典》的解释,文化是人类在社会历史发展过程中所创造的物质财富和精神财富的总和,特指精神财富,如文学、艺术、教育、科学等。我国的《辞海》对文化是这样定义的:广义指人类在社会实践过程中所获得的物质、精神的生产能力和创造的物质、精神财富的总和。

文化在不同学科中的定义侧重点也各不相同。从人类学的角度看,文化是"风俗习惯、文明和特定的时间的成果"。例如,中华文化、埃及文化等。当我们谈到希腊文化时,我们指的是 2000 年前希腊的风俗、文明和成果。美国语言学家、人类学家爱德华·萨丕尔(Edward Sapir)是从社会学的角度定义文化的,他指出"文化是社会传承下来的实践和信念,这两者决定了我们生活的结构"。荷兰学者 Geert Hofstede(1997)是从心理学的角度定义文化的,指出文化是"智慧的集体结晶,它区分了人的类别"。文化是"理智的软件"。而文化学家 Kroeber 和 Kluckhohn(1952)认为:"文化的基础核心构成了传统思想,尤其是附属于传统思想的价值观念。文化系统一方面可以看成是行为的产物,另一方面可以看成是深层行为的条件因素。"从中我们可以领会到文化的核心实际上是社会的思想和价值观念。

不论文化有多少不同的定义,有一点是明确的,即文化的核心是人。人们的生活,无论是物质的还是精神的,始终发生在特定的文化氛围中,而文化反过来又影响和形成人们的所思所想、所作所为。文化使得我们继承同一种文化遗产群体中的个体拥有的共同的知识、信仰、价值观、生活方式、行为方式、思维方式、道德规范等;文化教给我们如何看待世界,如何判断美丑、正误,如何待人接物,如何表达情感。文化因素隐含在我们生活中的各个方面,小到准备什么样的早餐,大到如何处理国际事务。可以说,文化无所不在。

Task 1

How do you understand culture? Which definition mentioned above do you think is the closest to your understanding?

_____

_____

_____

二、文化在语言学习中的重要性

　　语言学习不仅要求学习者掌握语言形式,更要求学习者了解和掌握目的语文化知识,并具备实际使用语言的能力。

　　事实证明,文化语用失误比单纯的语言错误更容易在实际交际过程中造成不良影响。因为听者很容易发现表面的语言错误,如语法错误、语音不准确等,一旦发现这种错误,听者最多认为说话者缺乏足够的语言知识,可以谅解,甚至会对说话人敢于交谈的勇气表示钦佩。而对于文化方面的语用失误,听者却不会像语法错误那样看待。如果一个能说一口流利外语的人出现语用失误,那么他很可能被认为缺乏礼貌或不友好。他在交际中的失误便不会被归咎于语言能力的缺乏,而会被看作是粗鲁的或富有敌意的。心理语言学家沃尔夫森(1983)表示了相似的观点,"在与外国人交往时,以外语为母语的人倾向于容忍发音和句法方面的错误;相反地,他们常常把违反讲话规则解释为态度不友好"。这表明一个人语言能力越强,在交际中出现的语用失误对听者所造成的伤害可能就越严重,成功的交际也就越不可能实现。中外文化交际中有以下四种较为常见的文化语用失误:

1. 不适宜的社交语用

　　这种语用失误常出现在对人的称呼和问候方式上,比如,一些学生直接使用西方人的姓称呼他们,如"Smith"、"Brown",而不冠以"Mr."、"Ms."、"Professor"等头衔,这往往令西方人很不舒服,甚至感到气愤和不解。而一些西方人对于中国人以"Where are you going?""Are you going to...?"为问候方式感到费解,他们认为这是在侵犯他们的隐私。

2. 文化误解

中国人喜欢对初来乍到的西方人给以善意的建议和提醒,但是西方人仿佛并不领情,他们认为这是对他们的判断力和智商的怀疑。而中国人的过分谦逊也让西方人不知所措,中国人很少心安理得地接受赞美,当西方人由衷地对其进行夸奖时,中国人往往会说"No, not at all good"而不是"Thank you very much"。

3. 不同价值观

"隐私"是中国人很难把握的一个概念,因为西方人眼中的隐私在中国人看来是完全可以公开的信息。比如,在中国询问他人新买的衣服的价格是很正常的,表示你对其眼光的认同,同时也表示你们的关系很好;而在西方人看来,这是相当不礼貌的。在中国,当我们去朋友家里拜访时,翻看主人的影集并加以评论是再正常不过的;可是对于西方人来讲,不经允许翻看他人的影集是对他人隐私极大的侵犯。

4. 文化定式

对于西方人和西方的文化有很多已经定型的错误理解。比如,有些人认为所有美国人都喜欢摇滚乐,所有美国人都很富有,所有美国人都喜欢吃麦当劳的快餐。实际上,西方文化中的人同其他文化中的人一样是形形色色的,过度定型化会使我们在学习外国文化的过程中因一叶障目而忽视了整个森林的博大和丰富。

总而言之,外语学习者在学习一门语言时是不应忽视目的语文化的。随着文化在语言习得中的重要性逐渐被肯定,语言学习者应掌握有效地获得文化知识的策略。寓语言学习于文化背景中的目的之一是发现并排除干扰语言交际的因素。不同文化层次上的语用失误贯穿于英语学习和使用的每个阶段。因此,不同阶段的语言学习应与不同层次的文化学习有机地结合起来,从而建立一个相应的文化认知系统,使英语水平得到全面提高。

Task 2

Case Analysis: *Read the following story and consider why Gorge and Janice were* depressed by their experience? Discuss with your partner.

Dinner with Friends

Janice is a young American engineer working for a manufacturing joint venture near Nanjing. She and her husband George, who is teaching English at a university, are learning Chinese and enjoying their new life. They have been eager to get to know Chinese people better so they were pleased when Liu Lingling, Janice's young co-worker invited them to her home for dinner.

When Janice and George arrived, Lingling introduced them to her husband Yang Feng, asked them to sit down at a table containing 8 plates of various cold dishes, served them tea and then disappeared with her husband into the kitchen. After a few minutes Lingling came back and added water to their tea. Janice offered to help in the kitchen but Lingling said she didn't need help. She invited the couple to look at their new CD player and their color TV and then disappeared again.

A half-hour later, she came back and sat down and the three began to eat. Yang Feng came in from time to time to put dish after dish on the table. Most of the food was wonderful but there was much more than they could eat. They kept wishing Yang Feng would sit down so they could talk to him. Finally he did sit down to eat a bit, but quickly turned on the TV to show them all its high tech features. Soon it was time to go home. Gorge and Janice felt slightly depressed by this experience.

三、文化学习的内容

研究发现,一些文化学习者往往都在学习一些本民族或本国的历史、地理、政治知识,很难提高实际语境中的跨文化交际能力。那么,文化学习究竟应涵盖哪些内容呢?是否应重点学习某些国家的文化呢?是否应该涵盖艺术和文学方面的知识呢?所学的文化知识是否应该与语言知识紧密相关呢?这些都是我们在文化学习过程中需要不断研讨和给出确切回答的问题。所以,明确文化学习的具体内容是学好文化的重要前提。

广义文化涉及的内容有政治、军事、经济、历史等大的方面,也有社交礼仪、节日文化、禁忌文化等风俗习惯。由于英语学习者的时间和精力有限,对于纷繁复杂的文化学习内容需要有所取舍,重点学习与英美国家有关的文化内容，简要地了解其他英语国家的文化，或世界范围内的文化。具体的文化学习内容可参见下表：

文化分类	文化内容
观念文化	1. 地理历史——英美地理、历史； 2. 艺术——美术、建筑、音乐； 3. 哲学——哲学(古代、近现代)； 4. 文学——英国文学、美国文学； 5. 科学技术——科学技术发展简史。
制度文化	1. 政治制度——英国政治制度,美国政治制度； 2. 法律制度——英国法律制度,美国法律制度； 3. 经济制度——英国经济制度,美国经济制度； 4. 生活习俗——英美生活习俗； 5. 礼仪——英美礼仪常识。
物质文化	1. 饮食——英美饮食； 2. 服装——英美服装流派。
语言文化	1. 词语内涵 2. 习语、谚语； 3. 语篇结构。

学习文化归根结底是为了更好地与来自该文化圈的人们交流，所以在文化学习内容的选择上应该注重容易掌握、适于学习、实用性强的文化知识和文化技能，比如英美国家的地理、历史知识，词汇和短语的文化内涵，社会习俗，非言语交际符号，价值观念和思维方式等。

Task 3

Which part of the cultural knowledge do you think is the most important in English learning? Talk with your partner and record your reasons below.

_____
_____
_____

四、文化学习策略

文化学习策略应根据具体的学习内容来选择,不同的文化内容需要辅以不同的学习策略才能达到事半功倍的效果。针对上文中提到的文化学习内容的分类,学习者应采用适宜的学习策略。

1. 了解英美国家的地理、历史知识

毋庸置疑,一种文化的传承源起并依赖于一个国家的地理、历史变迁,所以必须对其演变发展的过程加以学习。我们在英语学习中接触的主要是英美文化,有效地掌握英美国家的地理、历史知识将使文化学习更有据可依。对于这种客观性知识的学习主要靠扩大阅读量。学习者可以阅读一些历史人物传记、纪实性的文章,也可以观看一些纪录片,如《世界地理杂志》的影像资料。学习资料不必局限于英文书刊,汉语的书籍和影像资料同样有利于学习者积累知识、开阔眼界。

Task 4

Choose the correct answers to the following questions. These questions are based on general knowledge about the USA and UK.

① How many states are there in the U.S.?
  a. 49   b. 50   c. 51
② Which president freed the slaves?
  a. Thomas Jefferson b. George Washington c. Abraham Lincoln
③ Who was the civil rights leader who fought through nonviolent(非暴力的)action?
  a. Thomas Paine b. Martin Luther King Jr. c. John Kennedy
④ Who was the first person to walk on the moon?
  a. John Glenn b. Jin Lowell c. Neil Armstrong
⑤ Where's the White House located?
  a. New York b. Washington D. C. c. Houston

2. 挖掘词和短语的文化内涵

学习者应该意识到,即使最平常的词汇和短语,在特定文化背景下也可

以激发人们对不同形象的联想。比如,"同志"在汉语中是人们称呼彼此时经常使用的一个词,使人们联想到"友好"、"诚实"、"平等"等概念,而在英语国家中,人们却认为"comrade"一词具有政治色彩。与之相反,"individualism"一词在西方文化中被赋予很高的价值,人们提倡并尊重个性化和特立独行,而我们往往将"个人主义"一词作为"自私"、"以自我为中心"、"自负"的同义词。所以,在不同的文化背景下,表面意义相似的词和短语的文化内涵往往有天壤之别。

  词汇是最明显的承载文化信息、反映人类社会文化生活的工具。词语意义的文化差异是学好外语的一大障碍,因此,要注意词语的文化意义在目的语和母语之间的异同。由于人类的文化传统、生活习惯、经历和爱好有其相似性,英汉语言中部分词汇的文化内涵有其相似性;又由于受文学、艺术、环境、风俗等诸多因素的影响,两种语言的词汇文化内涵又不可能完全对等。也就是说,英汉词汇之所以不能完全对应,是因为文化差异的存在。不同国家、不同民族甚至不同地区的人对某些字的理解、好恶是不一样的。词汇的文化内涵举不胜举,语言和文化密不可分。一个国家的语言不能游离于它的文化而独立存在。一个国家的文化对这个国家的语言,尤其是词汇,有着全面而深刻的影响。在外语学习中,应加强对语言中所折射出来的文化知识的学习。以学习英文词汇和短语的文化内涵为目的,学习者可以应用以下策略:

(1) 使用英英词典

  相对于英汉词典,英英词典的解释更能反映出以英语为母语的人对某个词或短语的感情色彩和好恶程度。而在现实情况中,很多学习者最喜欢使用的仍然是英汉词典,这对增强文化差异的敏感性帮助不大。比如说:cadre 的中文意思为"干部",而英文释义则为:the key group of officers and enlisted personnel necessary to train a new military unit。两者相去甚远。如果不使用英英词典,就很难理解它们之间的区别。

Task 5

Rephrase the following words and phrases with your own words, and then check the meaning in an English-English dictionary to see whether you are correct or not.

① busboy: _____

② service station: _____

③ restroom: _____

④ to eat one's own words: _____

(2) 阅读英美报刊和文学作品

　　学习者应大量阅读英美报刊和文学作品。报刊是时事的载体;而文学作品是了解一个民族的脾性、心理状态、文化特点、风俗习惯、社会关系等最生动、最丰富的材料。文化内涵丰富的词在报刊和文学作品中比比皆是。The British Isles 和 Great Britain 在课文中都是指英国,而事实上 the British Isles 却是由两个大岛(即大不列颠岛和爱尔兰岛)以及几百个小岛组成的,Great Britain 则指英国的一部分,即大不列颠岛。上面所列出的这些词都带有其特定的含义,如果不了解社会文化背景,而仅仅从词汇本身出发,就不能理解其所包含的社会文化意义。

Task 6

Read the following paragraph, and pay attention to the underlined phrase. Do you know its connotation? Discuss with your partner and see what else he/she knows about it. And then try to find as much as possible about the phrase in the dictionaries or encyclopedias.

　　For the second year in a row, the General Electric Corporation is ranked number one in an annual survey of the 100 most powerful corporations in the world.

　　The survey, compiled and published by Forbes business magazine, shows General Electric of the United States ranked number one, followed in second and third place by the U.S. banking and financial services giants Citigroup and Bank of America. In fourth and fifth place are the British-based HSBC Banking Company and Daimler-Chrysler, the German-American auto-company.

(3) 关注有典故的词汇和短语

　　英语中有许多具有文化内涵的词,它们的形成与广泛使用有赖于一些众所周知的文学形象或历史事件,在汉语中我们称之为典故或成语。比如我们用"鸿门宴"这个词暗指用心险恶的布局,以使人落入事先安排好的陷阱。在英语文化中,这样的词不胜枚举:Cinderella(灰姑娘)一词来自于童话故事《灰姑娘》,讲的是一个心地善良的漂亮女孩儿受继母的虐待,过着悲惨的日子,后得到仙女的帮助,与王子结为夫妻。现在人们常用 Cinderella 一词指原本贫穷但得到好的机遇而飞黄腾达的人。Shylock(夏洛克)是莎士比亚戏剧《威尼斯商人》中的一个凶狠贪婪的人物,为了获取暴利,他在放债时提出了极为苛刻、违背人性的条件。现在人们看到心肠狠毒、唯利是图的小人,常称之为 Shylock。

Task 7

Do you know the meaning of the following expressions?

① to meet one's Waterloo
_____

② in a Catch-22 situation
_____

③ to open a Pandora's box
_____

④ to cry wolf
_____

⑤ to bell the cat
_____

(4) 了解谚语的深层含义

　　谚语是一种文化智慧的积累和经验的沉淀，英语中有许多谚语反映了西方文化的价值观念和行为准则。谚语的学习无疑会使学习者对西方文化了解得更加透彻。

Task 8

Do you know what the following English proverbs mean?

① Still waters run deep: _____
② Better untaught than ill taught: _____
③ Don't cross your bridges before you come to them: _____
④ Even a worm will turn: _____
⑤ It is the last straw that breaks the camel's back: _____
⑥ One tongue is enough for a woman: _____
⑦ Live and let live: _____
⑧ Birds of a feather flock together: _____

3. 关注社会习俗

　　学习者应关注社会习俗对人们行为的影响，并了解目的语文化中的人们在平常情况下和紧急状况下的行为方式。文化制约着人们的一切行为，包括语言行为。不同的文化背景有不同的语言习惯和行为方式。例如，在日常交往中英语国家的人喜欢谈论天气、地理位置等话题，而把年龄、工资、婚姻状况等作为禁忌的话题。再如，中国人在接受礼物时，习惯推辞几次才接受，当着客人的面打开礼物被认为是不礼貌的;而英语国家的人则习惯当场把礼物拆开,并且要赞美几句。

对于社会习俗的学习,最好的方法是身临其境地感受西方人待人接物的方式,但外语学习者却鲜有这样的机会。所以,通过观赏英文的影视剧来了解西方的社会习俗不失为一种好办法,影视作品通过直观地对西方人的生活、学习、工作、娱乐等方面的多角度描绘为我们提供了学习资料,只要在观赏过程中有目的、有意识地去关注西方的社会习俗,就会有所了解。

(1) 日常交际礼仪

交际双方第一次见面时通常要握手。此外,久违的朋友相见时,通常也要握手,拒绝握手是非常不礼貌的。通常是由年龄大或地位高的一方或者女子先伸手。

西方常用的问候语是"早上好"(Good morning)、"下午好"(Good afternoon)或"晚上好"(Good evening)。对不认识的人可说一声"Hello"(你好)表示友好,对方也会以"Hello"作为回答。有些问候在中国是合乎礼节的,而在西方却不被采用。如果你问候一个西方人说"你上哪儿去?"(Where are you going?)或说"你去哪儿啦?"(Where have you been?),他会认为你在打听他的私事。而如果你说"你吃过了吗?"(Have you had your dinner?),他可能会认为你想邀请他与你共同进餐。

在西方,当受到邀请时,如果对方是口头提出邀请的,你应即刻回应,如果当时不能决定,你可以说:"我今晚告诉你,行吗?"但不管是口头邀请还是书面邀请,都应当给予明确的回答。

中西方在日常生活中的习惯有诸多差异,上述只是几点基本的常识,要想与来自西方文化的人更好地交流,应多关注生活中的细节,掌握更多的西方日常生活礼节。

Task 9

How do the Americans respond under the following circumstances? Act out these situations in class. The teacher and other students may act as the other role. The time limit is 1 minute. In every situation, your response must adapt to the American social customs.

① Someone praises your new dress.
② You bump into someone on the street.
③ Someone bump into you and apologize to you.
④ You show up on one's birthday party and wish him/her happy birthday.

⑤ You make a toast on the wedding of your friend.
⑥ You are introduced to a professor.
⑦ You are introduced to your peer.

(2) 餐饮礼仪

　　以宴请的方式款待宾客,是涉外交往中一项常有的活动,是人际交往中一种重要的形式,因而礼节在宴请中占据着举足轻重的位置。国际上最主要的宴请方式有四种:招待会、茶会、工作进餐和宴会。招待会只备一些食品和饮料,不备正餐,不安排座次,是一种较为自由的宴请方式。茶会是一种更为简便的招待方式,一般上午10时或下午4时在客厅举行,客人可以一边品茶一边交谈。工作进餐是一种经常采用的非正式的宴请方式,它不请配偶及其他与工作无关的人员,大家边吃边谈,有时候要各自付费。宴会是较为隆重的正餐,一般来说,对衣着打扮的要求都会印在宴会请柬上。不论参加的是什么宴会,请柬的下角都会注明客人该穿的装束。参加较隆重的社交场合时,欧美人士主张男士们都穿一样的装束,如颜色相近的整套深色西装或黑礼服。西方习俗是男女交叉安排,以女主人的座位为准,主宾坐在女主人右上方,主宾夫人坐在男主人右上方。

　　西餐餐具的摆法也相对固定:正面放着汤盘,左手放叉,右手放刀,汤上方放着匙,再上方放着酒杯。餐巾放在空汤盘里或插在空酒杯里,面包、奶油盘摆在左上方。普通西餐的上菜顺序是:面包、汤、各类菜肴、布丁、咖啡或红茶。在正式餐会上,内容可能会更加丰盛。入座后摊开餐巾或离座前收起餐巾,均应以主人为先。

Task 10

Do you know some table manners in western countries? Answer the following questions and discuss with your partner.

① How should you place your napkin at table?

② How do you have dinner using knife and fork?

③ When you leave the table for a moment, but you still want to continue later, how should you place the knife and fork?

④ When you taste the soup, what is the proper manner?

⑤ Bread is the staple food in western countries, how should you eat bread properly?

(3) 西方禁忌文化

所谓禁忌就是那些因为传统习惯或社会风俗等而应避免使用的词语或忌讳的行为。每种语言中都有它的禁忌,如:英语国家忌数字 13。饭店里没有 13 号房间,高层住宅不设 13 层电梯,请客忌讳 13 人,每月的 13 日不举行重要的活动。又如,在一些西方国家,黑猫被视为禁忌动物。如果人们遇到黑猫穿过马路迎面走来,则避而远之。另外,英语国家有用鲜花送礼的习惯,其中也有一些禁忌,比如不送双数花,等等。英美社会中还有一些常见的迷信说法和禁忌,如:To get out of bed on the wrong side means you will have a bad day (下床方向错了,一天都不会顺利)。禁忌几乎无处不在,在文化交际中避免触及对方所忌讳的语言和行为是保证顺利交流的重要前提。

Task 11

The following sentences tell you about the taboos in some western countries. Translate them into Chinese.

① The bride should not see the husband on the morning before the wedding.

② To pass under a ladder brings bad luck.

③ Lighting three cigarettes from one match brings bad luck to the third person.

④ To break a mirror brings seven years' bad luck.

⑤ Opening an umbrella in the house is bad luck.

4. 掌握非言语交际的信息

除了社交过程中表达方式和待人接物上的巨大差别外,非言语交际(Non-verbal Communication)也是文化学习的重要内容之一。美国学者 Larry A Samovar(1981) 认为:"非言语交际指的是在一定交际环境中语言因素以外的,对输出者或接收者含有信息价值的那些因素。这些因素既可人为地生成,也可由环境造就。"对于来自于不同文化的人而言,由于语言不通,非言语交际信息往往在交际中起到更重要的作用。然而,非言语交际并不仅仅局限于手势、表情等,还包括不同文化对时间、空间、色彩的不同看法以及在听觉、嗅觉、视觉、触觉等感官方面的不同感知特点。

(1) 体态语

　　体态语指的是传递交际信息的表情和动作,主要包括身体各个部位的动作,如头部动作、面部动作、眼部动作、臂部动作和手部动作等等。由于不同文化传承的动作习惯不同,相同的动作在不同的文化中往往蕴含着截然不同的意义,这是需要学习者加以注意并用心领会的。例如,跟相识的人打招呼时,英语国家的人常扬一下头,而我们则习惯点头示意。西方人虽然也用点头表示相互认识,但认为扬头更为友善。

　　体态语渗透在人们举手投足、一颦一笑之间,是来自不同文化的人们需要用心观察才能彼此了解的。外语学习者熟练地掌握体态语所传达的信息,对于成功的跨文化交际将有极大的帮助。

Task 12

Do you know the different meanings of the following gestures in different countries? Fill in the table.

　　　　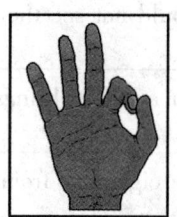

　　　(1)　　　　　　　　　　(2)

Gestures	Countries	Meanings
(1) thumbs up	the U. S.	
	Nigeria	
	Germany	
	Japan	

续表

Gestures	Countries	Meanings
(2) a circle with one's thumb and index finger	Most countries	
	Japan	
	France	
	Brazil	
	Germany	

Task 13

What information can you get from the gestures of the man in the following pictures? Discuss with your partner and exchange your ideas.

　　　　(1)　　　　　　　　　(2)

（2）副语言

　　"副语言"是指伴随话语发生的或对话语有影响的有声现象,是一些超出语言特征的附加现象,如说话时的音高、语调、音质等都属于此范畴。此外,诸如喊、叫、哭、笑、叹气、咳嗽、沉默等也可以被看作副语言现象。比如,说话时气喘吁吁暗示说话人比较紧张,嗓子沙哑透露说话人未休息好,说话尖溜溜的表示冷嘲热讽,整句话带鼻音可能表示对方生气了,某个字音拉得很长表示强调或暗示,压低嗓音表示谈话内容较为机密,结结巴巴说话则暗示对方在说谎或紧张,等等。这些是伴随话语而发生的或对话语有影响的,有某种意义,但是其意义并非来自词汇、语法或一般语音规则。学习掌握这些语言之外的副语言现象是透视说话者意图的关键。

Task 14

How do people in China and the U.S. understand "keeping silent" in different ways?

_____

_____

(3) 环境语

　　环境语也是非言语交际的一种重要形式。环境指的是文化本身所造成的生理和心理环境,包括时间、空间、颜色、声音、信号和建筑等。这些环境因素都可提供交际信息,所以环境语也可展示文化特性。下面以颜色为例,看看相同的颜色在中西方文化中的不同含义。汉语中"绿色"可引申出"生态良好"之意,因此就有了"绿意浓浓"等表达;而在英语中,指没有经验、知识浅薄时则用"green"来比喻,因此就有了 a green hand(生手,易上当受骗的人),green goods(新鲜货),a green man(新来的水手),a green old age(老当益壮),等等。汉语里"白手"是"一无所有"的意思,而英语里的 white hand 则有"pure"(纯洁)或"unstained"(清白)之意。要说"白手起家",只能用 start from scratch 或 build up from nothing 表示。而"he has white hands"绝不是说"他的手白",而是指"他是清白无辜的"。这些环境语也是文化学习内容的一部分,对提高我们的交际能力有举足轻重的作用。

Task 15

Translate the following English phrases into Chinese and compare the implied meaning of colors in both languages.

① red light district:＿＿＿＿＿＿＿＿＿＿＿＿＿＿＿＿＿＿＿＿＿＿
② red-tape:＿＿＿＿＿＿＿＿＿＿＿＿＿＿＿＿＿＿＿＿＿＿＿＿＿
③ catch sb. red-handed:＿＿＿＿＿＿＿＿＿＿＿＿＿＿＿＿＿＿＿
④ like a red rag to a bull:＿＿＿＿＿＿＿＿＿＿＿＿＿＿＿＿＿＿
⑤ black humor:＿＿＿＿＿＿＿＿＿＿＿＿＿＿＿＿＿＿＿＿＿＿

本章学习心得:

＿＿＿＿＿＿＿＿＿＿＿＿＿＿＿＿＿＿＿＿＿＿＿＿＿＿＿＿＿＿＿＿
＿＿＿＿＿＿＿＿＿＿＿＿＿＿＿＿＿＿＿＿＿＿＿＿＿＿＿＿＿＿＿＿
＿＿＿＿＿＿＿＿＿＿＿＿＿＿＿＿＿＿＿＿＿＿＿＿＿＿＿＿＿＿＿＿

附 录

附录一：英语学习情况调查问卷

英语学习情况调查问卷

（文秋芳）

同学们，你们好！为了了解你们的英语学习情况，请填写下面的问卷。你的回答只反映你的英语学习观念和策略使用情况，没有好坏对错之分。请记住在填写时，要根据自己的实际想法和做法，而不是其他人或理想中的想法和做法。谢谢合作！

一、外语学习观念

下面是人们对外语学习的一些看法，请大家根据每个数字所代表的含义选出其中一个写在句子的末尾，所填的数字一定要能如实代表你自己的看法。

1 = 我坚决不同意这个看法
2 = 我不同意这个看法
3 = 对这个看法我没有明确的答案
4 = 我同意这个看法
5 = 我坚决同意这个看法

1. 很好地计划自己的学习时间是学好英语的重要保证。（ ）
2. 选择有效的学习方法对学好英语很重要。（ ）
3. 有明确的长期和短期的学习目标对学好英语很重要。（ ）
4. 不断总结自己的进步并找出存在的问题对学好英语很重要。（ ）
5. 了解自己的个性特点，才能发挥长处，克服短处。（ ）
6. 有效调整自己的学习情绪才能提高学习效率。（ ）

7. 情绪不好的时候,没有必要强迫自己去学习。( )
8. 情绪好的时候,应该多学习;情绪不好的时候,应该少学习。( )
9. 增强自己的自信心是外语学习成功的重要保证。( )
10. 外语学习中遇到困难时,一定不能慌张。( )
11. 外语学习中不能自暴自弃,必须对自己有信心。( )
12. 在外语学习中碰到困难时,应该自己鼓励自己。( )
13. 经常反思自己的学习方法是否有效,对学习外语非常重要。( )
14. 记外语句型对学习外语非常重要。( )
15. 记单词对学好外语很重要。( )
16. 精读课文对学习外语很重要。( )
17. 背诵好的课文对学习外语很重要。( )
18. 理解课文最好的方法是翻译。( )
19. 反复朗读课文对学好外语很重要。( )
20. 进行大量的听力练习对学好外语很重要。( )
21. 要学好外语,阅读外文报纸、杂志、小说等比精读更重要。( )
22. 猜测是学好外语的一个重要方法。( )
23. 要想将所听的外语内容记下来,最好的方法是记中文意思。( )
24. 反复模仿好的录音带对练好语音语调很重要。( )
25. 进行大量的口语训练,对学好外语很重要。( )
26. 进行大量的写作练习,对学习外语很重要。( )
27. 要想写出好的英语作文,最好的方法是先用中文组织好想写的内容。( )
28. 说英语时,最好先用中文想好要说的内容。( )
29. 遇到不懂的单词和句子时,问同学和老师是最有效的方法。( )
30. 遇到不会表达的内容,最好回避它。( )
31. 没有把握表达正确的语言形式,最好不要用。( )
32. 遇到不懂的语言形式,最好的方法是跳过去,不去管它。( )

二、学习英语的策略

下面是人们常用的一些学习策略,请根据数字所代表的意思,选择其中一个填在句子的末尾,所选数字一定要能如实描述你的学习情况。请记住填写时,要根据自己的实际做法而不是你的想法或其他人的做法。

1 = 这个句子完全或几乎完全不适合我的情况
2 = 这个句子通常不适合我的情况

3 = 这个句子有时适合我的情况
4 = 这个句子通常适合我的情况
5 = 这个句子完全或几乎完全适合我的情况

1. 除了老师布置的作业外,我有自己的英语学习计划。（ ）
2. 为了使自己有足够的时间学习英语,我很好地安排自己的学习日程。（ ）
3. 我对改进自己的英语学习有明确的要求。（ ）
4. 我评价自己学习英语进步的情况,从而找出薄弱环节和改进的措施。（ ）
5. 我评价自己的学习策略,从而找出存在的问题和解决的方法。（ ）
6. 我根据学习任务的特点,选择不同的学习策略。（ ）
7. 我选择适合自己英语水平的材料来学习。（ ）
8. 我研究自己的个性特点,做到扬长避短。（ ）
9. 我有意识地选择策略来调节自己的学习情绪。（ ）
10. 我评估自己调节情绪策略的成效。（ ）
11. 当考试成绩不理想时,我总是暗暗鼓励自己千万不能泄气。（ ）
12. 我有意识地训练自己的毅力。（ ）
13. 情绪紧张时,我用深呼吸的方式调整情绪。（ ）
14. 遇到困难时,我自己安慰自己:别人也会感到困难。（ ）
15. 当阅读英语材料时,我争取弄懂文章里的每一处。（ ）
16. 我阅读英文报纸、杂志或小说。（ ）
17. 为了帮助对英文的理解,我把句子译成中文。（ ）
18. 我反复朗读英文课文。（ ）
19. 在阅读英语材料中碰到生词时,我从上下文中猜意思。（ ）
20. 读英文文章时,我先通读全篇了解文章的概要,然后再理解每个句子的意思。（ ）
21. 当我不懂句子意思时,我分析句子的语法结构。（ ）
22. 我背诵英语短文。（ ）
23. 我记英语阅读材料中出现的生词和短语。（ ）
24. 我跟别人用英语交谈时,尽量听别人讲。（ ）
25. 为了提高自己的听力理解能力,我主动听各种录音。（ ）
26. 我听英语广播。（ ）
27. 当听英语材料时,我争取听懂每一句话的意思。（ ）
28. 听英语时碰到生词,我会跳过生词继续听下去。（ ）
29. 听英语时碰到生词,我会尽量记住生词的发音,然后根据发音在字典上查找该词。（ ）
30. 听英语时,我用中文记住所听的内容。（ ）

31. 听英语时,我只注意所听材料的意思。( )
32. 听英语时,我注意说话人所用的词语。( )
33. 跟别人用英语交谈时,我尽量主动多说话。( )
34. 我看英语电视或电影。( )
35. 当与别人讲英语时,我回避自己不熟悉的话题。( )
36. 我尽量抓住机会,用英语与别人交际。( )
37. 我自己对自己说英语。( )
38. 我说英语时,首先用中文组织意思,再翻译成英语。( )
39. 我主动地用英语记笔记、留言、写信或写日记。( )
40. 我用英语写作文时,先用中文组织意思,再翻译成英语。( )
41. 当我查字典时,我看一个词的各种意思及所给的例句。( )
42. 当在字典上查到某个生词时,我只找出与课文内容有关的意思。( )
43. 为了改进自己的语音语调,我反复听外国人录制的录音磁带。( )
44. 遇到不懂的单词,我就查字典。( )
45. 遇到不懂的句子,我就问同学或老师。( )
46. 遇到不会用英语表达的内容,我就回避。( )
47. 遇到不会用英语表达的内容,我就问老师或同学。( )
48. 当听不懂对方说的英语时,我会向对方询问。( )
49. 当听不懂对方说的英语时,我装作听懂了。( )
50. 没有把握说对的,我就不说。( )

附录二：学习策略应用调查问卷

学习策略应用调查问卷

(Andrew D. Cohen & Julie C. Chi)

姓名：_____ 性别：_____ 级别：_____级

此问卷的目的是使语言学习者了解自己的英语学习情况，并找到能帮助其掌握一门外语的学习策略。请查看表示各种学习策略运用情况的选项，将代表选项的字母填到随附的选项卡上。

不同的运用情况分别是：

A. 我使用这个策略，并且喜欢用它
B. 我已使用这个策略，并且还要再用
C. 我从来没有用过这个策略，但我很感兴趣
D. 这个策略不适合我

一、听力策略的应用

增加我和目标语言接触的策略

1. 参加使用目标语言的课外活动。
2. 收听使用目标语言的广播节目，观看使用目标语言的电视节目及电影。
3. 在饭店和商店听工作人员使用目标语言。
4. 听人们用目标语言谈话，争取抓住谈话的主旨。

熟悉目标语言发音的策略

5. 练习目标语言的发音，并熟悉这些发音。
6. 寻找目标语言中词和短语的发音与熟知的发音的联系。
7. 模仿目标语言本族讲话人的谈话方式。
8. 向目标语言本族讲话人询问不熟悉的发音。

准备用目标语言交谈的策略

9. 特别注意语言的特殊方面，比如，某些音的发音方式。

10. 根据已知谈话内容预测要交谈的内容。

11. 事先了解背景材料,为倾听使用目标语言的讨论和表演做准备。

倾听使用目标语言谈话的策略

12. 听传达主要意思的关键词。

13. 注意听说话人强调的词语。

14. 注意谈话人停顿的时间和长短。

15. 注意说话人谈话中的语音升降调。

16. 练习略听,即听话时留意某部分而忽略其他部分。

17. 努力理解听到的内容,而不要字字翻译。

18. 注意谈话的上下文。

19. 注意听某个细节,看是否能够理解。

不能理解使用目标语言谈话的某些或大部分内容时的策略

20. 听不清时,请说话人重复谈话内容。

21. 当他们谈话太快时,请他们放慢语速。

22. 当第一次不能理解谈话内容时,请求澄清。

23. 把说话人的语调作为线索,去理解谈话内容。

24. 根据已交谈的内容,猜测谈话的主题。

25. 根据自己的经验了解主要意思。

26. 观察说话人的姿势和肢体语言,有助于了解谈话的内容。

二、词汇策略的应用

学习词汇的策略

27. 注意新单词的结构。

28. 把新单词分成可以分辨的几个部分。

29. 把词汇按词性分类。

30. 把新单词与你所熟悉的词汇的发音联系起来。

31. 利用新单词的发音来记忆。

32. 在脑海中反映新单词的形象。

33. 列出与新单词相关的词汇。

34. 用新单词造句。

35. 把动词所代表的动作演示出来。

36. 用制作卡片的方式来学习新单词。

复习词汇的策略

37. 经常复习已学会的单词,以巩固记忆。
38. 定期复习已学会的单词,以避免遗忘。

回忆词汇的策略

39. 观察词汇中有意义的部分,来回忆词汇的意思(例如:前缀、后缀)。
40. 尽力回忆第一次听到或看到某个单词时的场景,或者回忆该单词在书中所在的页数和一些特殊符号。
41. 在脑海中拼写新单词。

应用词汇的策略

42. 以各种方式来应用新词汇。
43. 以不同的方式练习应用新词汇。
44. 尽量学习和应用英语中词汇的惯用法。

三、口语策略的使用

练习口语的策略

45. 练习对自己说一些新的表达。
46. 在不同的场合下练习新的语法结构,以建立信心。
47. 思考英语国家的人会怎样说,并以同样的方式进行表达。

进行会话的策略

48. 时常寻找机会同英语国家的人进行交谈。
49. 尽量使用目标语言开始对话。
50. 把对话引向自己熟悉的话题。
51. 事先计划好自己想要说的话。
52. 以在对话中进行提问作为参加对话的方式。
53. 根据已经谈论过的事情预测将要被谈论的话题。
54. 尝试讨论自己不熟悉的话题。
55. 鼓励其他人改正自己表达中的错误。
56. 在英语国家的人表达要求、道歉或抱怨的时候,注意他们的语言表达,并将其模式化。

想不出恰当表达时的策略

57. 向会话搭档寻求帮助。
58. 使用同义词等其他方式进行表达。

59. 使用自己的母语,但以目标语言的结构方式进行表达。

60. 如果不知道恰当的表达方式则杜撰新词或进行猜测。

61. 使用手势传达意思。

62. 如果知道对方能够理解自己的意思,就时不时地插用自己的母语。

四、阅读策略的应用

提高阅读能力的策略

63. 尽可能多地阅读用目标语言写的材料。

64. 在目标语言中找到有趣的东西来阅读。

65. 找到适合自己水平的阅读材料。

66. 阅读前做好计划:如何去阅读文章,检查自己进展如何,然后看一下自己的领会程度。

67. 对于学术文章,首先快速浏览获取主旨,然后再进行细致阅读。

68. 对于故事和对话,进行反复阅读,直到完全理解。

69. 注意文章结构,尤其是标题和副标题。

70. 阅读的同时在脑海中或者文章空白处进行即时总结。

71. 对于文章的发展做出预测。

遇到不能理解的单词和语法结构时的策略

72. 通过文章的上下文来猜测大致的意思。

73. 使用字典来获取单词的准确意思。

五、写作策略的运用

基本写作策略

74. 练习正确的书写格式。

75. 提前列出写作大纲,监督写作进度,并检查你想说的是否已准确地表达出来。

76. 试着练习书写不同体裁的文章(例如:私人便条、书信、学期论文等)。

77. 尽可能多地记质量高的笔记。

学术文章的写作策略

78. 当不知道正确的表达方式时,尽量找另外一种方式表达(例如:用近义词描述一下此观点)。

79. 在继续往下写之前,看看已经写过的内容。
80. 用一些辅助材料帮你查找或修改词语(例如:字典、百科全书等)。
81. 直到文章全部撰写完之后再修改文章。

在写完草稿后应使用的策略

82. 把文章修改两至三遍,力求提高语言的准确度及丰富文章的内容。
83. 尽量听取别人的反馈意见,尤其是以此目标语言为母语的人。

选项卡

	A	B	C	D		A	B	C	D
1					42				
2					43				
3					44				
4					45				
5					46				
6					47				
7					48				
8					49				
9					50				
10					51				
11					52				
12					53				
13					54				
14					55				
15					56				
16					57				
17					58				
18					59				
19					60				
20					61				

续表

	A	B	C	D		A	B	C	D
21					62				
22					63				
23					64				
24					65				
25					66				
26					67				
27					68				
28					69				
29					70				
30					71				
31					72				
32					73				
33					74				
34					75				
35					76				
36					77				
37					78				
38					79				
39					80				
40					81				
41					82				
—	—	—	—	—	83				

附录三:学习风格调查问卷

学习风格调查问卷

(Andrew D. Cohen, Rebecca L. Oxford & Julie C. Chi)

同学们,你们好!为了了解你们的学习风格,请填写下面的问卷。你的回答只反映你的学习风格和倾向,没有好坏对错之分。请记住在填写时,要根据自己的实际情况而不是你的想法或其他人的想法。

请填完所有条目。填写时给出你的第一反应,然后马上做下一条目。请在每个条目后面的括号里标出相应的数字。谢谢合作!
0 代表"从不";1 代表"很少";2 代表"有时";3 代表"经常";4 代表"总是"

一、如何认知	
1. 如果写下来,我会记得更牢。	( )
2. 上课时,我记详细的笔记。	( )
3. 当听的时候,我的脑海里会出现图像、数字或文字。	( )
4. 我喜欢从电视或录像中学习,而不愿接触别的媒体。	( )
5. 我在工作或学习时,利用彩色标记。	( )
6. 我需要书面的工作或学习指导。	( )
7. 我要看着说话人才能理解他的意思。	( )
8. 老师写板书可以帮助我理解授课内容。	( )
9. 表格、图标和地图可以帮助我理解谈话内容。	( )
10. 我能记住别人的脸,但记不住他们的名字。	( )
	A. 总分( )
11. 如果与别人讨论,我会记得更牢。	( )
12. 我愿意通过听课的形式学习,不愿意采取阅读的方式学习。	( )

续表

13. 做事时,我需要口头指导。	(	)
14. 背景声音可以帮助我思考。	(	)
15. 工作或学习时,我喜欢听音乐。	(	)
16. 即使我看不到说话人,我也能理解他所表达的意思。	(	)
17. 我记得住别人的名字,但记不住他们的长相。	(	)
18. 我很容易就能记住听过的笑话。	(	)
19. 我可以辨认出别人的声音(例如电话里的声音)。	(	)
20. 看电视时,我主要是听内容,而不太看屏幕。	(	)
	B. 总分(	)
21. 我情愿直接做事,而不是先看指导书之类再做事。	(	)
22. 工作或学习时,我需要不时休息一下。	(	)
23. 我工作或学习时,喜欢吃东西。	(	)
24. 要我选择坐着还是站着的话,我会选择站着。	(	)
25. 一动不动地坐很久会让我感到紧张。	(	)
26. 我在走动的时候思维活跃。	(	)
27. 上课时,我习惯玩弄或者啃咬钢笔。	(	)
28. 摆弄某种物件可以帮我记住别人所说的话。	(	)
29. 说话时,我会挥动双手。	(	)
30. 上课时,我会在笔记本上画很多图画(涂鸦之作)。	(	)
	C. 总分(	)
二、如何选择学习环境		
1. 我与其他人一起学习比独自一人学习效果好。	(	)
2. 我可以通过加入别人谈话的方式结识新朋友。	(	)
3. 我在课堂上学习比家教辅导学习效果好。	(	)
4. 对我来说,接近陌生人很容易。	(	)
5. 与人交流让我感到充满活力。	(	)
6. 我喜欢先体验,后理解。	(	)
	A. 总分(	)

续表

7. 我的心理世界(内心所想)让我充满活力。	( )
8. 我喜欢一个人的或一对一的游戏和活动。	( )
9. 我的兴趣不多,但我很专注。	( )
10. 和一群人一起工作,让我觉得很累。	( )
11. 当我身处人群时,我会沉默地倾听。	( )
12. 动手之前,我想先了解我要做的事。	( )
	B.总分( )
三、如何把握可能	
1. 我有丰富的想象力。	( )
2. 我试图找出很多的可能性去解释事情发生的原因。	( )
3. 我为未来仔细准备。	( )
4. 我喜欢自己探索,不喜欢事事都听别人的解释。	( )
5. 在课堂讨论时,我会发表自己的观点。	( )
6. 我很乐意接受同龄人的建议。	( )
	A.总分( )
7. 我专注于所处的态势,而不去想怎么会出现这样的态势。	( )
8. 使用仪器或设备(例如电脑或录像机)前,我会阅读说明书。	( )
9. 我相信具体事实,不相信新的、未经检验的观点。	( )
10. 我喜欢按部就班的介绍方式。	( )
11. 我不喜欢同学改变我们合作学习活动的计划内容。	( )
12. 我仔细按照说明书做事。	( )
	B.总分( )
四、如何处理学习任务	
1. 我喜欢仔细计划语言学习的内容,及时或提早完成功课。	( )
2. 我的笔记、活页和其他学习材料都很规整。	( )
3. 我喜欢弄清楚事物在目的语中的含义。	( )
4. 我喜欢知道规则的使用方法和原因。	( )
	A.总分( )

续表

5. 如果我在做其他的事,我会忽略上件事的完成期限。	( )
6. 我通常可以容忍很多东西堆在桌子上,最后再整理。	( )
7. 我并不想弄清楚所有的事。	( )
8. 我觉得不应该马上对一件事下结论。	( )
	B. 总分( )
五、如何接受信息	
1. 我喜欢简短的答案,不喜欢冗长的解释。	( )
2. 我会忽视看起来无关紧要的细节。	( )
3. 对我来讲,看宏观计划和大图片比较容易接受。	( )
4. 明白主要意思对我来说就足够了。	( )
5. 当讲一个很久以前的故事时,我会忘记很多具体细节。	( )
	A. 总分( )
6. 我需要很具体的例子才能完全理解整体意义。	( )
7. 我注意具体的事实或具体信息。	( )
8. 我擅长捕捉听到的新短语或新词。	( )
9. 我喜欢做听力的缺词填空练习。	( )
10. 讲笑话的时候,我能记住细节但会忘记妙语部分。	( )
	B. 总分( )
六、如何加工信息	
1. 我能很容易地对信息进行总结。	( )
2. 我能很快地对别人说的话进行释义。	( )
3. 我制定大纲的时候,先考虑关键的问题。	( )
4. 我喜欢做把他人的想法进行汇总的活动。	( )
5. 通过观察整体形势,我能很容易地理解他人。	( )
	A. 总分( )
6. 当我不认识每一个词时,理解就很困难。	( )
7. 我讲故事或解释一件事情的时候要花很长时间。	( )
8. 我喜欢关注语法规则。	( )

续表

9. 我擅长处理复杂的推理或猜谜游戏。	(　　)
10. 我擅长注意任务中最小的细节。	(　　)
	B. 总分(　　)
七、如何记忆	
1. 学习时,我尽量注意新资料的所有特征。	(　　)
2. 当我记忆零碎的语言材料时,我很容易就能回想起记忆的内容,就像我已经把它们存在大脑的不同区域一样。	(　　)
3. 当学习新语言知识时,我能够很好地区分语音、语法形式词和短语。	(　　)
	A. 总分(　　)
4. 学习新内容时,我会用去除或缩减差别而专注相似点的方法收集资料。	(　　)
5. 我会忽略那些让我在某语境中增加语言准确性的细微语言差别。	(　　)
6. 相似的记忆互相混淆,我会把新学来的东西与原有知识混合。	(　　)
	B. 总分(　　)
八、如何处理多种知识输入方式	
1. 即使有干扰信息存在,我也能够在已知语境中挑出相关的重要信息。	(　　)
2. 无论使用目的语口头表达还是书面表达,我都要确保语法准确。	(　　)
3. 我不仅注意语法,而且还会注意到语言的正式性、得体性和礼貌性。	(　　)
	A. 总分(　　)
4. 说话或写作时,对语法的关注程度取决于信息内容。	(　　)
5. 对我来说,在口头表达和书面沟通时,既注意交际性又注意语法准确性很难。	(　　)
6. 用长句时,我会分神,从而忽视语法的问题。	(　　)
	B. 总分(　　)

参考文献

[1] Anderson L. W., Krathwohl D. R. A Taxonomy for Learning, Teaching, and Assessing: A Revision of Bloom's Taxonomy of Educational Objectives [M]. New York: Longman, 2001.

[2] Austin, J. L. How to Do Things with Words [M]. Oxford: Clarendon Press, 1962.

[3] Bachman, L. F., Palmer, A. S. Language Testing in Practice [M]. Oxford: Oxford University Press, 1996.

[4] Bachman, L. F., Palmer, A. S. Language Assessment in Practice: Developing Language Assessment and Justifying Their Use in the Real World [M]. Oxford: Oxford University Press, 2010.

[5] Bell, R. T. Translation and Translating: Theory and Practice [M]. London: Longman, 1991.

[6] Bloom, B. S. (Ed.), Engelhart, M. D., Furst, E. J., Hill, W. H., Krathwohl, D. R. Taxonomy of Educational Objectives: The Classification of Educational Goals. Handbook 1: Cognitive Domain. New York: David McKay, 1956.

[7] Burgess, S., Head, K. How to Teach for Exams [M]. England: Pearson Education Limited, 2005.

[8] Chomsky, N. Aspects of the Theory of Syntax [M]. Cambridge, Mass: MIT Press. 1965.

[9] Dudley-Evans, T., St John, M. Developments in ESP: A Multi-Disciplinary Approach [M]. Cambridge: Cambridge University Press, 1998.

[10] Flavel, J. H. Meta-cognition and Cognitive Monitoring: A New Area of Cognitive-Developmental Inquiry [J]. American Psychologist, 1979 (34).

[11] Genesee, F & Upshur, Johna A. Classroom-based Evaluation in Second Language Education [M]. Cambridge: Cambridge University Press, 1996.

[12] Goodman. K. S Learning to Read in Different Languages[J]. Journal of Typographic Research, 1970(4): 103-110.

[13] Grellet, F. Developing Reading Skills[M]. New York: Cambridge University Press, 1981.

[14] Halliday, M. A. K. & R. Hasan. Cohesion in English [M]. London: Longman, 1976.

[15] Hymes, D. Foundations in Sociolinguistics: An Ethnographic Approach [M]. Philadelphia: University of Pennsylvania Press, 1974.

[16] Hofstede, G. Cultures and Organizations: Software of the Mind: Intercultural Cooperation and its Important for Survival [M]. New York: McGrawHill, 1997.

[17] Holec, H. Autonomy and Foreign Language Learning[M]. (First published 1979, Strasbourg: Council of Europe.) Oxford: Pergamon, 1981.

[18] Hughes, A. Testing for Language Teachers[M]. Cambridge: Cambridge University Press, 2008.

[19] Hutchinson T, Waters A. English for Specific Purposes [M]. Cambridge: Cambridge University Press, 1987.

[20] Hymes, D. Competence and performance in linguistic theory[M]. In R. Huxley, E. Ingram (eds.). Language Acquisition and Methods. New York: Academic Press, 1971.

[21] Jakobson, R. Closing Statement: Linguistics and Poetics[A]. In Sebeok, T. A. (ed.) Style in language [C]. Mass: MIT Press, 1960.

[22] Krashen, S. Principles and Practice in Second Language Acquisition[M]. Oxford: Pergamon, 1982.

[23] Kroeber, A., Kluckhohn, C. Culture: A Critical Review of Concepts and Definitions[M]. Peabody Museum Papers 47,1. Cambridge. Harvard University Press, 1952.

[24] Larsen-Freeman D. Teaching Language: Form Grammar to Grammaring [M]. Bosten: Heinle, Heile, 2003.

[25] Martin, J. R. A contextual theory of language, in The Powers of Literacy — A Genre Approach to Teaching Writing [M]. Pittsburgh: University of Pittsburgh Press, 1993.

[26] Miller, C. Genre as Social Action [J]. Quarterly Journal of Speech, 1984,

70(1).

[27] Newcomb, L. H. , , Trefz, M. K. Toward teaching at higher levels of Cognition[J]. NACTA Journal,1987, 31(2).

[28] O'Malley J. M. , Chamot. A. U. Learning Strategies in Second Language Acquisition[M]. Cambridge: Cambridge University Press, 1990.

[29] Oxford R. L. Language Learning Strategies: What Every Teacher Should Know[M]. New York: Newbury House, 1990.

[30] PACTE. Building a Translation Competence Model[A]. In F. Alves(ed.) Triangulating Translation [C]. Amsterdam: John Benjamins, 2003: 43 – 66.

[31] Samovar, L. A. , et al. Understanding Intercultural Communication[M]. Wadsworth Publishing Company, 1981.

[32] Sandra Silberstein. Techniques and Resources in Teaching Reading[M]. Shanghai: Foreign Language Education Press. 2002.

[33] Schaffner, C. Running before Walking? Designing a Translation Programme at Undergraduate Level[A]. In Christina Schaffner Beverly Adab(ed). Developing Translation Competence[C]. Amsterdam: John Benjamins B. V. 2000.

[34] Schiffrin, D. The Handbook of Discourse Analysis [C]. London: Blackwell, 2001.

[35] Schmitt, N. An Introduction to Applied Linguistics[M]. 北京: 世界图书出版社, 2010.

[36] Sperber, D. & Wilson, D. Relevance: Communication and Cognition (2nd) [M]. Oxford, UK: Basil Blackwell, 2001.

[37] Strevens, P. ESP after Twenty Years: A Re – Appraisal [A]. In Tichoo M. (ed.). ESP: State of the Art [C]. Singapore: SEAMEO Regional Language Centre, 1988.

[38] Thompson, G & Hunston, S. System and Corpus—Exploring Connections [M]. 北京: 世界图书出版社, 2010.

[39] Urquhart, S. & Weir, C. Reading in a Foreign Language: Process, product and Practice[M]. New York: Longman, 1998.

[40] Verschuren. J. Understanding Pragmatics [M]. London: E. Arnold, 1999.

[41] Weir, C. J. & Bygate, M. Meeting the Criteria of Communicativeness in a

Spoken Language Test[J]. Journal of English and Foreign Language, No. 10 - 11, Central Institute of English and Foreign Languages, Hyderabad, India. 1992:27 - 43.

[42] Wellman, H. M. Origins of Metacognition. In D. L. F. - Pressley, G. E. McKinnon, & T. G. Waller (Eds.), Metacognition, Cognition and Human Performance (Vol. 1,). Orlando, Florida: Academic Press, 1985.

[43] Wolfson, N. An Empirically - based Analysis of Complimenting behavior in American English[J]. In N. Wolfson & E. Judd (Eds.), Sociolinguistics and Language Acquisition (pp. 82 - 95). Rowley, MA: Newbury House.

[44] Zimmerman B. J. A Social Cognitive View of Self - regulated Learning[J]. Journal of Educational Psychology, 1989.

[45] 安会云,吕琳,尚晓静. 学习风格研究综述[J]. 现代中小学教育,2005(4).

[46] 巴赫金全集:第四卷[M]. 石家庄:河北教育出版社,1998.

[47] 包惠南,包昂. 中国文化与汉英翻译[M]. 北京:外文出版社,2004.

[48] 毕继万. 跨文化非语言交际[M]. 北京:外语教学与研究出版社,2004.

[49] 程晓堂,郑敏. 英语学习策略[M]. 北京:外语教学与研究出版社,2002.

[50] 戴翰林. 学习的科学[M]. 徐州:中国矿业大学出版社,2004.

[51] 戴曼纯. 情感因素及其界定——读 J. Arnold (ed.)《语言学习中的情感因素》[J]. 外语教学与研究,2000(6).

[52] 丁言仁. 第二语言习得研究与外语教学[M],上海:上海外语教育出版社,2004.

[53] 付 瑶. 场独立性和场依存性认知风格在外语教学中的意义[J]. 济宁师范专科学校学报,2006(6).

[54] 郭德俊. 动机心理学:理论与实践[M]. 北京:人民教育出版社,2006.

[55] 郭海端. 大学英语教学中学生自主学习能力的培养[J]. 浙江海洋学院学报(人文科学版),2005(1).

[56] 贺小红. 学习风格的心理要素对学生学习的影响及策略[J]. 教育理论与实践,2005(6).

[57] 何勇斌. 外语听力学习中的情感因素[J]. 郑州航空工业管理学院学报(社会科学版),2005(2).

[58] 胡壮麟,朱永生,张德禄,李战子. 系统功能语言学概论[M]. 北京:北

京大学出版社,2008.
[59] 华厚坤,赵海洪. 试论第二语言习得中的动机[J]. 江苏大学学报,2003(1).
[60] 黄燕,等. 大学英语六级考试精讲与测试——写作篇[M]. 北京:机械工业出版社,2004.
[61] 教育部高等教育司. 大学英语课程教学要求[M]. 北京:清华大学出版社,2004.
[62] 蒋萍. 自主学习与大学英语教学[J]. 新疆教育学院学报,2005(1).
[63] 靳玉乐. 自主学习[M]. 成都:四川教育出版社,2005.
[64] 康淑敏. 学习风格理论——西方研究综述[J]. 山东外语教学,2003(3).
[65] 雷沛华. 国外外语学习风格理论研究概览[J]. 枣庄学院学报,2005(4).
[66] 李华东,栾述文,袁洪婵. 新世纪英语口语教程[M]. 北京:外语教学与研究出版社,2002.
[67] 李玲. 学习风格理论研究及其对英语教学的启示[J]. 齐齐哈尔大学学报,2006(2).
[68] 李哲. 第二语言习得研究[M]. 济南:山东大学出版社,2000.
[69] 刘安平,唐树良. 采用自主学习模式,提高大学英语教学质量[J]. 邯郸学院学报,2005(1).
[70] 刘琴. "以学生为中心"的教学模式与提高自主学习能力[J]. 延安教育学院学报,2005(2).
[71] 陆根书,于德弘. 学习风格与大学生自主学习[M]. 西安:西安交通大学出版社,2003.
[72] 陆忆松. 非英语专业新生自主性学习调查研究[J]. 浙江教育学院学报,2005(3).
[73] 马丁·韦德尔,刘润清. 外语教学与学习——理论与实践[M]. 北京:高等教育出版社,1995.
[74] 麦红宇. 情感因素对大学英语听力教学的影响[J]. 桂林师范高等专科学校学报,2006(4).
[75] 毛颖. 大学生英语自主学习研究[J]. 理工高教研究,2005(1).
[76] 苗菊. 翻译能力研究——构建翻译教学模式的基础[J]. 外语与外语教学,2007(4).

[77] 潘淑敏. 英语学习策略——成功之路[M]. 北京:高等教育出版社,2007.

[78] 潘亚玲. 外语学习策略与方法[M]. 北京:外语教学与研究出版社,2004.

[79] 庞维国. 自主学习——学与教的原理和策略[M]. 上海:华东师范大学出版社,2003.

[80] 庞晓青. 大学英语自主学习的课堂教学模式与策略[J]. 沧桑,2005(Z1).

[81] 邵瑞真. 教育心理学[M]. 上海:上海教育出版社,2000.

[82] 邵志洪. 词的理据在跨文化交际中的模糊性[J]. 外语教学与研究,1993(2).

[83] 施良方. 学习论[M]. 北京:人民教育出版社,2003.

[84] 束定芳,庄智象. 现代外语教学——理论、实践与方法[M]. 上海:上海外语教育出版社,1996.

[85] 谭美云. 听力微技能:精听与泛听[J]. 文教资料,2006(13).

[86] 田兴斌. "自主学习"方式与大学英语教学改革[J]. 铜仁师范高等专科学校学报,2005(2).

[87] 王东,高永华. 口才艺术[M]. 北京:光明日报出版社,1991.

[88] 王俊霞. 非英语专业大学生自主学习能力与大学英语教学[J]. 齐齐哈尔大学学报(哲学社会科学版),2005(3).

[89] 王丽维. 元认知策略在英语听力教学中的应用[J]. 中国成人教育,2007(2).

[90] 王守仁,何宁. 新编英语口语教程[M]. 上海:上海外语教育出版社,1998.

[91] 王守元,苗兴伟. 英语听力教学的理论与方法[J]. 外语电化教学,2003(4).

[92] 文秋芳. 英语学习策略理论研究[M]. 西安:陕西师范大学出版社,2003.

[93] 吴三香,徐柳明. 大学一年级新生英语自主学习能力的培养[J]. 泰山乡镇企业职工大学学报,2005(2).

[94] 谢金良. 西方文学典故词典[M]. 北京:中国展望出版社,1986.

[95] 燕国材. 非智力因素与学习[M]. 上海:上海教育出版社,2006.

[96] 严明. 大学英语自主学习能力培养模式研究——体验的视角[M].

哈尔滨:黑龙江大学出版社,2009.
[97] 颜晓华.认知语境的构建与沉默的意义解读[J].湘潭师范学院学报(社会科学版),2009(4).
[98] 杨　晋.英语学生焦虑感和听力理解的关系[J].外语研究,2000(1).
[99] 张殿玉.英语学习策略与自主学习[J].外语教学,2005(1).
[100] 张维友.英语学习策略与技巧教程[M].重庆:重庆大学出版社,2004.
[101] 张燕军.英语自主式学习的必要性、可行性及具体措施[J].东南大学学报(哲学社会科学版),2005(5).
[102] 支永碧,吴延平.现代几种主要的语言观及其对外语教育的启示[J].国外外语教学,2007(1).
[103] 朱永生.语境动态研究[M].北京:北京大学出版社,2005.
[104] 朱中都.场独立性与场依赖性风格对外语学习的影响[J].外语与外语教学,2002(4).